I0793726

IMAGES
of America

WILLIAMS

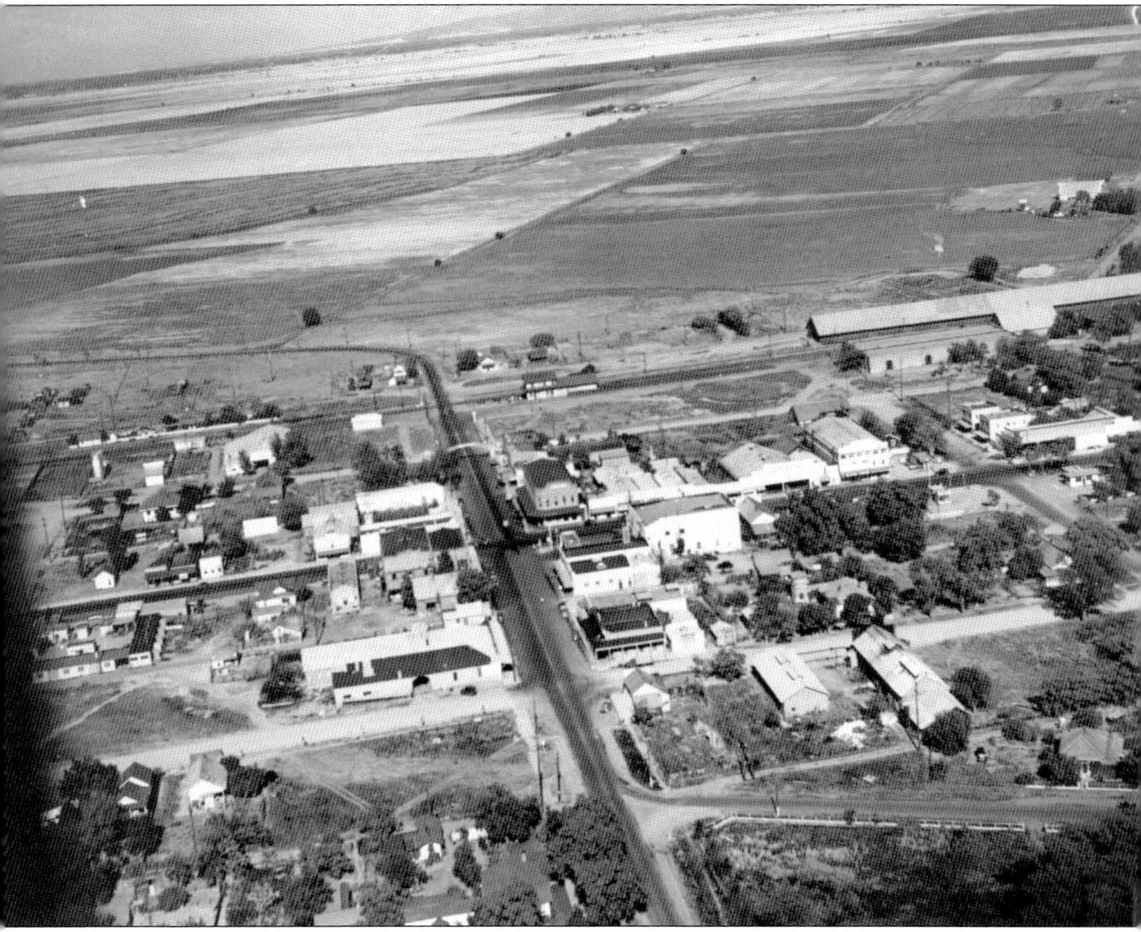

This 1936 *San Francisco Examiner* aerial photograph shows Williams before the city hall was built. Looking east, Highway 20 can be followed through town. (Gary Teragawa.)

On the Cover: The Texaco station was built at the corner of Seventh and F Streets in 1926. In 1932, H.H. Crutcher was named manager. Standing in front of the station are officers Charles Woods and Arch Matzka. In the center is H.H. Crutcher with Florence Green's children, in no particular order, Nate, George, and Leonard in the rumble seat. (Sacramento Valley Museum.)

IMAGES
of America

WILLIAMS

Patricia Ash

ARCADIA
PUBLISHING

ISBN 978-0-7385-9524-5

Published by Arcadia Publishing
Charleston, South Carolina

Printed in the United States of America

Library of Congress Control Number: 2012934811

For all general information, please contact Arcadia Publishing:
Telephone 843-853-2070
Fax 843-853-0044
E-mail sales@arcadiapublishing.com
For customer service and orders:
Toll-Free 1-888-313-2665

Visit us on the Internet at www.arcadiapublishing.com

This book is dedicated to Henry "Hank" Rhoades in thanks for preserving my childhood in Williams through the eye of his camera. Thanks for the memories.

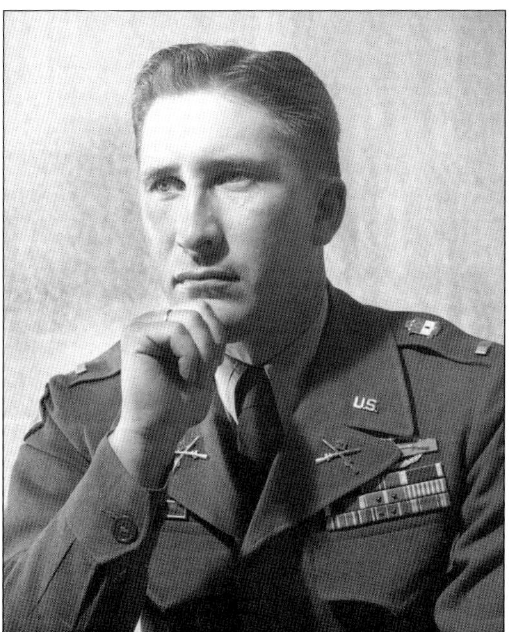

(Henry W. Rhoades family.)

Contents

ACKNOWLEDGMENTS

I want to thank Charles Yerxa Jr., president of the Colusi Historical Society, for encouraging me to go forward with this project. Thanks also to the Sacramento Valley Museum Board of Directors for its support.

To the ladies at the Colusa County Library, who allowed me to attach myself to the microfiche for my research, and to the staff of the Sacramento Valley Museum for allowing me to scan photographs for hours, I sincerely thank you.

I owe a big thank-you to Don Manor, Marjorie Marengo, Mike Ferraiuolo, Wanda Bowen, Bill Barrett, Susan Leardini, and Doug Gassaway for confirming identities and places in photographs and to Bill Manor for having the patience to answer my questions.

Thank you also to the Allen sisters for all of your information and photographs of early Williams, the Mountain House, and the stories of the Schuckman family. I would also like to thank Rusty Brookins and Rick Starnater for explaining the mechanics of early harvesters and equipment.

To my friend Jeanne Ann Del Pero, who spent hours and hours scanning photographs and negatives that belonged to her father, Henry "Hank" Rhoades, I owe you big time. A special thank-you also goes to Gion Gibson, great-grandson of Joseph Gibson, founder of the Gibson Ranch. With his generosity of photographs and my knowledge of their historical facts, we made a pretty good team. Thank you, Gion, for believing that your photographs should be seen and not locked away in a library, for it is only because of your beliefs that it is possible to show the world what a wonderful place the Gibson Ranch was as well as the people who lived and worked there.

Finally, to my family and friends who saw me through this process, and to my husband, Kevin, for his continued support, guidance, and professional opinions through the eye of a photographer I am forever indebted. To Arcadia Publishing for helping me realize a lifetime dream of writing the history of my hometown, thank you! You will never know how much I appreciate all of you.

Introduction

W.H. Williams made his first trip to Colusa County in 1851. He returned in 1853 to settle on 160 acres in a small valley west of Williams, joining the first white family to settle there, the Martin Britton family. It was Britton who was responsible for naming it Spring Valley.

W.H. Williams sowed barley and wheat as an experiment in 1854 and expanded his plantings over the next few years. It was not long before he moved to the valley floor, building a modest house where his mansion eventually stood. In 1861, he married Sarah Carey, the first of two wives, with whom he shared three daughters, Harriet May, Lulu, and Ella. He invested in the sheep business and was soon raising 1,000 head of sheep and was the owner of 7,360 acres, with a little less than half of those acres under fence.

The town of Central had a few settlers located just south of where Williams now lies, and when it was seen that the railroad was making its way up the valley, Williams had the land surveyed, had lots blocked out, and proceeded to buy and sell the property. Williams was underway.

As the railroad made its way north, a good-sized settlement was taking shape. Buildings made from the brick and clay found in the neighborhood began to spring up, replacing wooden structures. Warehouses were built and were substantial and capable of taking care of receiving and shipping grain for years to come. In the following years, the grain industry would see thousands of tons shipped to market, first by rail and then by truck, as it is today.

In 1876, the town was named after W.H. Williams, who sold the right-of-way to the railroad and went from being postmaster of Central to postmaster of Williams. The town of Williams began to flourish in 1877 but suffered many devastating fires that wiped out the town between 1877 and 1879.

One of the largest fires, on June 16, 1877, consumed much of the downtown, wiping out the Odd Fellows Hall, Nelks' Wagon Shop, the Hudson and Boardman Livery Stable and Blacksmith Shop, and Hyman and Sussman's General Store, which was housed on the bottom floor of the Odd Fellows Hall. Rebuilding began immediately, and by September 1877 the Odd Fellows held a ceremony laying the first brick of their new lodge. It was said to be in the neighborhood of $8,000 to build, with moneys put up by W.H. Williams, J.C. Stovall, and Capt. William Ash.

In an article from the *Central News* from 1877, a citizen was quoted as saying, "So you see, things will soon be as they were before the fire, the courage of the citizens of Williams will not allow the burning of a few buildings to check the progress of the town."

W.H. Williams went from having a modest house in the early 1800s to building a grand home at the cost of $10,000 in 1875, with bricks being brought in from Marysville. He filled the home with elegant furnishings and lit the home with gas fixtures. When the railroad began bringing people to the new territory, Williams opened his home as a place to stay until the Williams Hotel was built in 1876 at a cost of $40,000, located downtown at the corner of Seventh and E Streets. The new hotel had a dining room that could seat 100 people and was also the home of several businesses. On the northwest corner of Seventh and E Streets and adjoining the newly rebuilt Odd

Fellows Hall, an opera hall was built to hold 500 people. It was also home to a reading room, a smoking room, a large bar, and a stage that saw many performers as well as Chatauqua groups.

Word soon reached the East Coast and beyond of mineral springs located in the hills of western Colusa County, and trains were arriving with carloads of folks seeking the medicinal waters. The springs that were the biggest draw were Bartlett, Allen, Cooks, Wilbur, Fouts, Hough, and Sulphur. The stage ran regular routes daily after the first of June and three times a week in the off-season. Owning a stage line was a lucrative business during those years. There were two in the beginning: the Miller Brothers and Smith and Jones. With the stages came the need for stage stops.

One of those stage stops was the Mountain House, owned and operated by German immigrant August Schuckman, who fulfilled a lifelong dream to be an innkeeper. He had heard that the Twenty Mile House would be a good place because it was on the main road leading to Bear Valley and the coast. In 1871, he made a deal for the Twenty Mile House, which is where he stayed until around 1879, when August traded it to the Stovall Wilcoxson Company for the Mountain House—about a mile west—and $1,000. It included a hotel and barns and was well equipped to handle the public at a good location on the fork of two roads, one being to Sulphur Creek the other to Bartlett Springs.

Not only did the springs bring people to the mountains, but they also provided a very viable business of shipping out the coveted mineral water to be placed on the train at Williams. Freight wagons loaded with goods for the springs returned loaded with water. There were as many as 30 wagons snaking their way over the curved roads at any given time, with many teamsters also making their way back and forth over the hills every week. The freight business was booming, and it was not uncommon to ship out 60,000 bottles of water from the springs in one season along with flasks of quicksilver and gold, which added to the activity west of Williams.

Dry land farming soon gave way to irrigated crops and the raising of rice. Grapes were grown along with oranges and other citrus fruits, mules were raised and bound for Hawaii, and Williams was exporting more chickens via the railroad than any other town between San Francisco and Redding. Making their way to the railroad station, as well, were huge slabs of stone from the quarry located northwest of town. It supplied stone to build the finer hotels and government buildings over the years, and it was reported that none of the buildings built with stone from the Colusa County quarry succumbed to the Great San Francisco Earthquake of 1906.

Over the next 100 years, Williams would grow and change with the hard work of the folks who invested their efforts in a small town at the crossroads. It is not without the dedication and pride of the people who rolled up their sleeves and gave so much of themselves and their businesses that they would have sustained. They went the extra mile to support their troops, from saving their fruit pits during World War I to saving tin in World War II and buying more war bonds than other towns in the area. They gave unselfishly to improve the community and supported the schools and youth programs throughout the years.

One

The Early Settlers

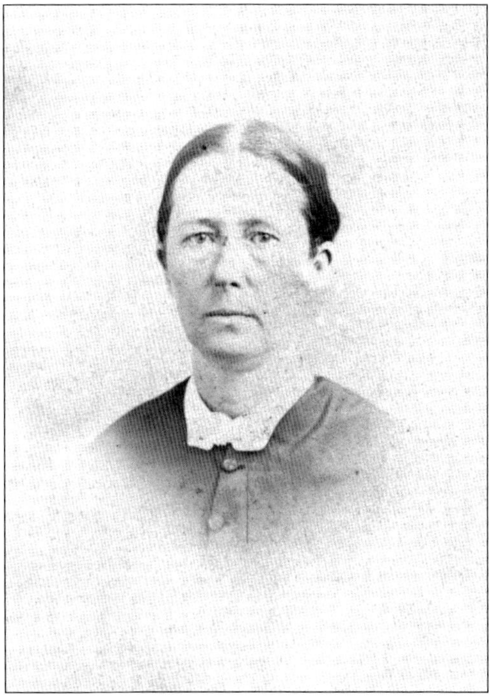

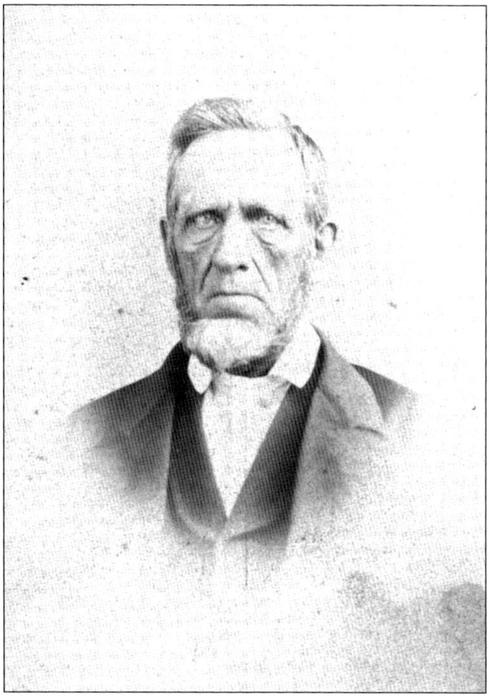

Martin A. Britton and his wife, Zerilda, were the first white settlers in Spring Valley west of Williams. Martin Britton named Spring Valley for the lush green fields of the valley. The Cortina Band of the Wintun tribe of Native Americans had already been residents of the valley, and from letters written by Britton, they peacefully coexisted and were even hired by the settlers to work for them. W.H. Williams moved into the valley approximately one year later to dry land farm, raise sheep, and make Spring Valley his home for approximately 20 years. An account by Britton notes that, while taking his grain to Colusa, there were three residences between Spring Valley and Colusa in 1855. (Author's collection.)

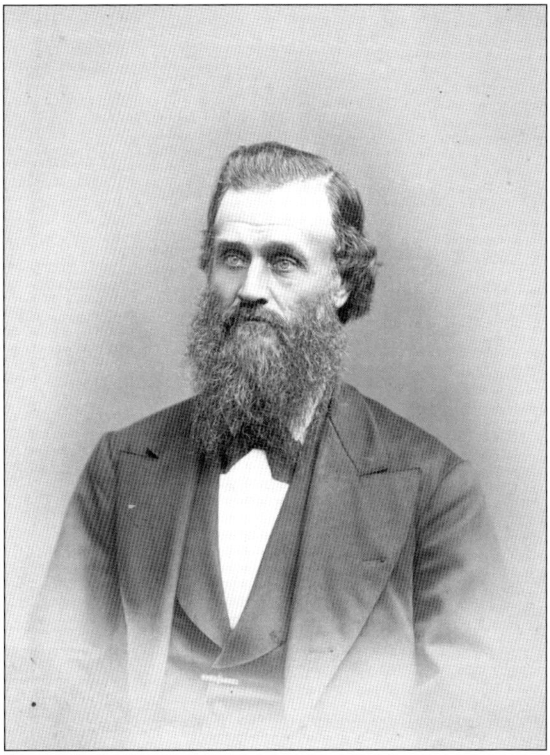

William Henry Williams was born in Maryland in 1828 and settled in Spring Valley in 1854. He took up dry land farming, raised sheep, and with every successful crop, bought more land. With the prospect of the coming railroad, he purchased land along the proposed site and gave the railroad a full interest and partnership in one half of the townsite in exchange for the railroad making Williams a stopping point. (Sacramento Valley Museum.)

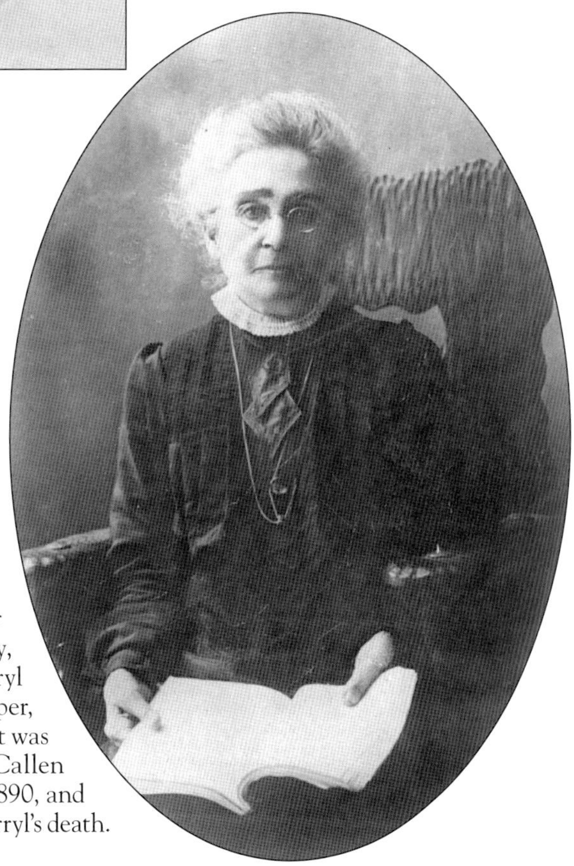

Sarah Carey, shown to the right, married W.H. Williams in 1861, and together they had four daughters, Harriet May, Lulu, Laura, and Ella. Lulu married Daryl Callen, and together they ran a newspaper, the *Williams Farmer*, beginning in 1887. It was the predecessor to the *Central News*. Callen sold half of his interest to G.W. Gay in 1890, and Lulu Callen leased out the paper after Darryl's death. (Sacramento Valley Museum.)

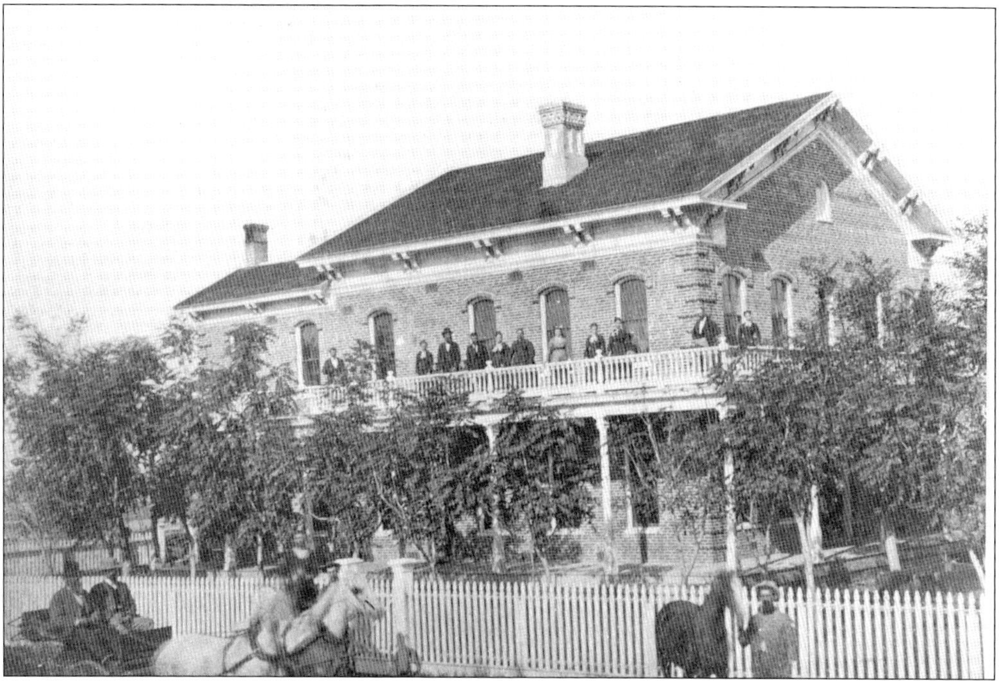

W.H. Williams built the Williams House in 1875, with the bricks hauled from Marysville. The window and door frames came from around Cape Horn with the makings of the Bower's Mansion in Carson City. It served as a hotel until the Williams Hotel was built one block away a year later. (Sacramento Valley Museum.)

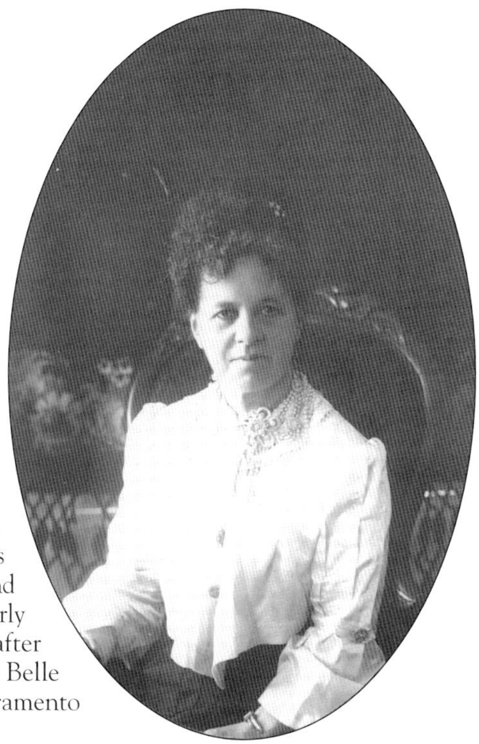

W.H. Williams met his second wife, Mary McEvoy, 31 years his junior, while she was employed at his hotel. Williams divorced Sarah to marry McEvoy, and they had six children, four of whom died at an early age. Mary passed away at the age of 78 in 1937 after residing in Williams for 56 years. Her daughters Belle Moore and Margurite Hotaling survived her. (Sacramento Valley Museum.)

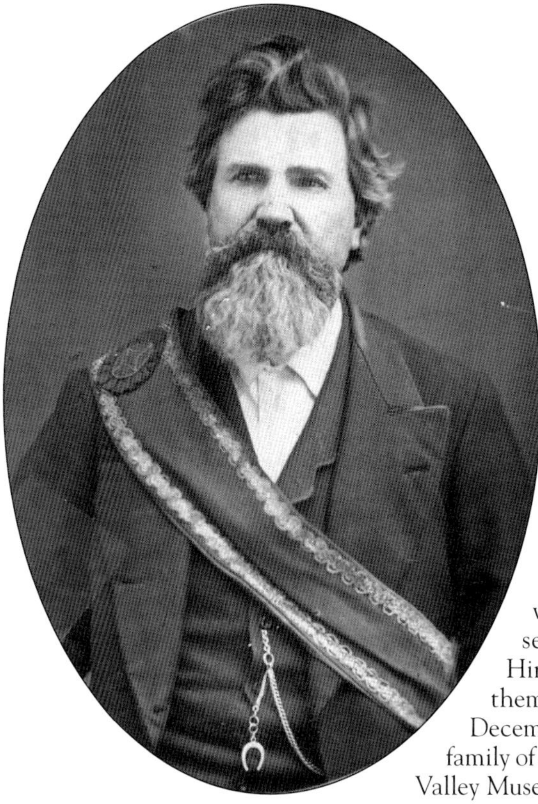

Jesse Curl Stovall (1822–1902) married Mary Moore in Sonoma on March 3, 1859. That same day, the couple made their way to western Williams, where they had purchased grazing land from the state. The grand house was built with lumber brought in from Marysville, and the nearest trading was in Colusa at that time. The Stovalls had seven children, Cordelia, William, James, Hiram, and Charles; Mary and Jesse preceded them in death. Tragically, the home burned on December 24, 1966, and the Judge Seymour Vann family of seven perished in the fire. (Left, Sacramento Valley Museum; below, Jean Terkildsen.)

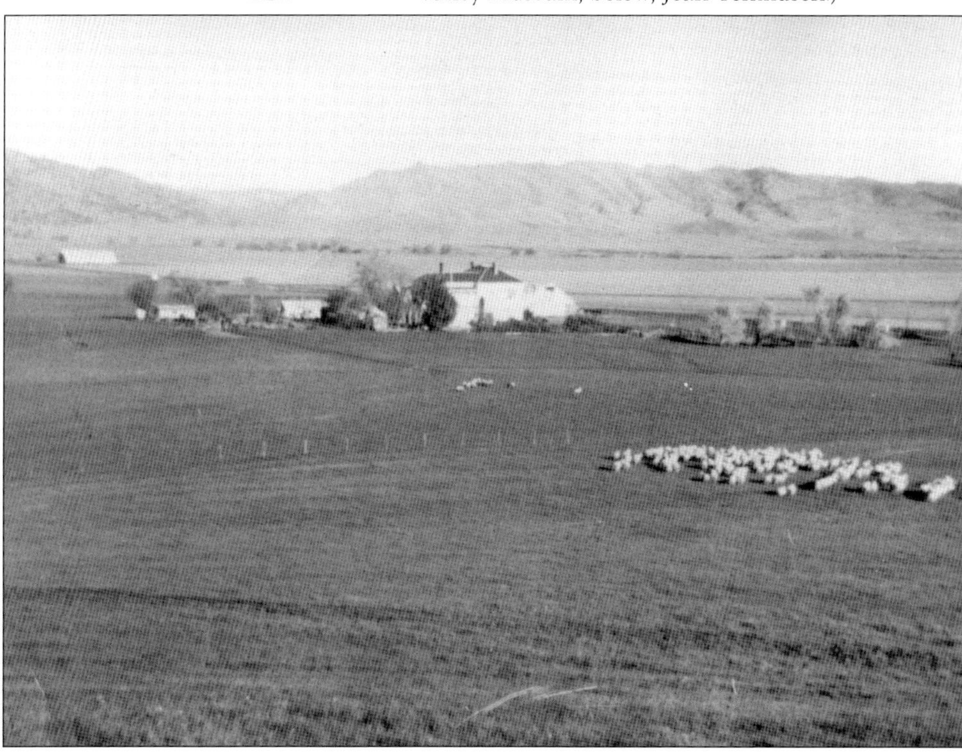

Capt. William Ash, the youngest of 15 children, was one of the early boosters of Williams. At the time of the Modoc/Klamath Indian wars in 1872, a militia company was organized, and he was commissioned captain, a name that stayed with him throughout his life. Along with W.H. Williams and H.C. Stovall, he built the first Odd Fellows Hall after their meeting place was burned and all was lost at the time of the Heyman and Sussman fire. (Ash family collection.)

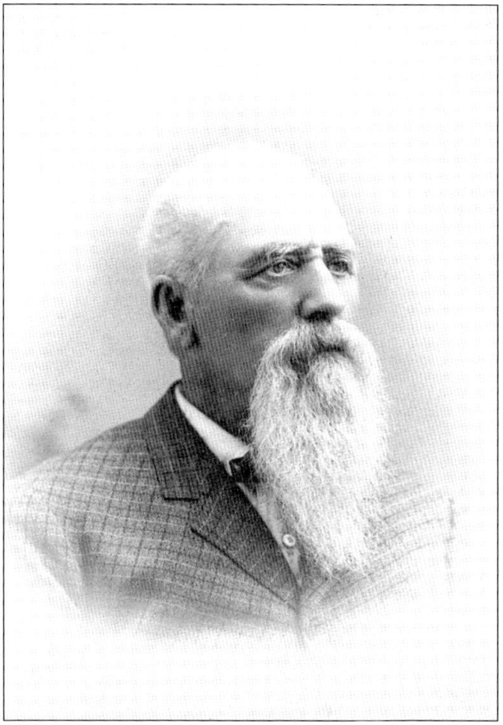

The home of Captain Ash was located in the Berlin area on 6,000 acres. Along with his spacious home was his aviary, which was 100 by 100 square feet and held one of the largest collections of native Californian and foreign birds in the state. He also owned two ranches in Willows, land in Colusa, and acreage in the foothills, amounting to over 11,000 acres. In 1904, he built the Ash Hotel in Arbuckle. At the time, it was the finest hotel in Colusa County. (Robert Ash.)

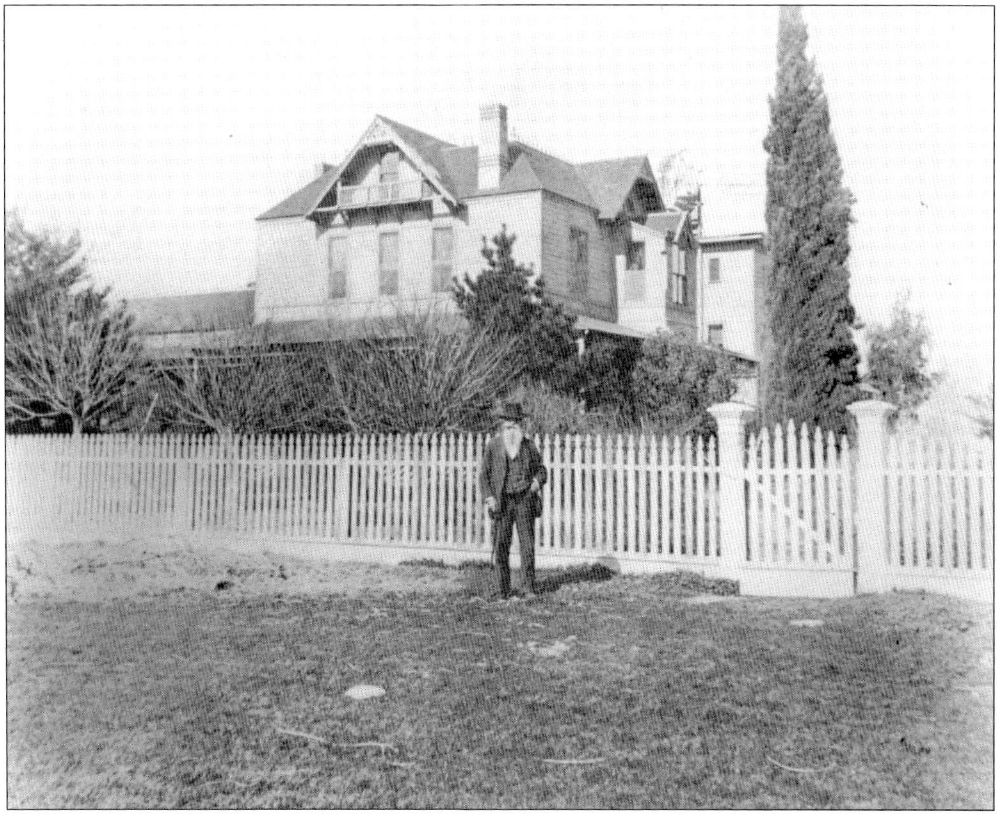

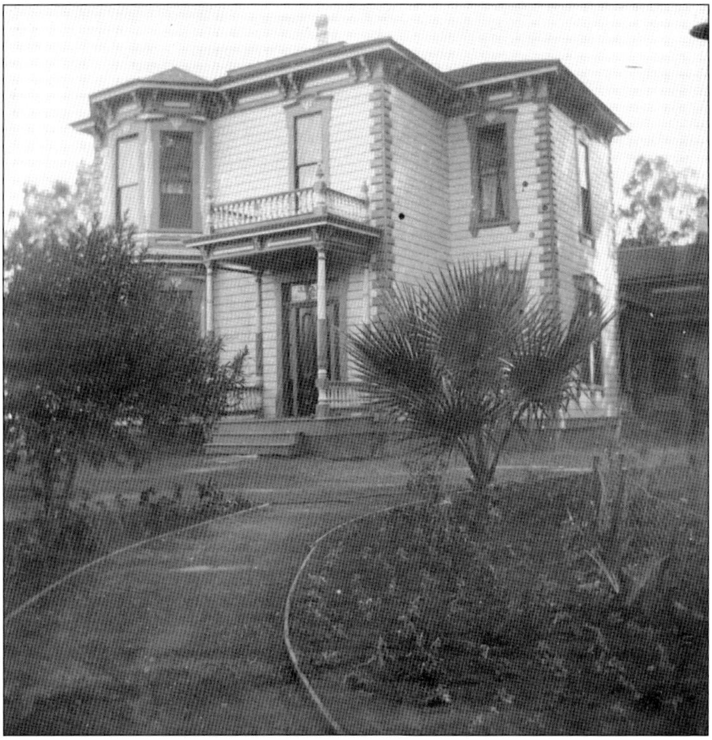

The Freshwater district of Colusa County was the home of John F. Abel Sr., who settled here in August 1869. He was the proud father of 10 and the owner of 800 acres. Also shown here are the families of the Abel unit with John Abel front and center. (Both, Annette Abel La Grande.)

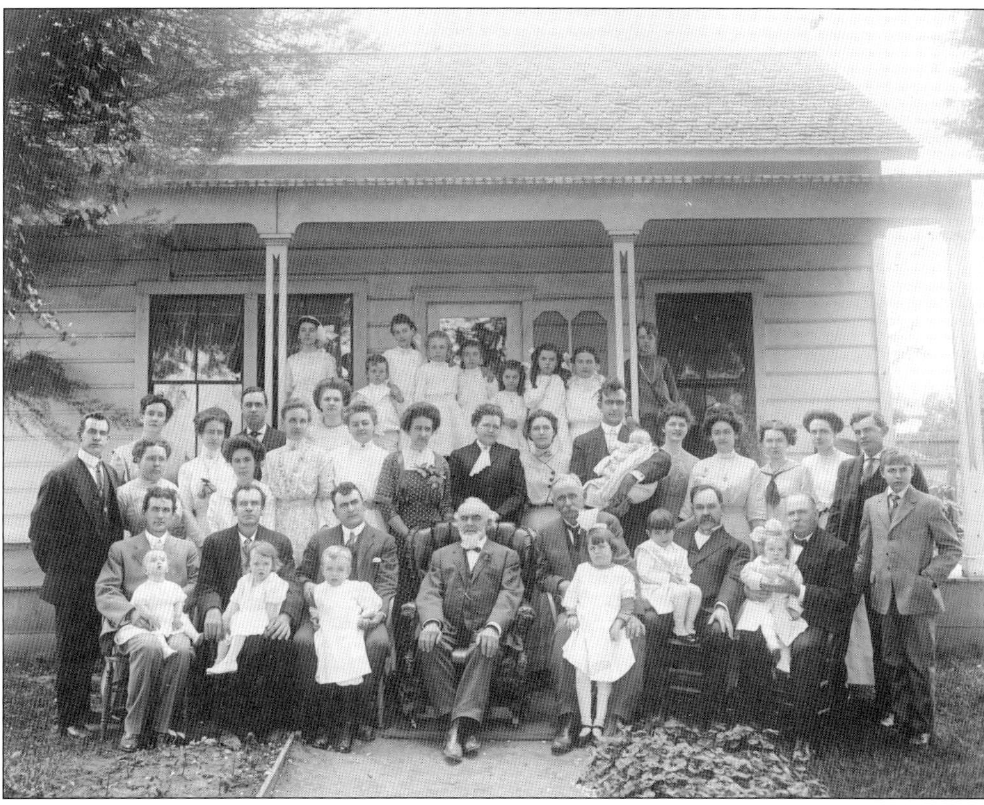

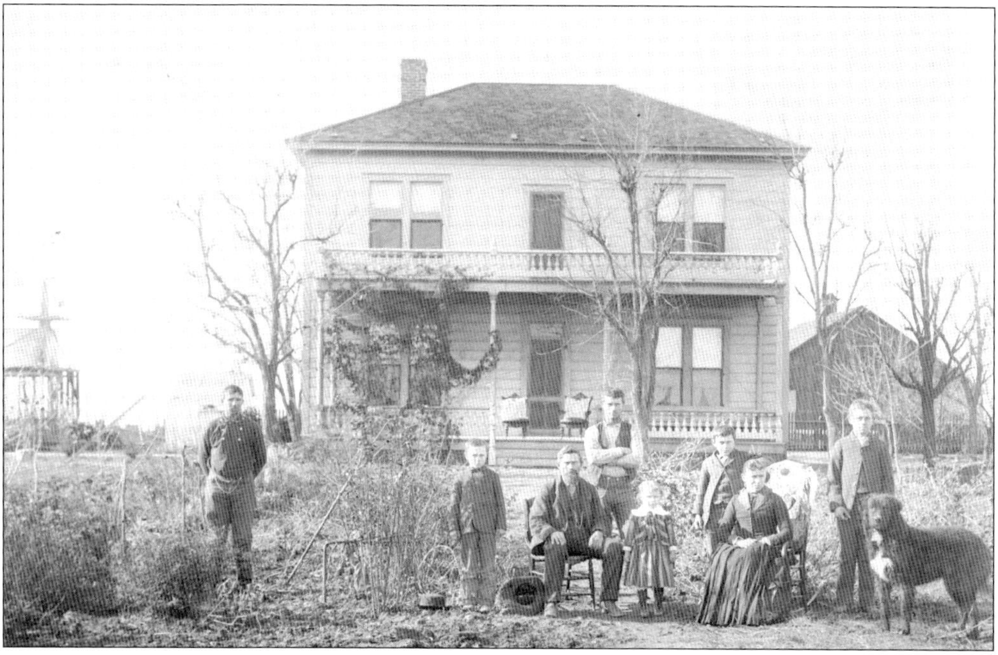

The ranch home of August Schaad is located on Lone Star Road and has remained in the family to this day. This 1885 photograph shows, from left to right, (standing) William Evans; sons Charlie, Fred, Clarence, and Albert; (sitting) parents August and Caroline with daughter Carrie in the middle. (Schaad-Fouch family collection.)

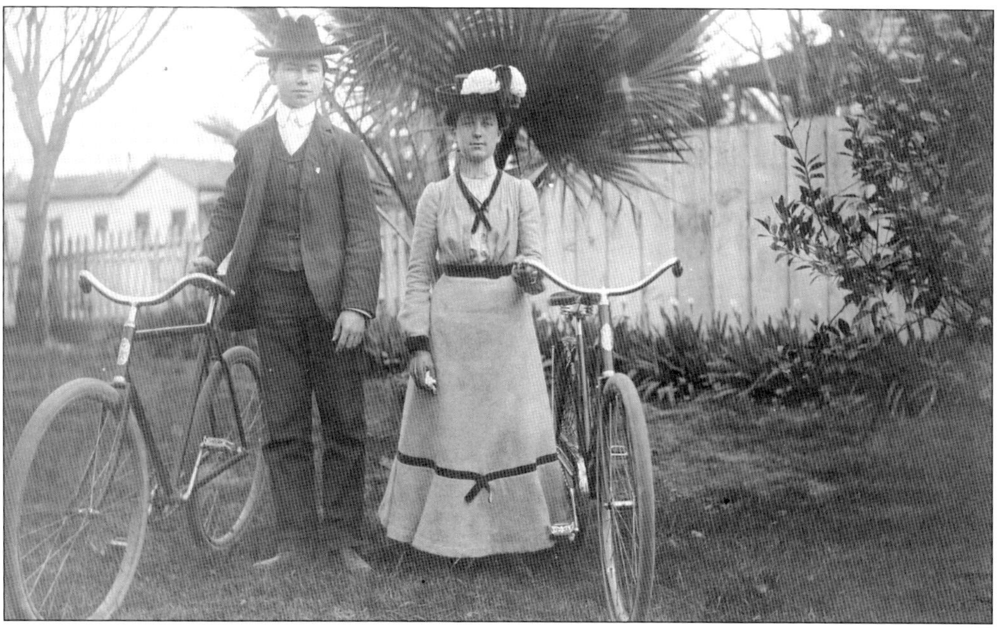

Carrie would later marry Bert Fouch, shown here in 1904. Bert was employed at the Bank of Williams at the age of 15 and went on to own the Farmer's Warehouse in Williams that was managed by Charlie Schaad. The warehouse suffered a fire in 1944 that was started by a passing train. Bert and Carrie raised three daughters, Augusta, Harriet, and Bertell, and their house still stands on the southwest corner of Ninth and D Streets today. (Schaad-Fouch family collection.)

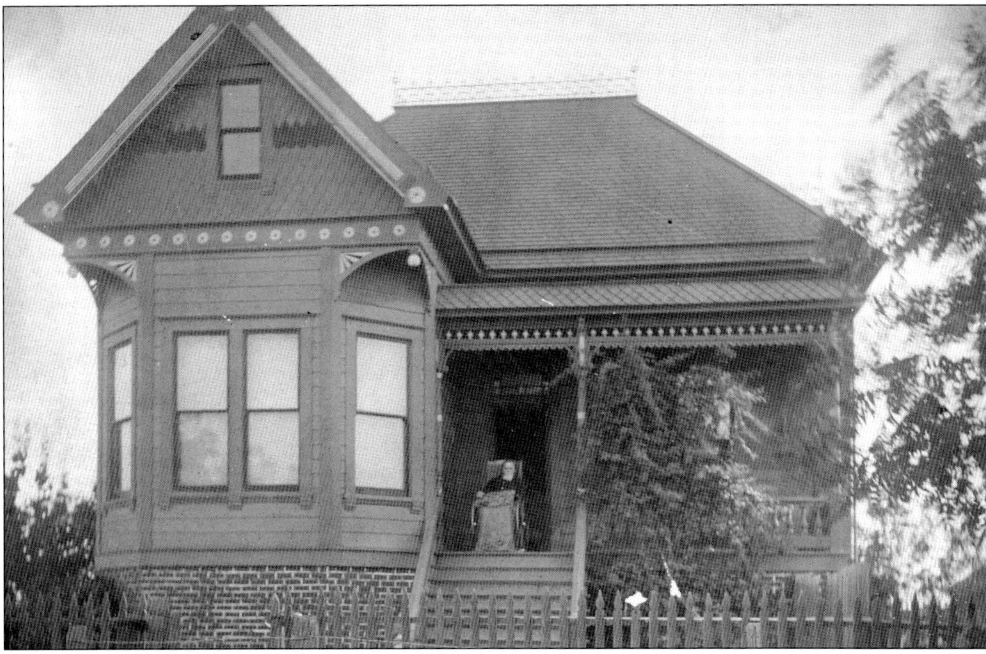

The Miller home was built around 1895 at the corner of Ninth and D Streets by John and Sarah Miller and was the residence of Dora Miller Reister when she was growing up. John Miller is pictured sitting on the front porch. After World War II, the home was given to Nevil Reister when he married his wife, Betty, and they made it their home until the early 1980s, when they moved next door. The old house was removed from its foundation during a tornado around that same time. The bricks from the foundation came from the Williams brick foundry, where the school grounds are now. (Diane Lucas.)

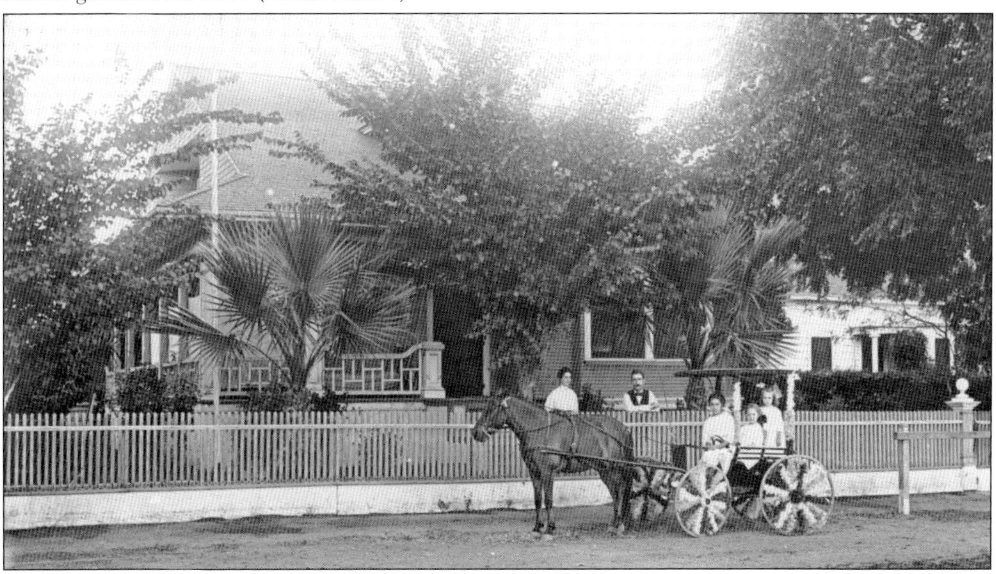

George and Jennie Comstock stand behind the fence and admire their three daughters. In no particular order are Janette, Virginia, and Elizabeth. George Comstock married Jennie Brim in November 1895. Comstock was a member of the community for 38 years and a leading businessman before his death in 1928. (Sacramento Valley Museum.)

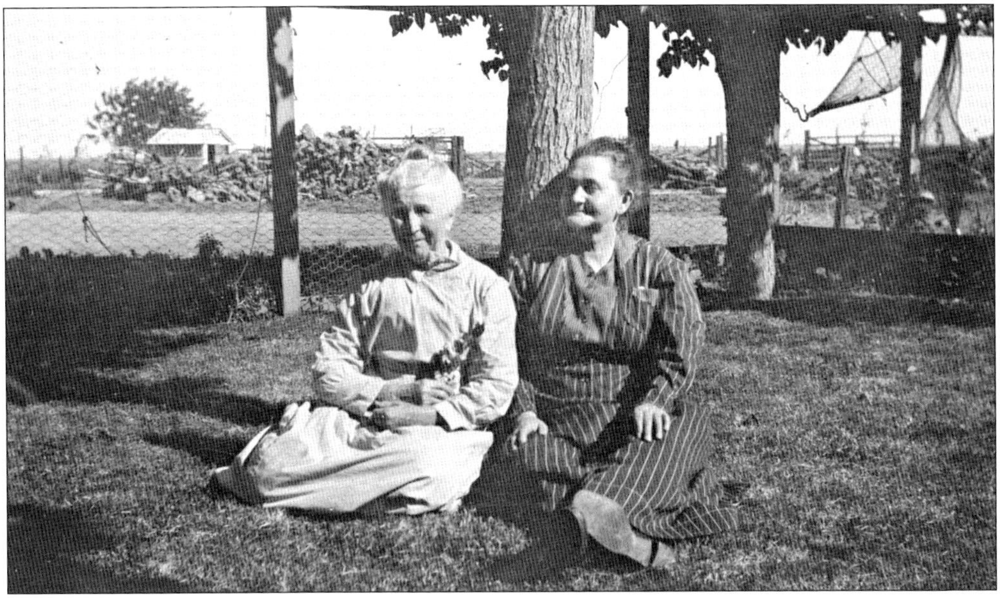

Sarah Gibson is seated on the right next to her neighbor and friend Elizabeth Wakefield Blevins. The Blevins family also lived in the Freshwater district of Williams. Sarah and Joseph Gibson raised three children, Gion, Nara California, and Josie, on the ranch. When Joseph died, son Gion lived with Sarah, and she helped to raise Gion's two children, Samuel and Rebecca. Sarah Gibson passed in 1923. (Gibson family collection.)

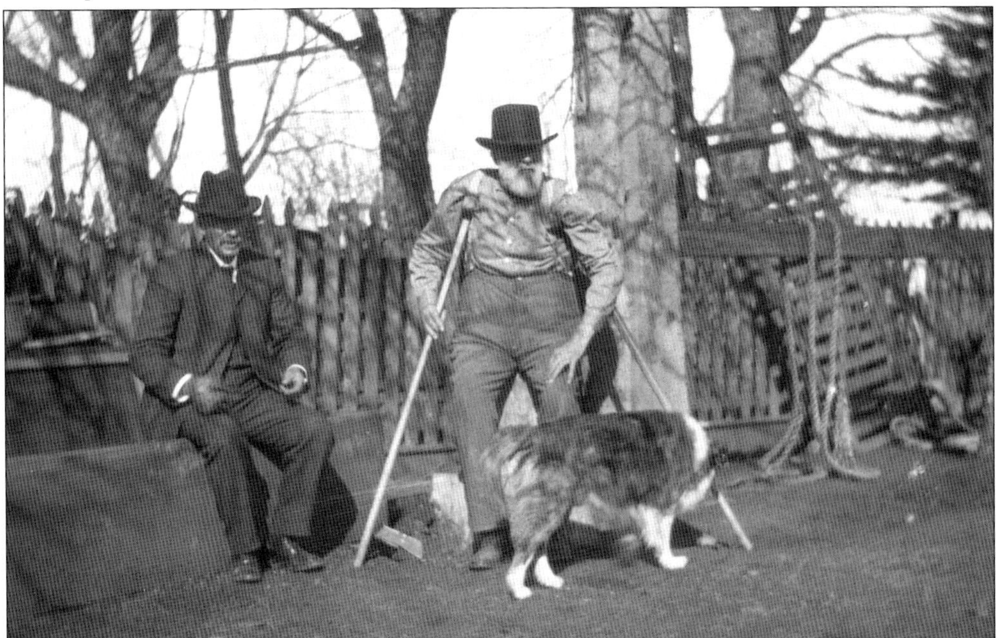

Shown here are Dr. Frank Pirky (left) and Joseph Sitton Gibson. Gibson was one of the first pioneers of Williams. In 1853, he settled in the Freshwater district, which is where he met Sarah Larch, who had come to Colusa to visit. He followed her when she returned to Missouri and married her; they then returned to Williams. Genealogy documents show that Sarah was the great-great-granddaughter of Daniel Boone. Joseph died in 1906 at the age of 80. (Gibson family collection.)

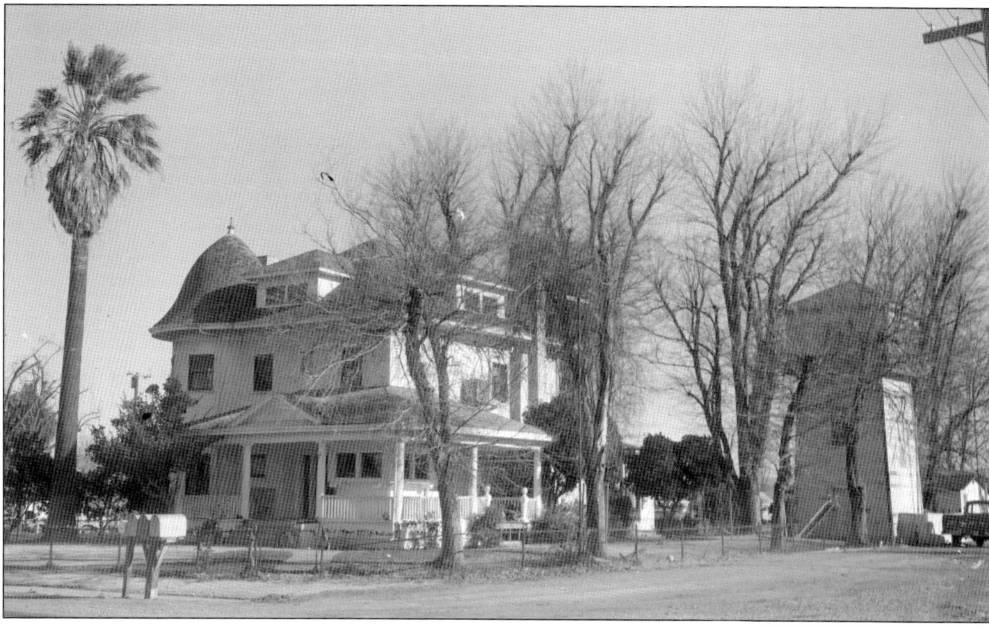

The Mendenhall home was built in 1905 and took three months to complete. It was the home of John Lindsey Mendenhall and his wife, Millie, who had a registered Shetland pony–breeding business. John Mendenhall was a member of the city council and served as mayor. He was also a Williams School Board member and was active in the promotion of Williams. The Mendenhalls had the distinction of having the first lighted tennis court in Williams. (Henry W. Rhoades family.)

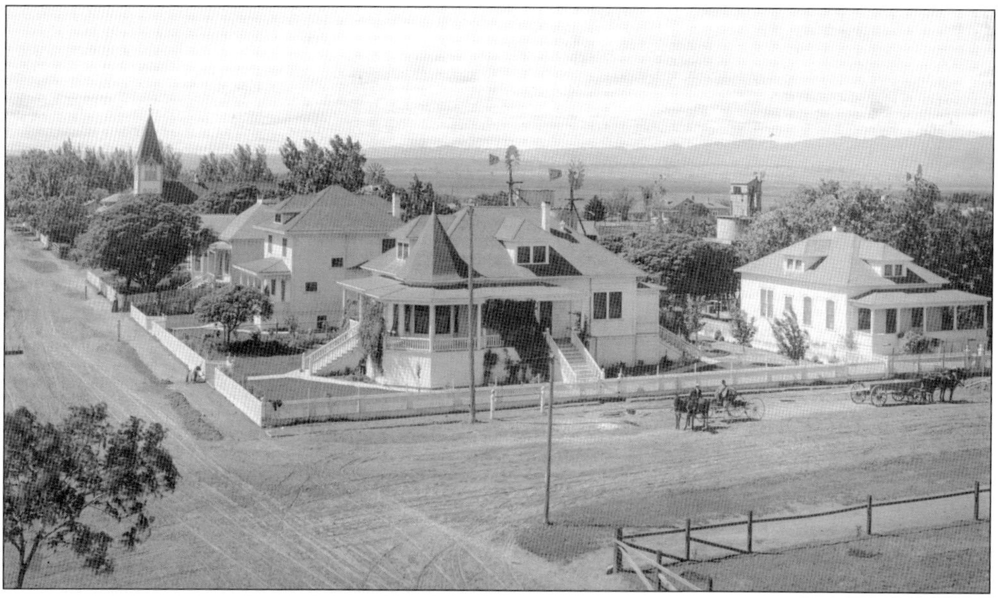

This bird's-eye view of the homes at Seventh and F Streets on property originally owned by J.O. Zumwalt shows three homes facing left, all of them built by Henry Heckhard Rettereth, father of Oma Retterth Tuttle, one of the first graduates of Williams High School. As shown in the photograph, the forms for the sidewalks are being constructed, and lumber is being off-loaded. The house on the corner, known as the "Stovall Place," was one of many built by the Stovall families. Just north would be the Williams Home with the split-rail fences. (Sacramento Valley Museum.)

Two

The Town during the First 100 Years

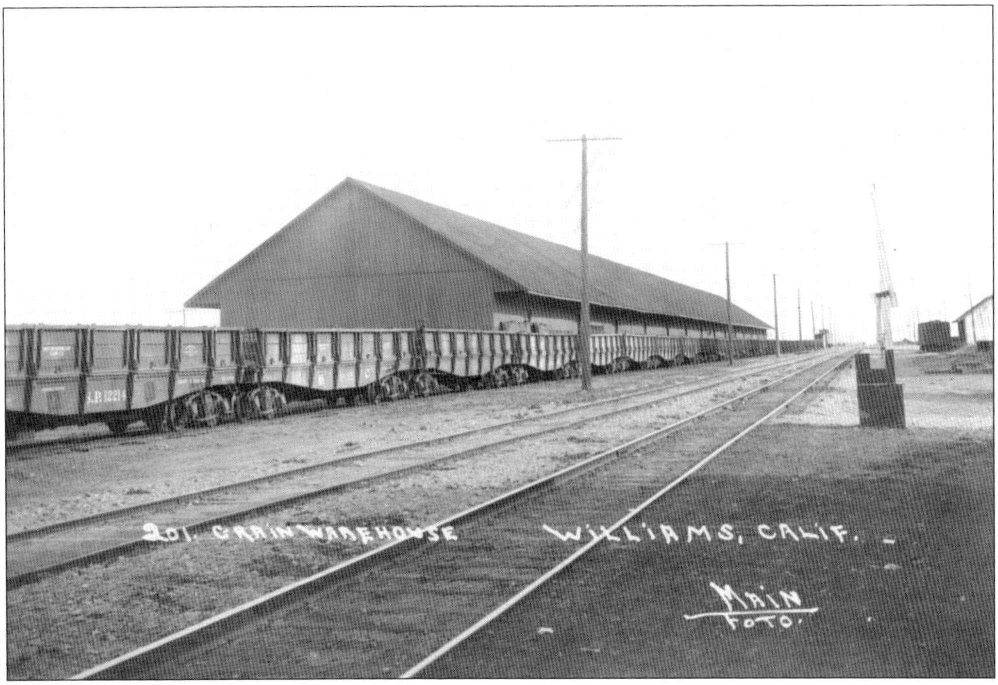

J.C. Stovall and his partner George Wilcoxson constructed a 600-by-60-foot wooden structure at a cost of $12,000 and employed eight men. In one instance, 5,000 sacks were off-loaded from one farm in one day alone. Stovall and Wilcoxson owned 40,000 acres and were instrumental in other businesses in Williams. The wood structure still stands today and is owned by Depue Warehouse. (Gayle Vaughn.)

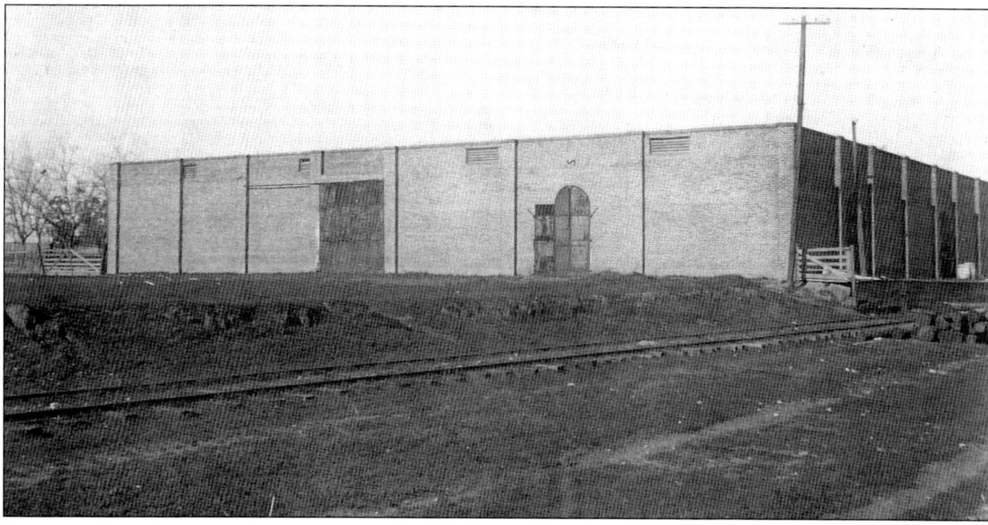

Situated directly across the tracks was the Williams Warehouse, which was built as a pull-through facility in 1880. Using bricks from the town's foundry at a cost of $10,000, it was 170 by 100 feet, well ventilated, and used for almost 100 years. Along with the warehouse, a flour mill was incorporated in 1879 and valued at $25,000. The owners were J.C. Stovall, H.P. Eakle, W.H. Williams, John Stanley, and J.O. Zumwalt. (Sacramento Valley Museum.)

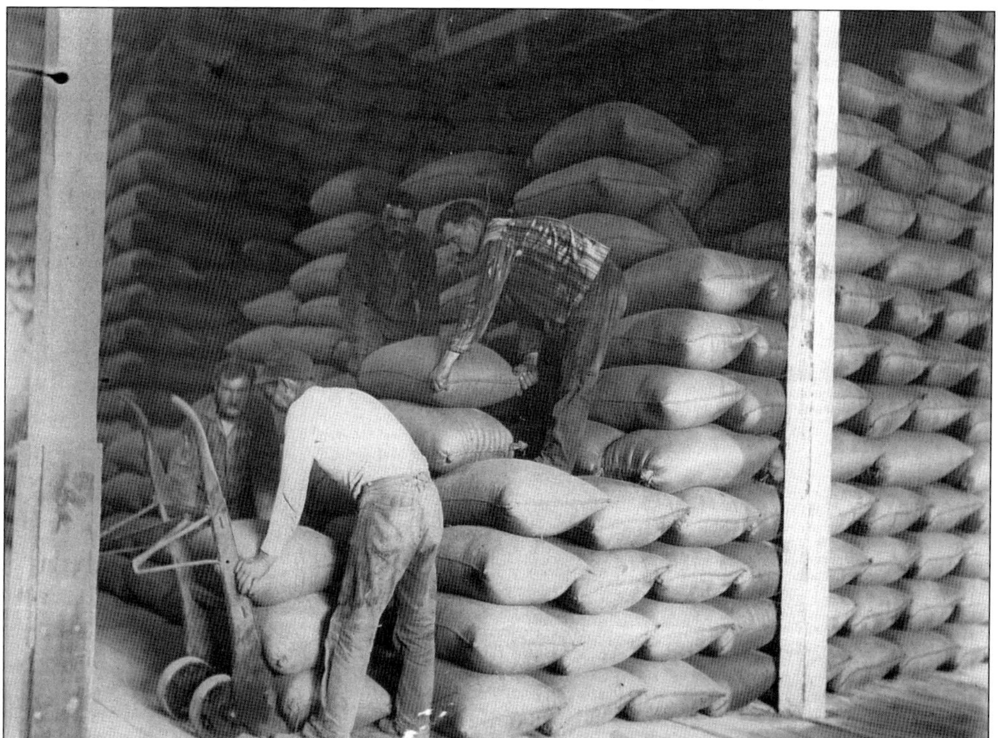

The Williams Warehouse employed four full-time men stacking sacks until they were shipped out via the railroad. During an average week, shipments would take in 2,500 to 3,000 sacks. The heaviest shipment was from the Steve Eakles's ranch, which consisted of 174 sacks, weighing nearly nine tons. (Sacramento Valley Museum.)

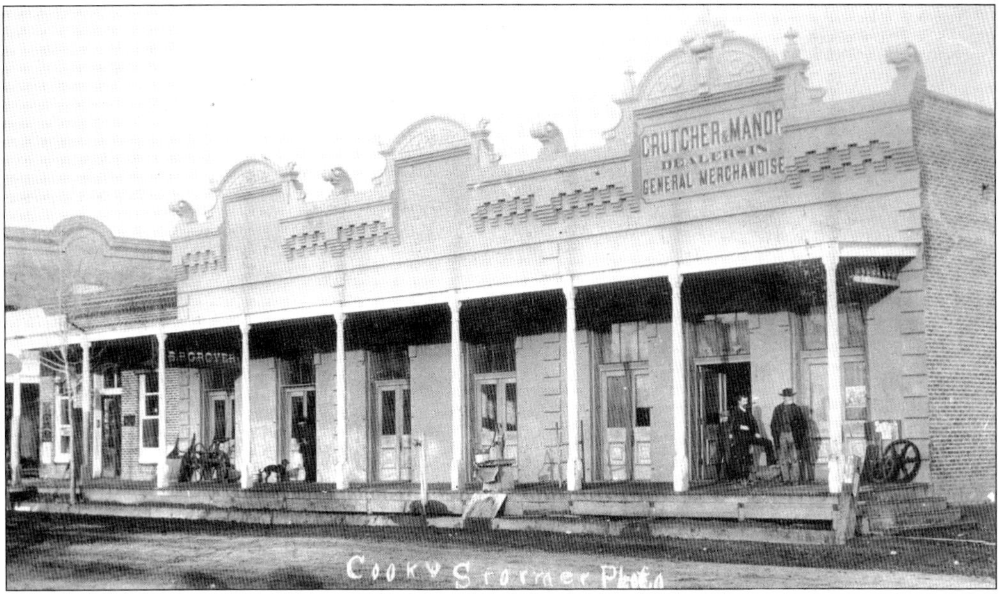

Crutcher and Manor General Merchandise was founded by J.W. Crutcher and A.B. Manor. After a fire in 1883 wiped out the original business along with Fouch's Drugstore in what was known as the Stanley building, both businesses moved two blocks east, sharing the block with the Bank of Williams and Grover's hardware. The business of Crutcher and Manor continued until after the death of Manor and then became George Comstock's. (Sacramento Valley Museum.)

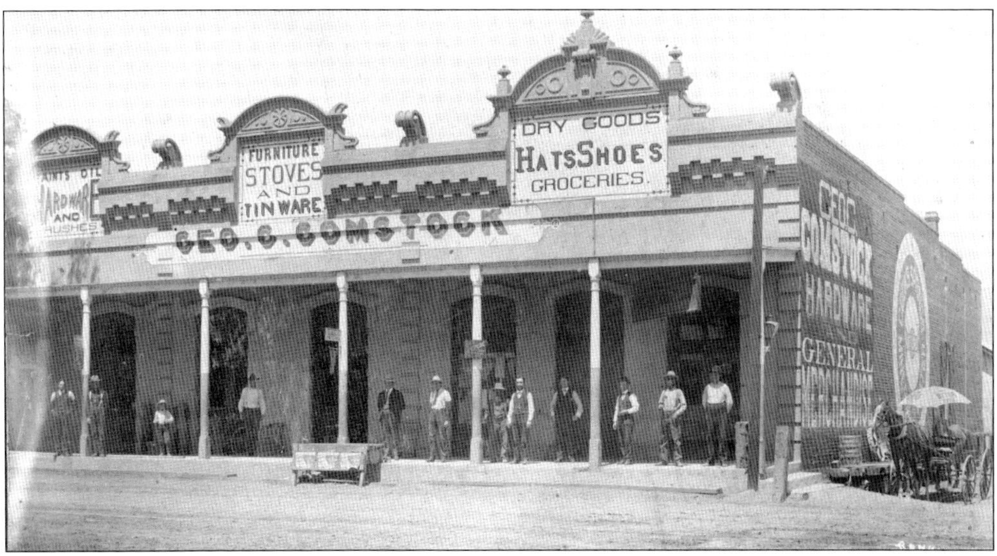

The George Comstock Hardware and General Merchandise store relocated to the Crutcher and Manor building after the death of A.B. Manor. This 1902 photograph shows Comstock's store, which became known as a major mercantile business for the county. When it burned in 1919, it left a huge hole in the Williams economy and was also a big loss for the county. (Sacramento Valley Museum.)

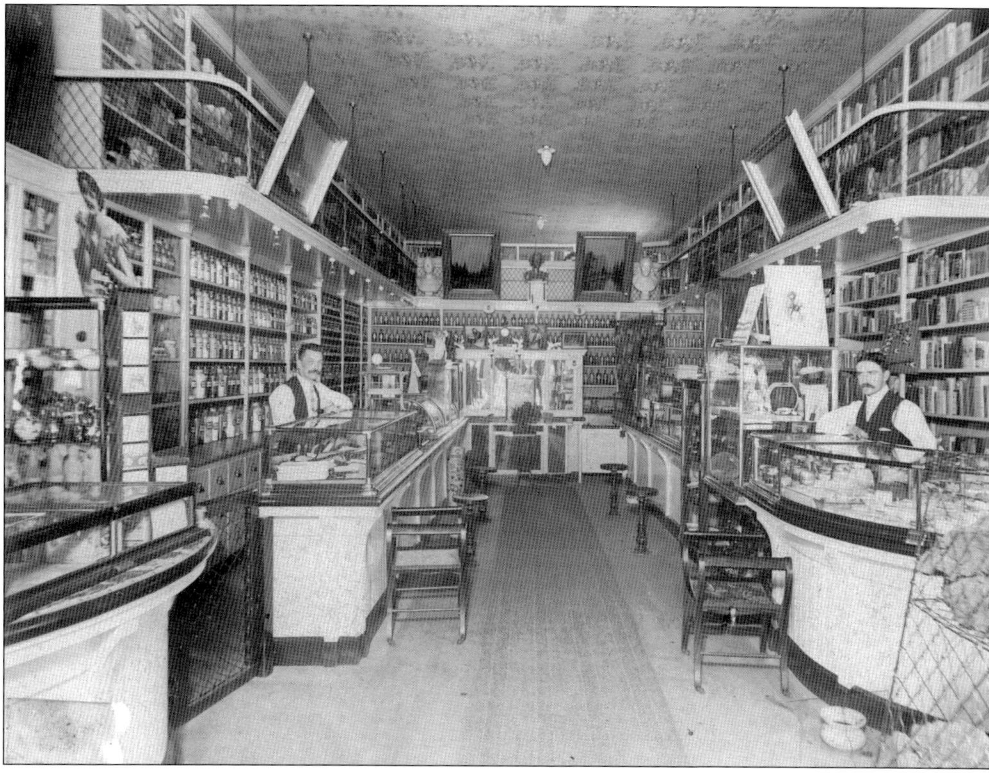

The inside of the Comstock store rivaled any of those in larger cities. His inventory was extensive and carried everything a person could want or need, as evidenced in these photographs. Over the next 20 years, the look of George Comstock's store changed, and the photograph below, taken in 1916, shows the menswear section of the store. (Both, Sacramento Valley Museum.)

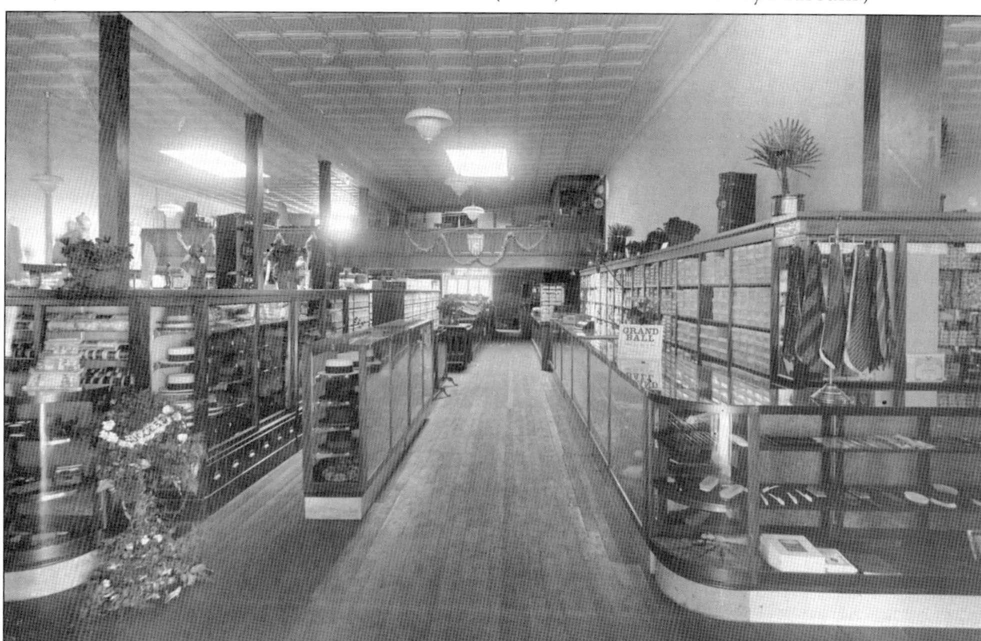

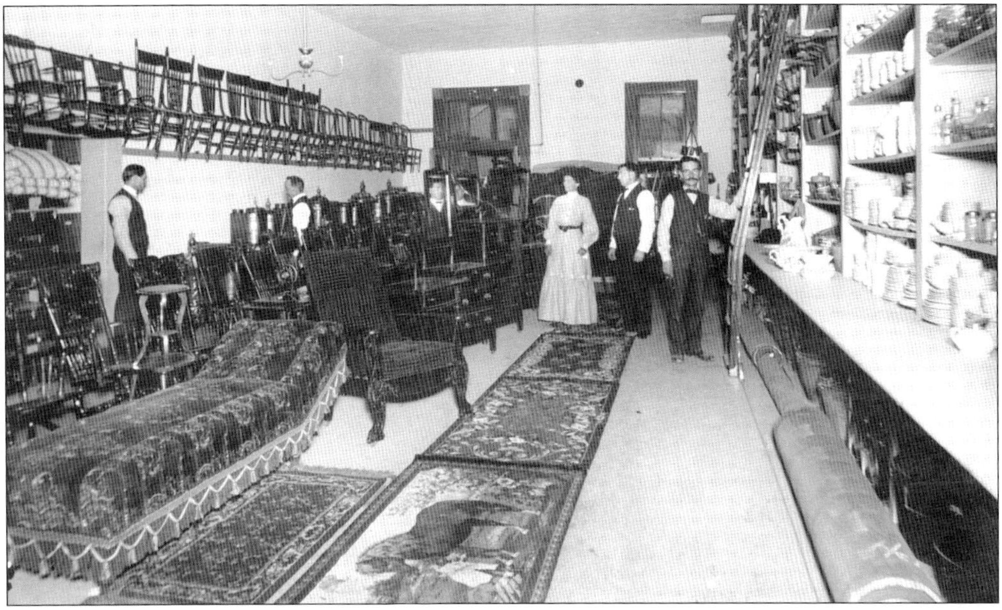

Even household furniture was sold at the Comstock store, with some of the finest collections of rugs anywhere. When Comstock burned, an estimated $100,000 worth of inventory was lost. Valiantly fought by citizens and the volunteer fire department, the fire consumed the building due to inadequate water pressure. (Sacramento Valley Museum.)

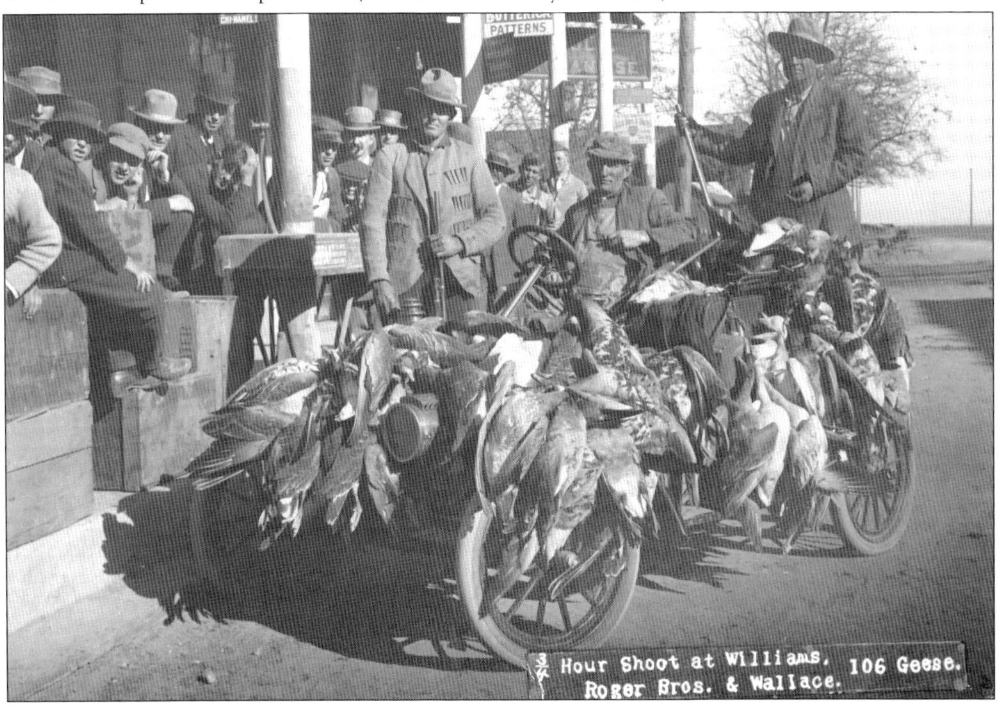

This famous photograph was taken in front of Comstock's and shows store manager Frank Wallace standing with shotgun, Will Rogers seated behind the wheel, and Cliff Rogers standing on the back of the car after a 45-minute shoot that netted the hunters 106 geese. George Comstock is shown in the back with the cigar. (Ash family collection.)

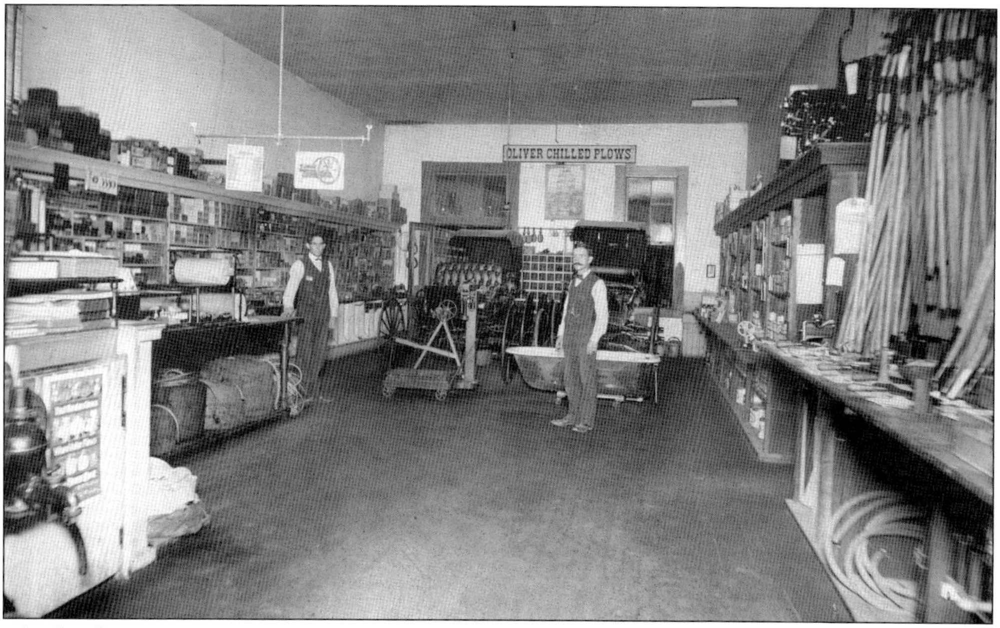

The hardware store was owned by B.P. Grover and was established in 1887. Grover owned a residence in San Francisco and ran a very lucrative business. He sold everything from shovels to buggies, and the store was lauded as "systematically arranged and scrupulously clean." In 1893, Elbert Brim and George Comstock became owners of the store. A year later, Comstock purchased Brim's interest and became sole owner. (Sacramento Valley Museum.)

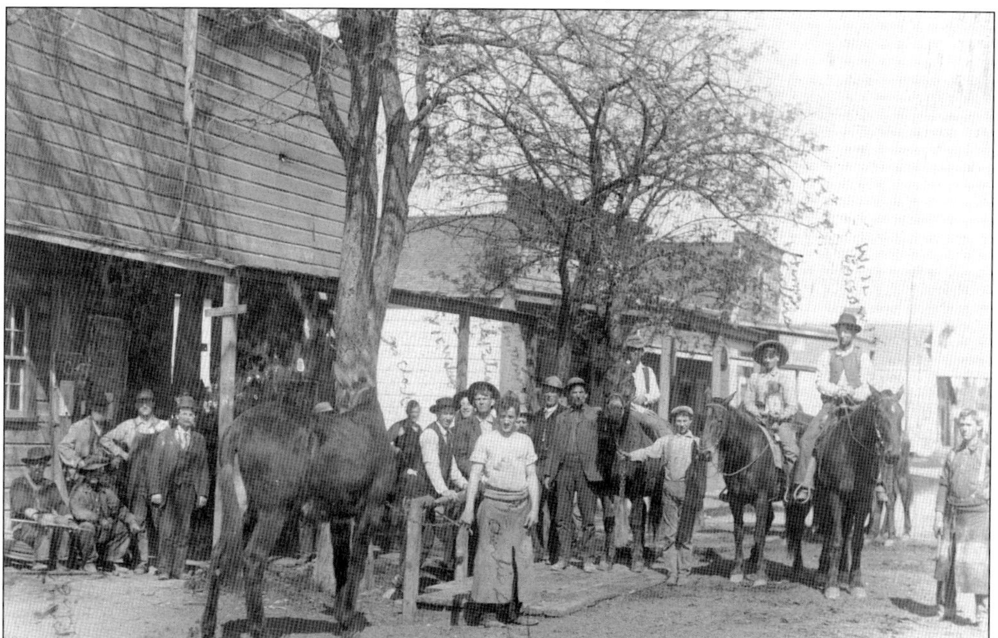

The town's menfolk are shown gathered at the blacksmith shop around 1909. A young Bill Stokes is standing in front with blacksmith chaps on. Stokes later operated a blacksmith shop in Colusa for many years. On horses to the far right are, from left to right, Ben Cullers and William Gassaway. (Author's collection.)

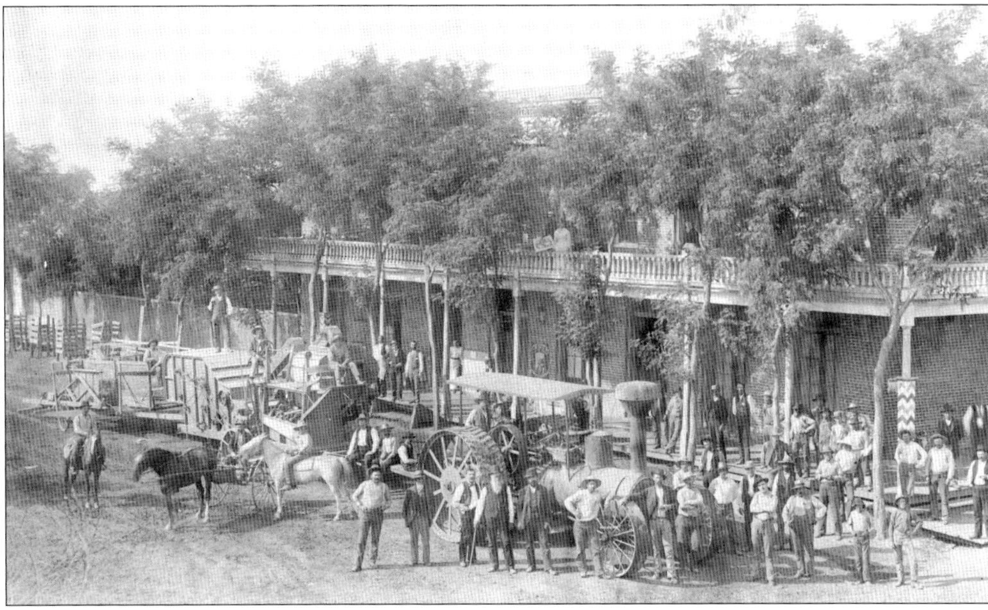

The Williams Hotel was used as a backdrop for many photographs of Williams. Built at a cost of $40,000, it was thought to be one of the finest hotels in the valley. Farmers are showing off a tractor-drawn harvester as W.H. Williams stands front and center with his hat, vest, and cane. (Sacramento Valley Museum.)

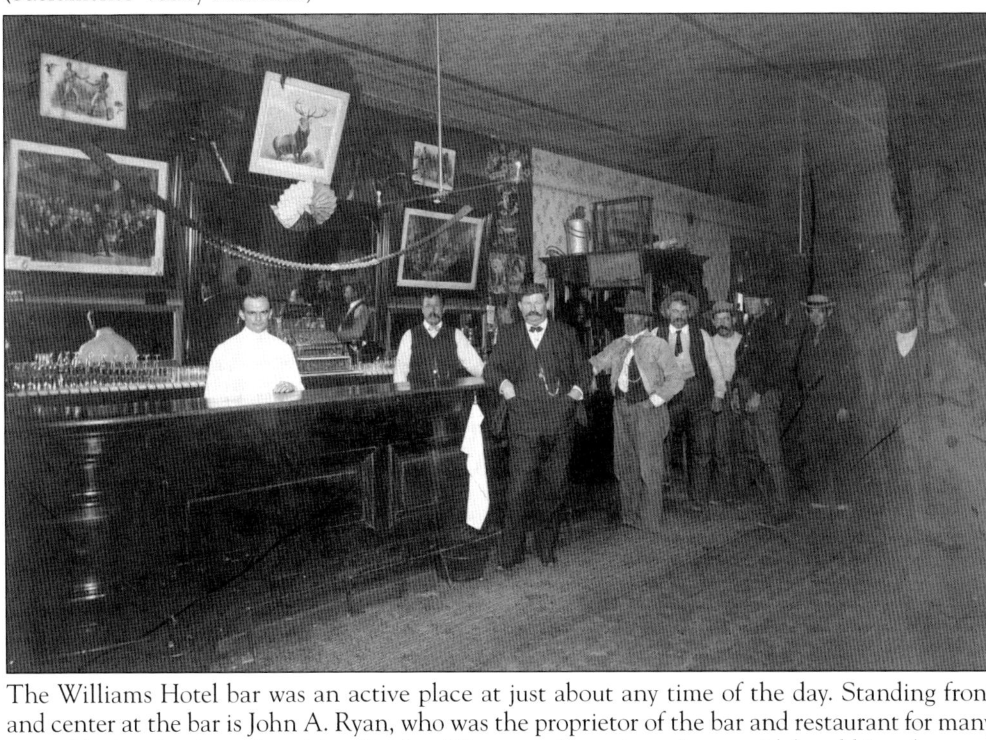

The Williams Hotel bar was an active place at just about any time of the day. Standing front and center at the bar is John A. Ryan, who was the proprietor of the bar and restaurant for many years. Notice the sign advertising Bartlett Water on the register. It was widely sold in saloons to ward off the aftereffects of alcohol. At one time, there were 16 saloons operating in Williams. (Annette Abel La Grande.)

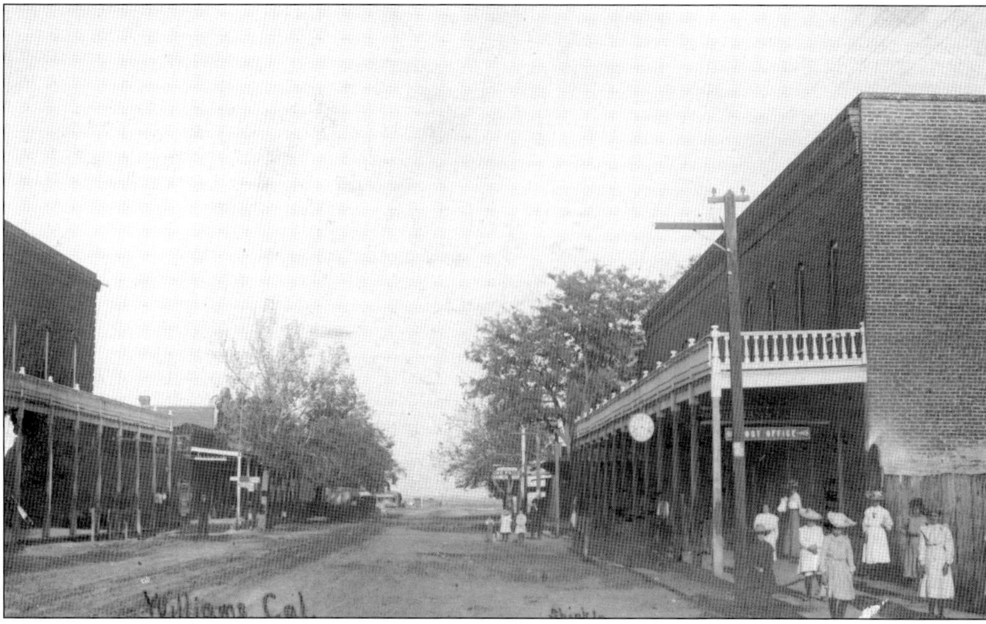

The hotel shown on the right was also home to several businesses throughout the years. At the time of the fire in 1923, an ice cream parlor, real estate office, grain office, millinery shop, post office, newspaper office, and the offices of H.D. Lynch and Marguerita Williams Welch were lost. (Gilbert Allen family.)

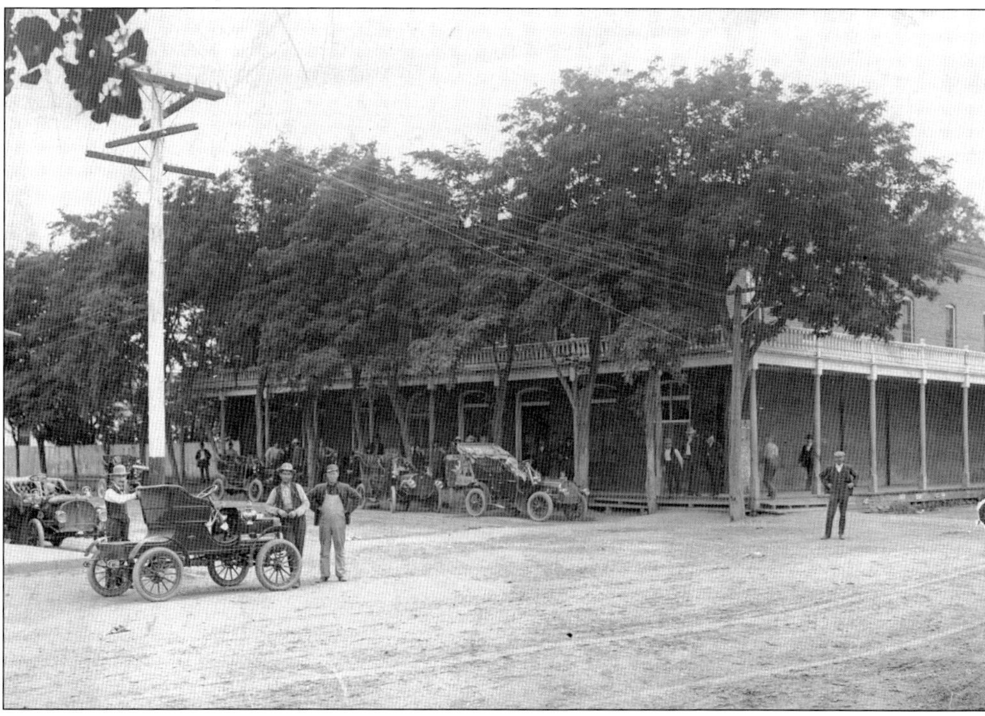

The Williams Hotel was always a hub of activity, as seen in this photograph showing six automobiles parked in front. George Comstock is seen on the far left with his hand on the car. The date of the photograph is unknown. (Gilbert Allen family.)

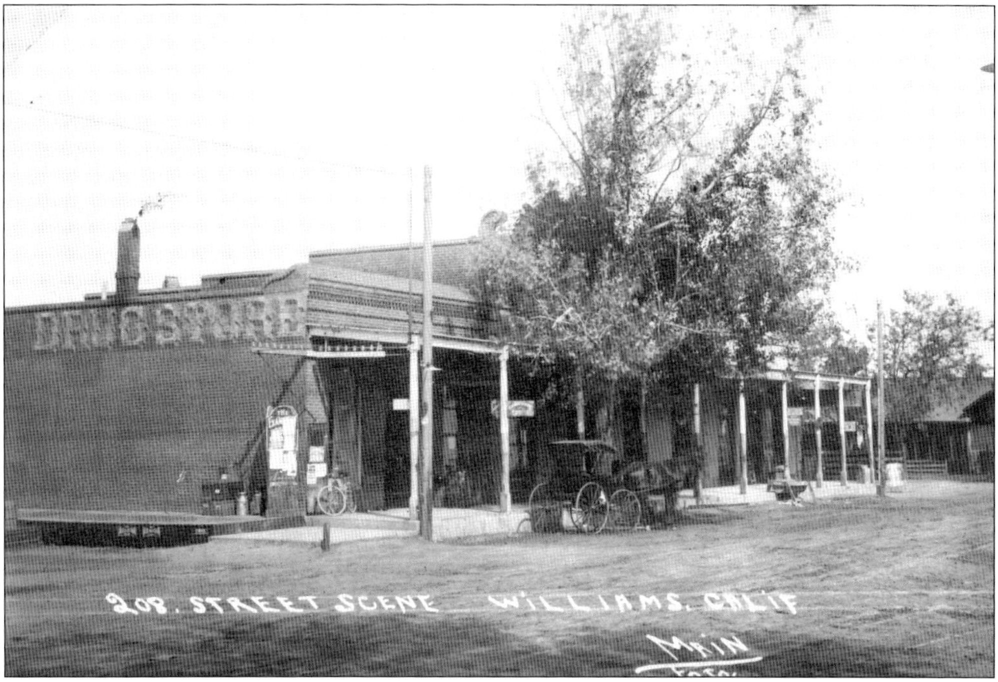

Fouch's Drugstore was founded in 1879 and owned by the Fouch family until 2003, when it was sold to another drugstore family, the Davisons from Colusa. Once threatened by fire in 1919 when the Comstock store burned, it was only saved due to the diligence of the town's citizens, who threw wet sacks onto the building. (Gilbert Allen family.)

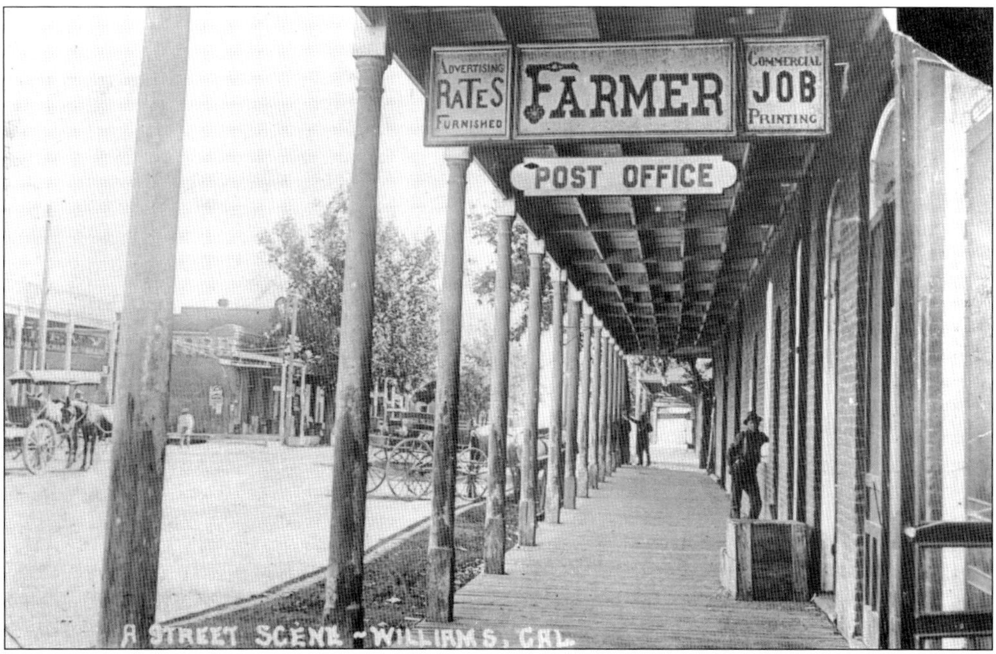

The *Williams Farmer* was first established in 1882 as the *Central News*. After Daryl Callen's death, Lulu Callen leased the business before selling it to Dick Smith and his brother Harry in 1919. They ran it for many years. (Author's collection.)

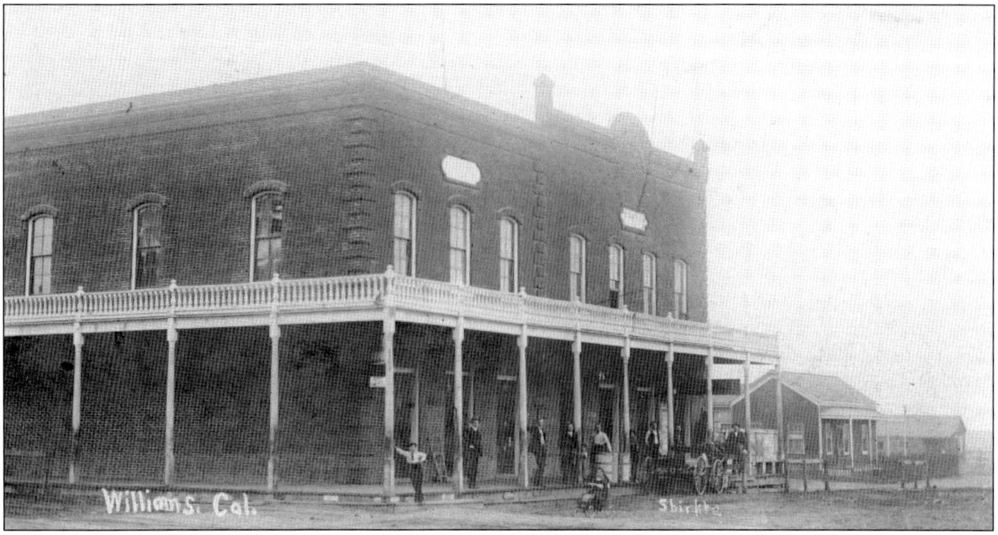

W.H. Williams, J.C. Stovall, and Capt. William Ash built the Odd Fellows Hall Central Lodge No. 229, shown above, in 1877 at a cost of $8,000. It was a meeting place for various lodges and religious denominations and was built from brick clay found on the site of the Williams Grammar School. In 1885, it was enlarged to include an opera hall that was equipped for 500 people to enjoy theatrical performances, dances, and socials. The first motion picture ever presented in Williams was shown on a screen here. Several stores occupied the downstairs, such as Heyman and Sussman, whose first store (where the city hall now stands) was destroyed by fire. The opera hall and lodge building was torn down in 1939 to make way for an up-to-date service station. (Above, Sacramento Valley Museum; below, Jauregui family collection.)

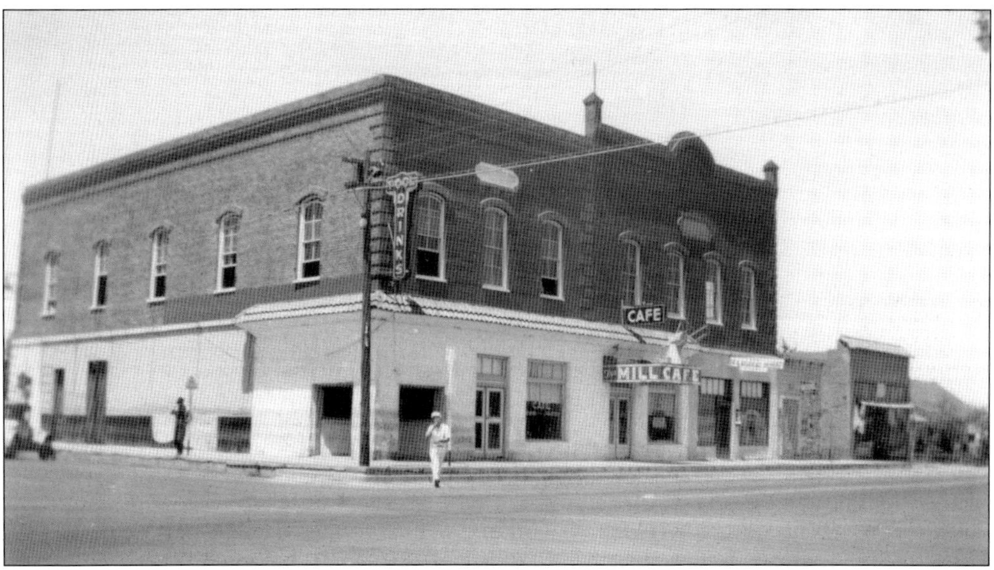

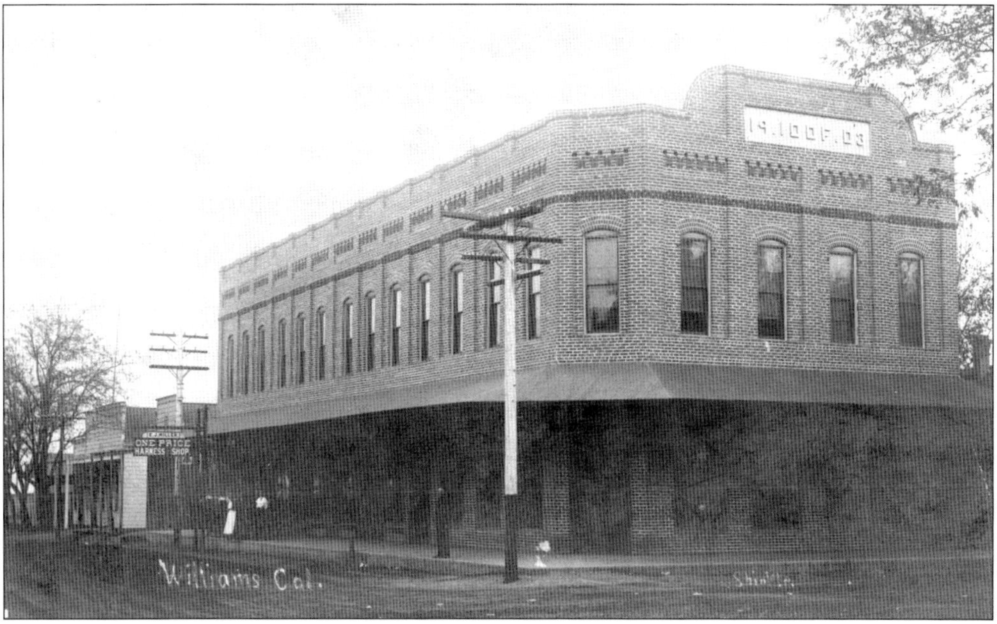

The third home of the Odd Fellows Hall was dedicated on February 19, 1904. By this time, of the seven charter members of the lodge, only Captain Ash and Henry Husted were still active. Billed as the pride of every citizen of Williams, the fellowship of Colusa County Odd Fellows lodges grew to a membership of over 600. It was remodeled in the 1920s with an inside staircase and a kitchen extension on the second floor over the staircase. (Susan Leardini.)

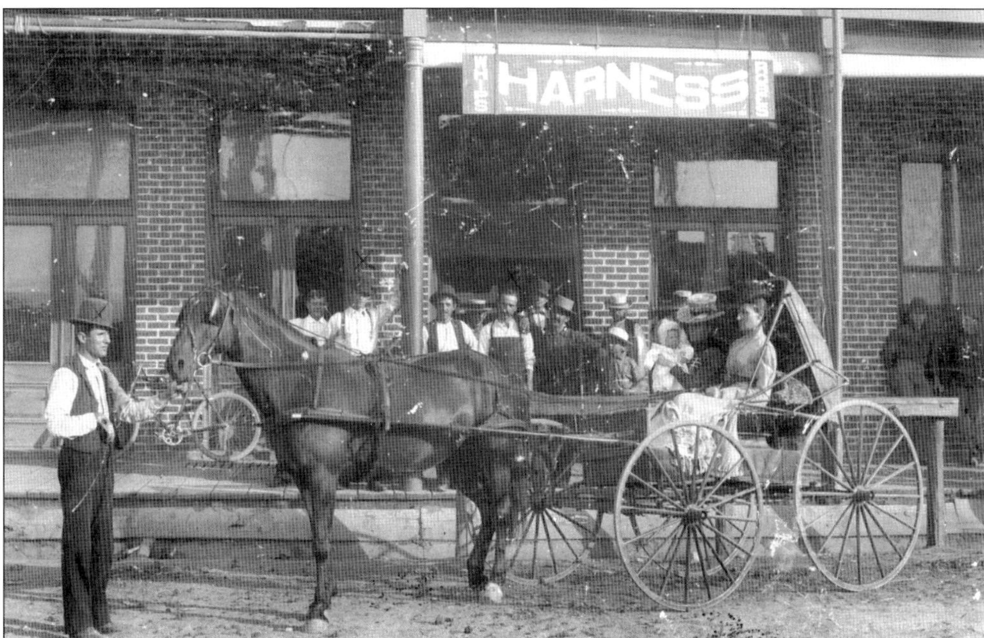

Bob Mayfield is pictured around 1903 or 1904 standing in front of his harness shop, which was located on the ground floor of the Odd Fellows Hall. Pictured from left to right (marked with Xs) are Bob Mayfield, proprietor; Art Mayfield, brother; and Will Mayfield, brother; (seated in buggy) Alice Mayfield, mother; Danley Mayfield, and child. (Sacramento Valley Museum.)

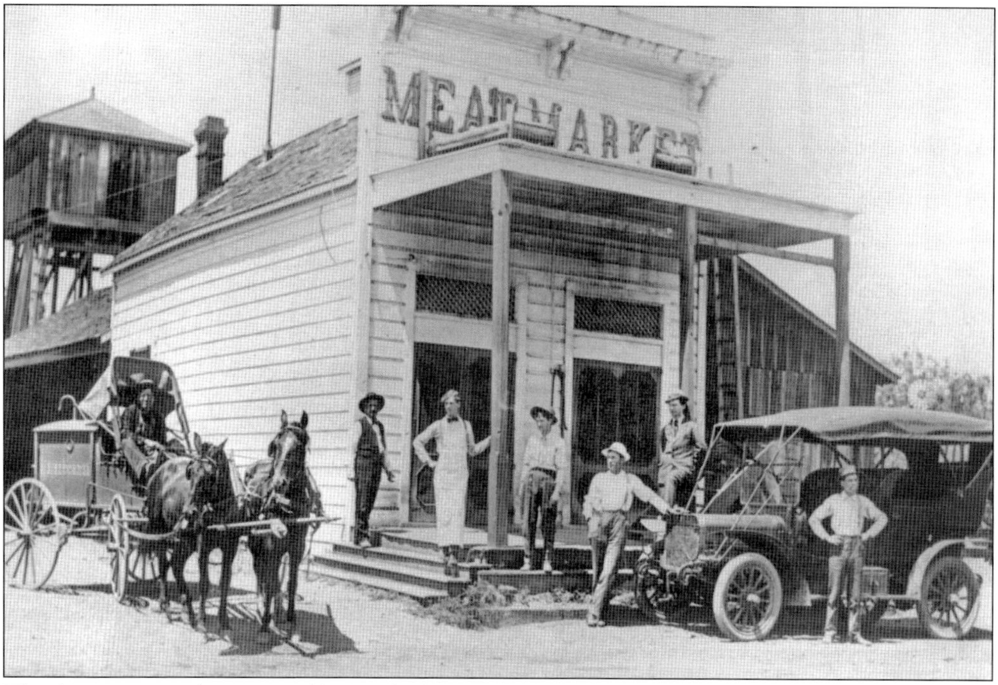

The first meat market originally stood where the city hall is now. J.E. Mitchell of Williams and Henry Houchins of Grimes bought it from Ira Albert Fouch on March 1, 1904. In 1917, it was known as J.E. Mitchell and Son. It was then sold to Harry Lamorree, an employee of the business since 1918. In 1923, Joe Mitchell's son Edgar bought out Lamoree's interest. (Author's collection.)

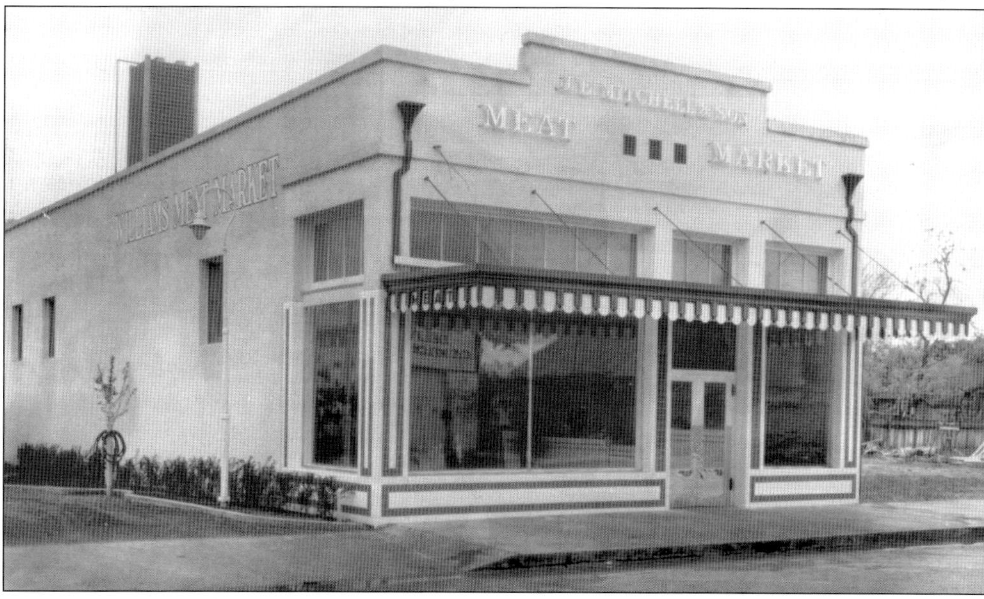

In 1928, Joe Mitchell built a new butcher shop with a cold storage plant, which had the capacity of handling a carload of beef at a time. Built of tile and cement, it was fireproof and up-to-date in every respect. In 1956, under the ownership of John Colman and Herb Murphy, the business closed. Coleman started his career in 1919 under J.E. Mitchell, and Murphy had worked as a butcher for over 50 years. (Sacramento Valley Museum.)

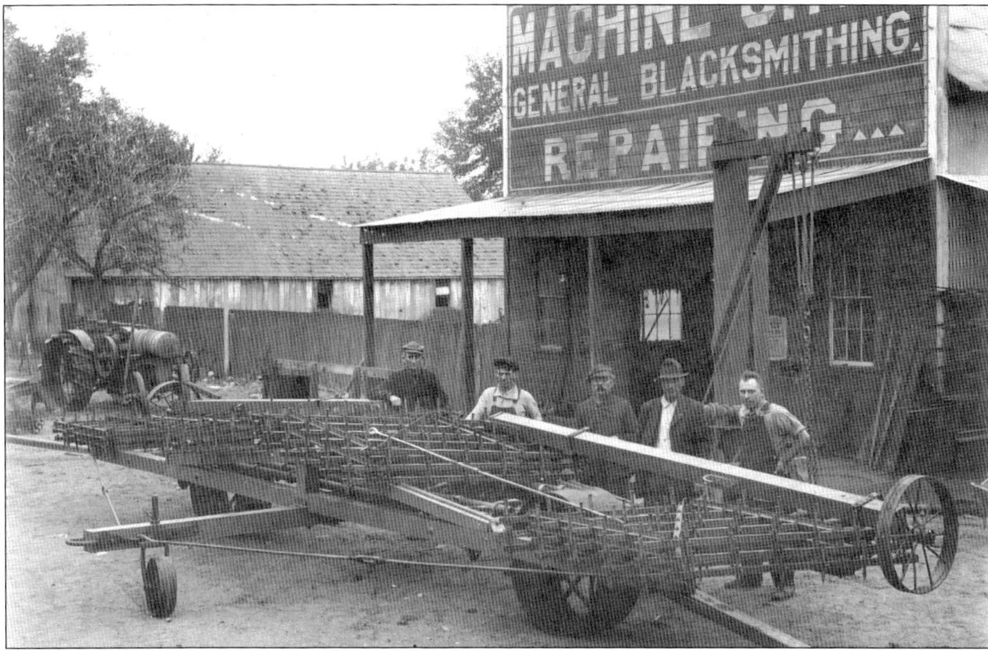

The H.T. Miller and Son Blacksmith Shop was later named the Williams Machine Shop. They once used 13 tons of iron to manufacture 170 harrow sections, which were hitched to a tractor or behind an eight-horse team in order to prepare the fields for planting seed in 1919. (Sacramento Valley Museum.)

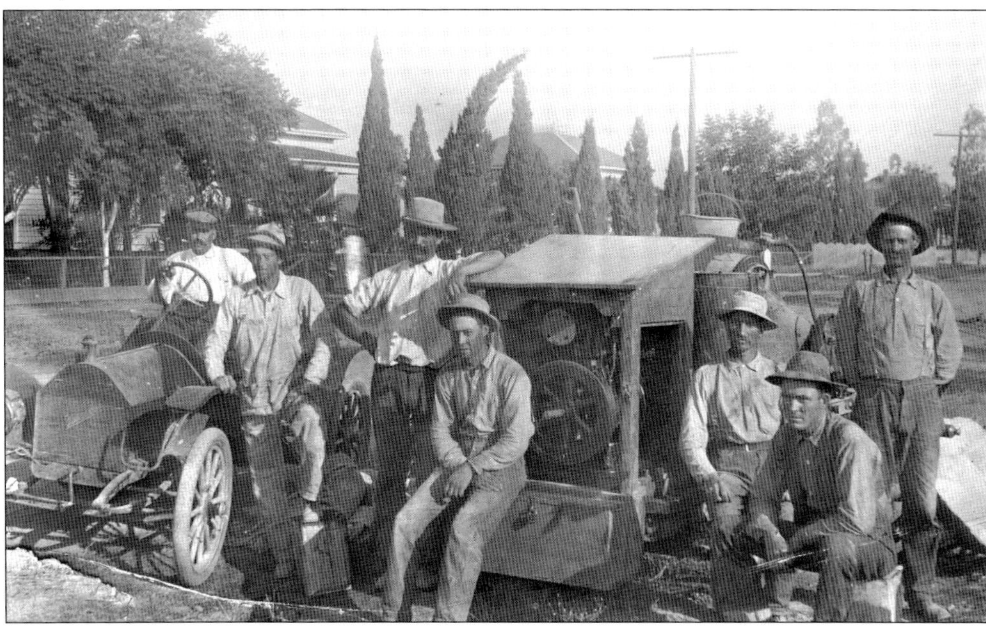

One of the earliest cement businesses in Williams was that of Schaad and Anthony, which installed most of the older sidewalks in town. This 1910 photograph shows Charles Lemuel Schaad in the auto to the left. Sitting on the right is Asa Saunders Anthony, his brother-in-law and partner in the business. The Schaad and Anthony stamp is still visible on many sidewalks, such as in front of Louis Cairo's. (Henry W. Rhoades family.)

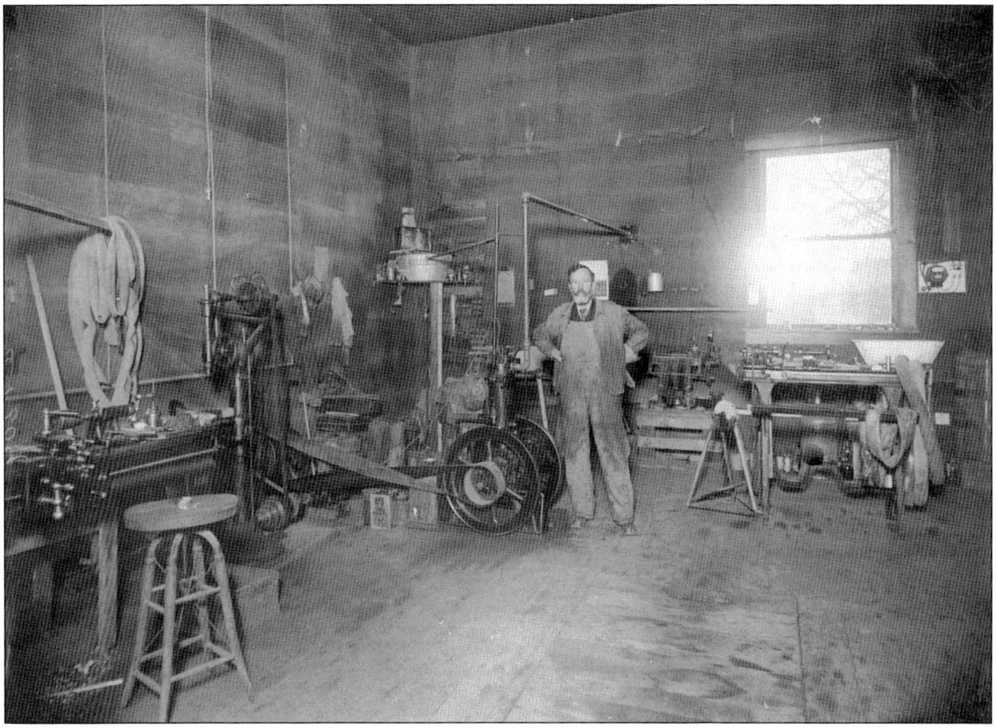

Northey's Garage was established 1900 and operated until 1914. J.L. Kimball then purchased it and operated a tin and plumbing shop. (Sacramento Valley Museum.)

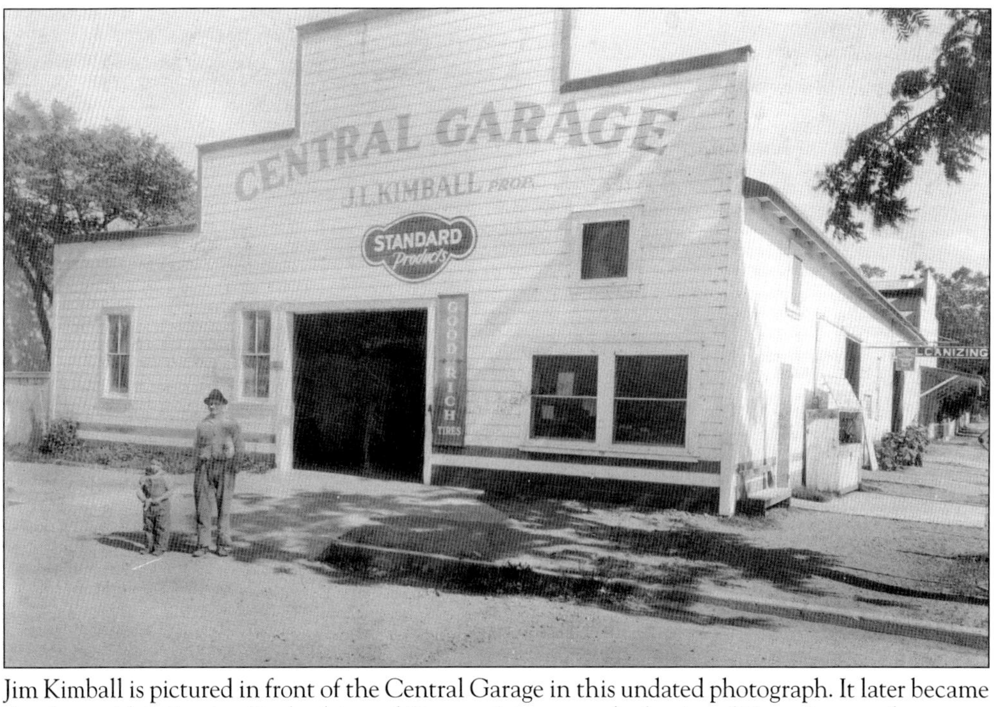

Jim Kimball is pictured in front of the Central Garage in this undated photograph. It later became the Armocido's Pontiac Dealership and Garage. It is currently the site of Napa Auto at the corner of Seventh and F Streets. (Sacramento Valley Museum.)

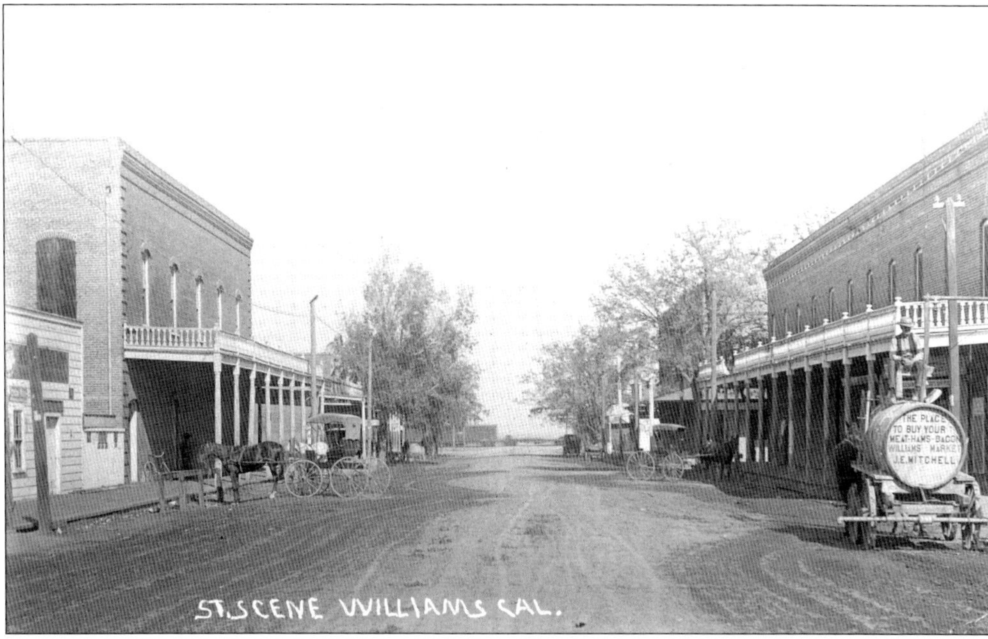

This street scene was taken looking east toward the track. On the left is the opera house, and on the right is the Williams Hotel. The water wagon is advertising Jim Mitchell's meat market with an attendant filling it with water. In the distance are a railcar and flatcar on the track. (Gilbert Allen family.)

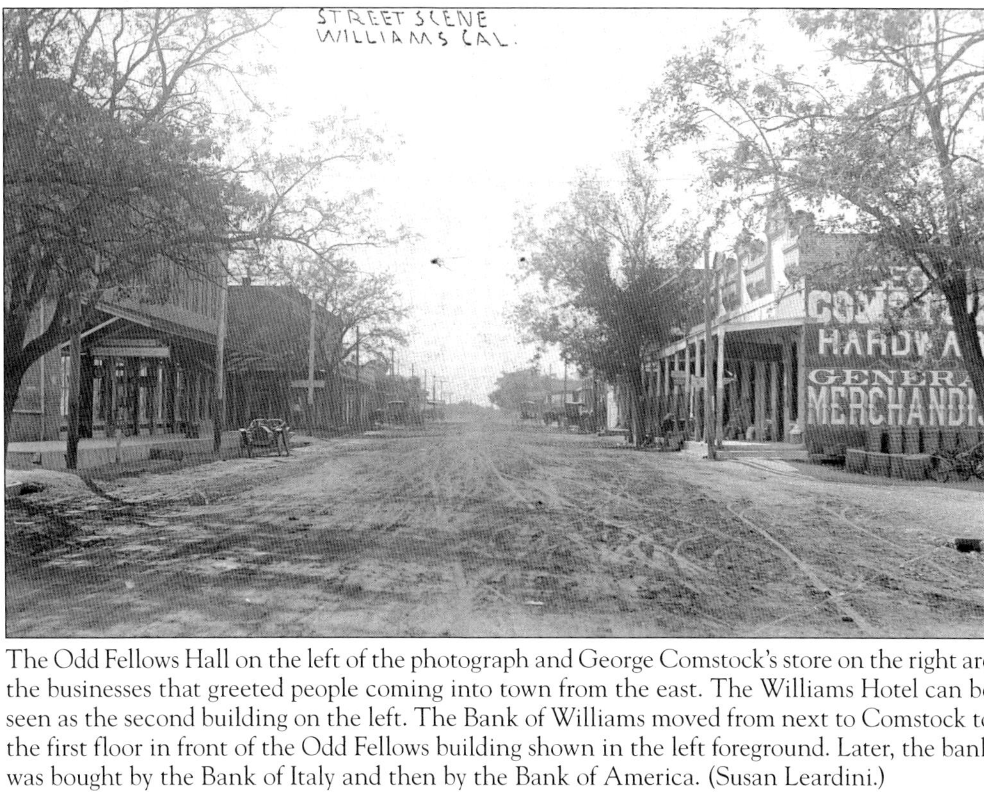

The Odd Fellows Hall on the left of the photograph and George Comstock's store on the right are the businesses that greeted people coming into town from the east. The Williams Hotel can be seen as the second building on the left. The Bank of Williams moved from next to Comstock to the first floor in front of the Odd Fellows building shown in the left foreground. Later, the bank was bought by the Bank of Italy and then by the Bank of America. (Susan Leardini.)

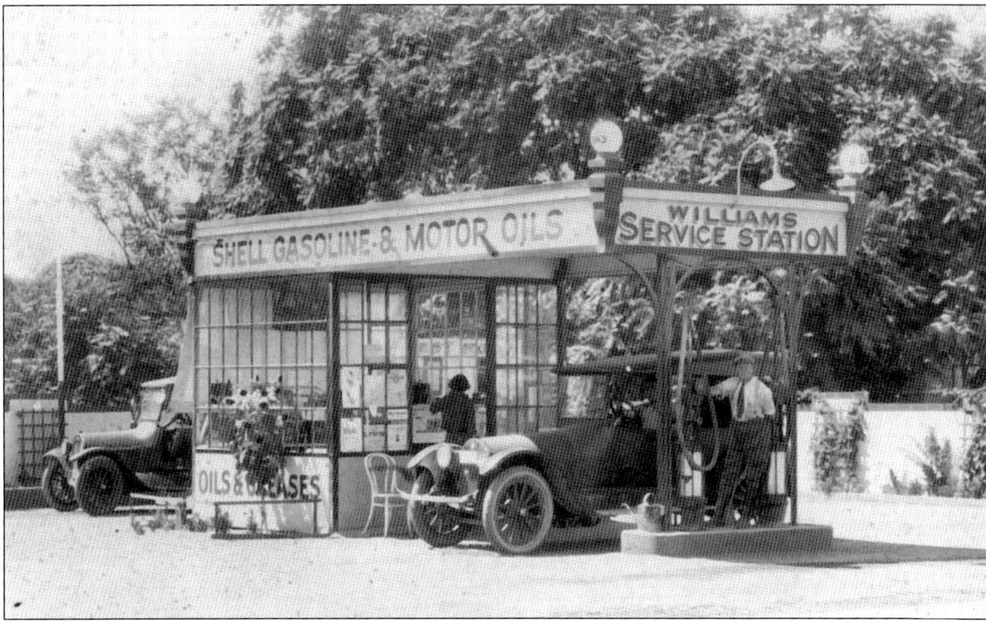

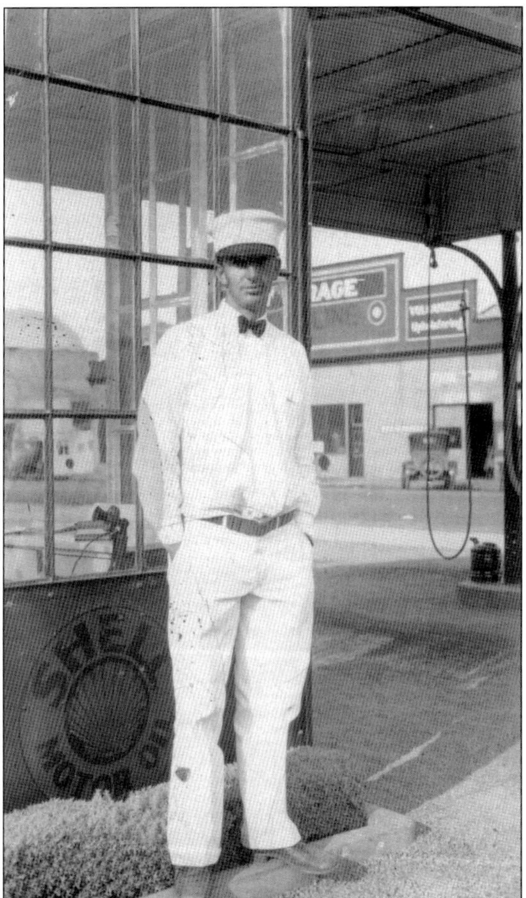

Williams was home to seven service stations located within a two-block section of town at one time. Once the Williams Oil Station, this early photograph shows the first Williams Shell Station, which was located on the north corner of Seventh and F Streets. In 1923, Shell renovated the station and updated the lot. Taken at the same location, a young Elbert "Tuffy" Gassaway is employed by Shell in the early 1930s. Looking over his shoulder is the east side of the block between E and F Streets. (Above, Annette Abel La Grande; left, author's collection.)

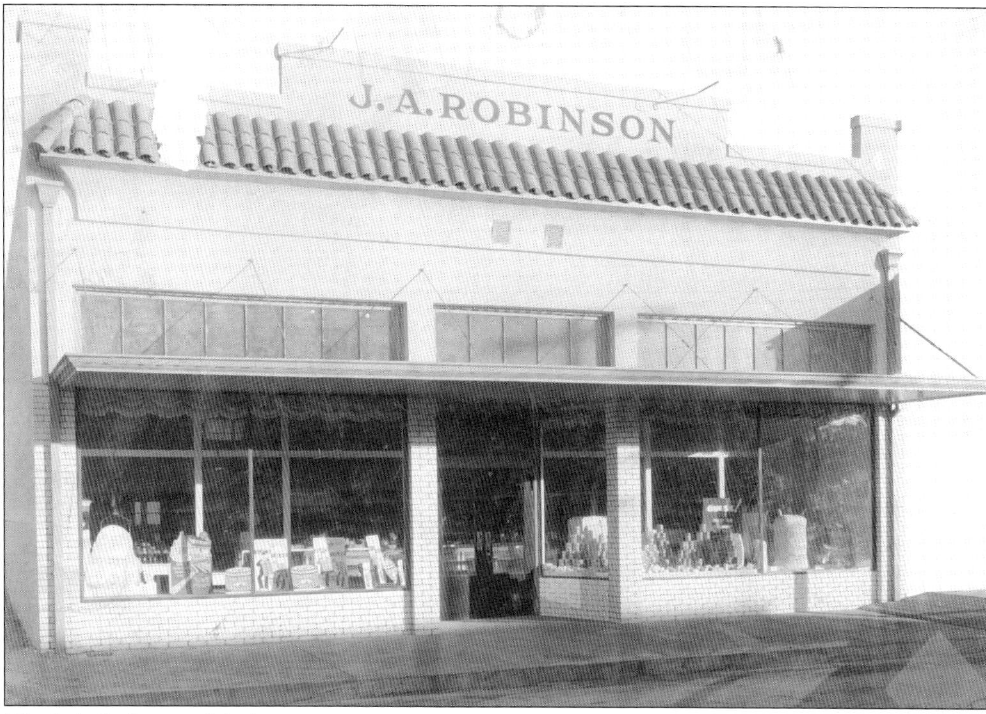

The J.A. Robinson Market was erected in 1931 and operated for many years on E Street. Owner J.A. Robinson was the former manager of the G.H.S. Cash Store and specified that the building would be as fireproof as possible. It was sold to Safeway in 1937, and the store operated under the Safeway logo until the mid-1950s. It still operates as a market today. (Sacramento Valley Museum.)

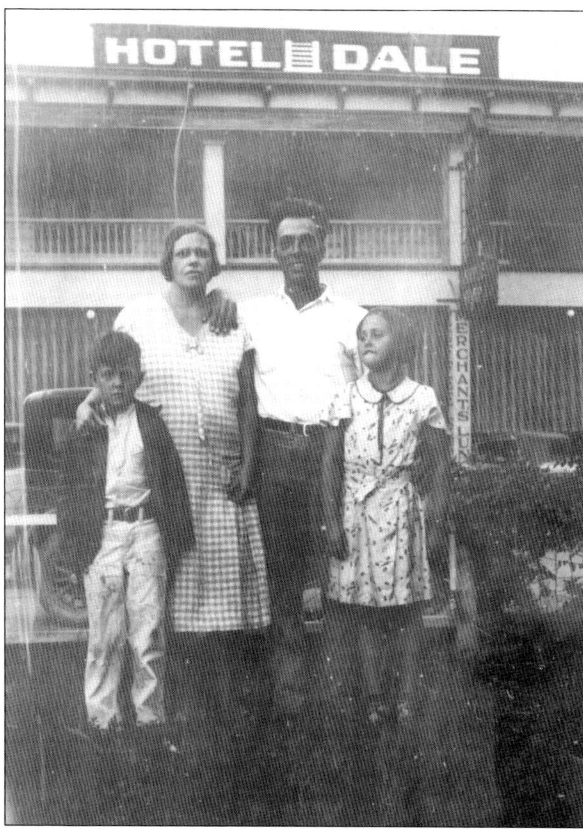

John Sylvia and his family stand in their front yard, which was located across the street from the Hotel Dale just north of the Williams Hardware. The photograph was taken prior to 1932, when the name was changed to the Hotel Gardner. The Hotel Gardner burned in September 1933 after a series of small fires plagued the business. Shown in this photograph are John and Vera Silva with their son Richard and daughter Shirley Silva Jauregui. (Jauregui family collection.)

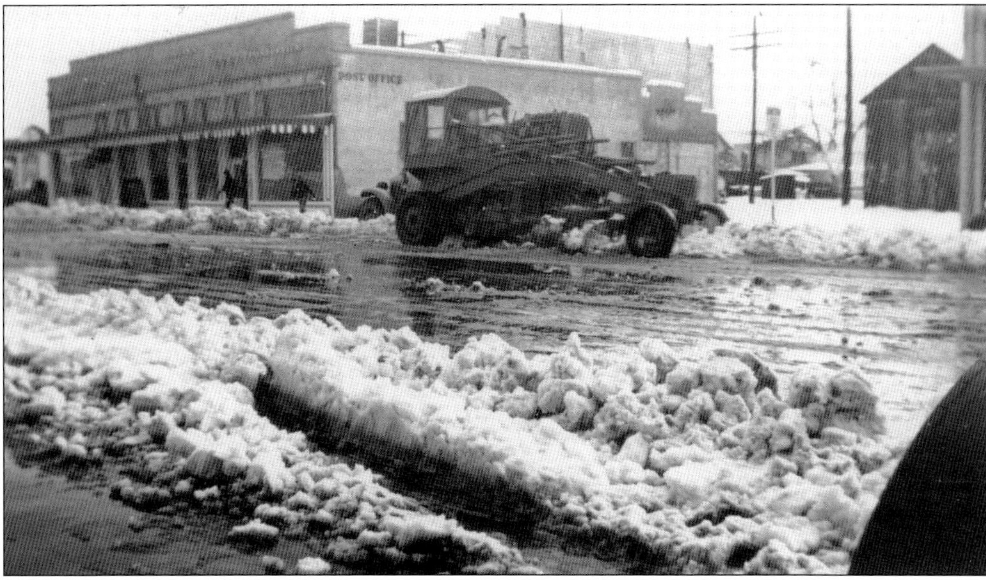

Snow in Williams does not occur often, but when it does, it is an exciting event. In January 1937, it snowed for two days and left 14–15 inches of white flakes, the most ever recorded since 1875. Schools were closed, roads were impassable, barns and buildings collapsed, and there was jubilation from the youngsters. Shown here are the Williams Post Office, Harry Harlan's Menswear, Mitchell's meat market, and the Masonic Hall in the background. (Jauregui family collection.)

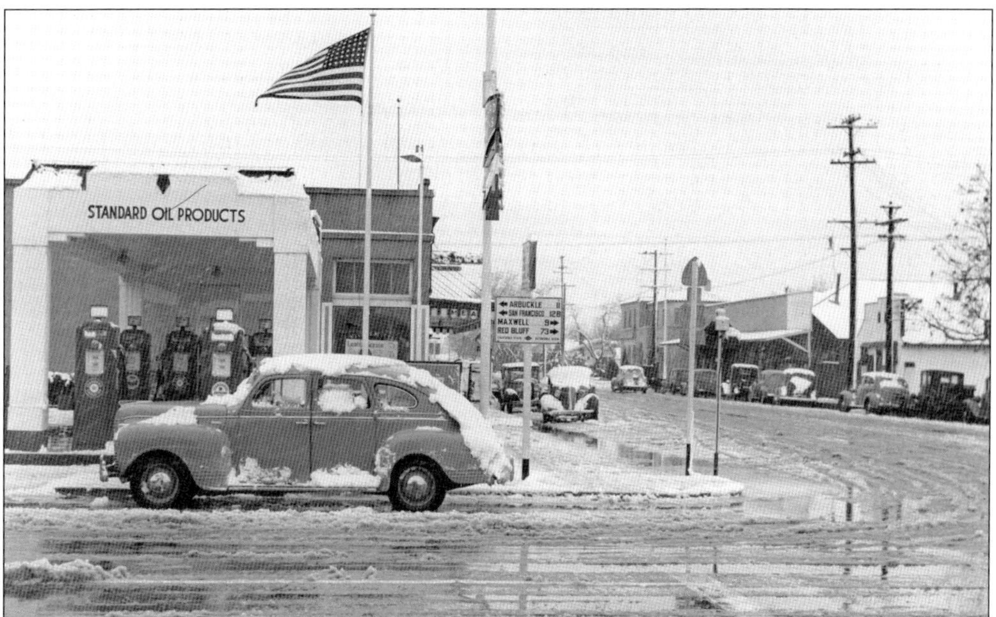

Looking westward from the intersection of Seventh and E Streets just as the snow was beginning to fall, the Standard Station and the meat market are on the left side. On the right are Doctor Marsh's office, the library, and a garage. City hall is in the background. (Abernathy family collection.)

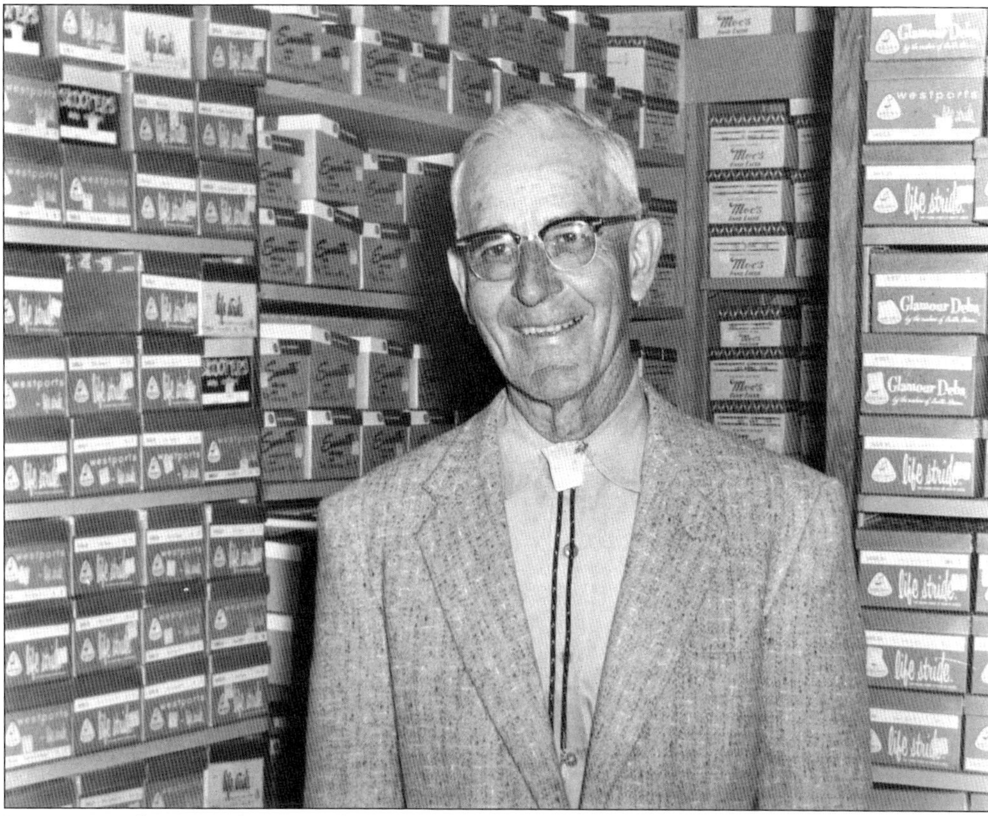

Everett Worsley started out as a harness maker and purchased the moving picture businesses at the Williams and Maxwell Opera Houses in 1913. In Williams, he bought out E.L. Miller and later founded the Worsley's Department Store in 1914. (Henry W. Rhoades family.)

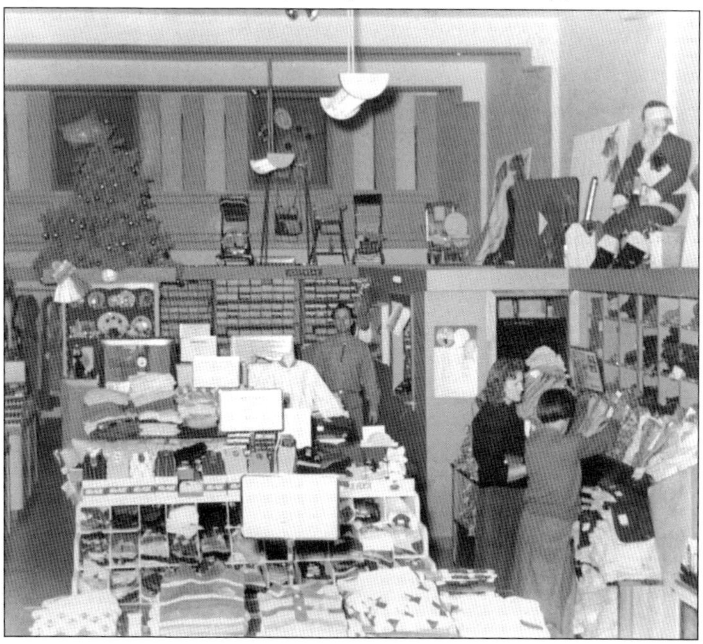

The Worsley business then went to his son Raymond and Raymond's wife, Shirley. Shown is the interior of the Williams store around the late 1950s. Raymond Worsley is pictured facing the camera, and the clerk is waiting on Stella Endeman. Worsley's carried the necessities as well as the luxury items. Later, they opened the Boat Fair and sold ski boats as well as accessories. Eventually, Worsley's Department Store expanded to Colusa. (Henry W. Rhoades family.)

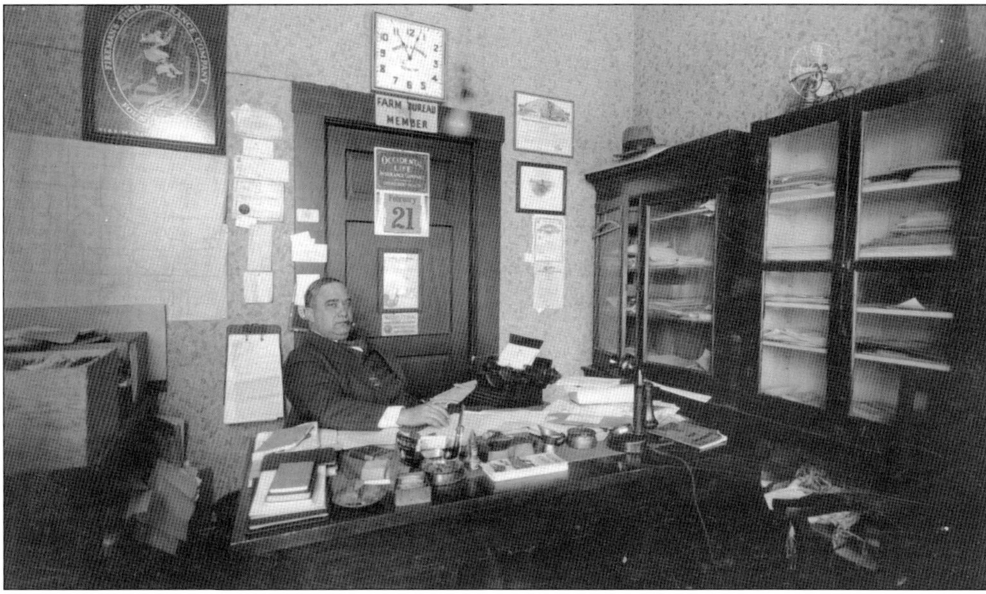

One of the leading businessmen of Williams was Henry "Hank" Atwood. He was an insurance salesman and was also the local real estate agent. Never without his cigar, Atwood was a very big part of the advancement of Williams. Pictured in his office in 1936, he was appointed as city judge of Williams, previously handled by the city clerk. He continued his business for over 30 years. (Jone Smith.)

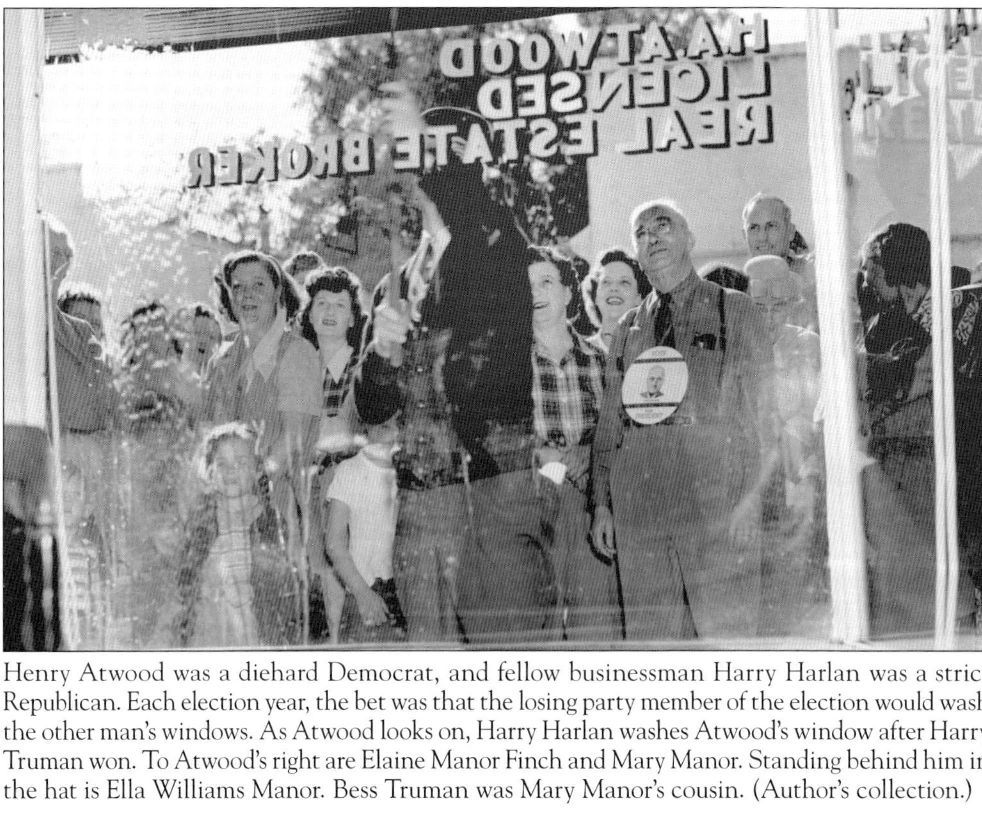

Henry Atwood was a diehard Democrat, and fellow businessman Harry Harlan was a strict Republican. Each election year, the bet was that the losing party member of the election would wash the other man's windows. As Atwood looks on, Harry Harlan washes Atwood's window after Harry Truman won. To Atwood's right are Elaine Manor Finch and Mary Manor. Standing behind him in the hat is Ella Williams Manor. Bess Truman was Mary Manor's cousin. (Author's collection.)

The C and S Service Station and Auto Park was the first motel in Williams. It was built in 1927 and owned and operated by Herbert Christy and his son Donn. The auto park started with five cottages and then expanded to occupy five lots. They installed the first car wash of the area, and the father and son team was also in the business of appliance sales and repairs, beginning in 1928. (Author's collection.)

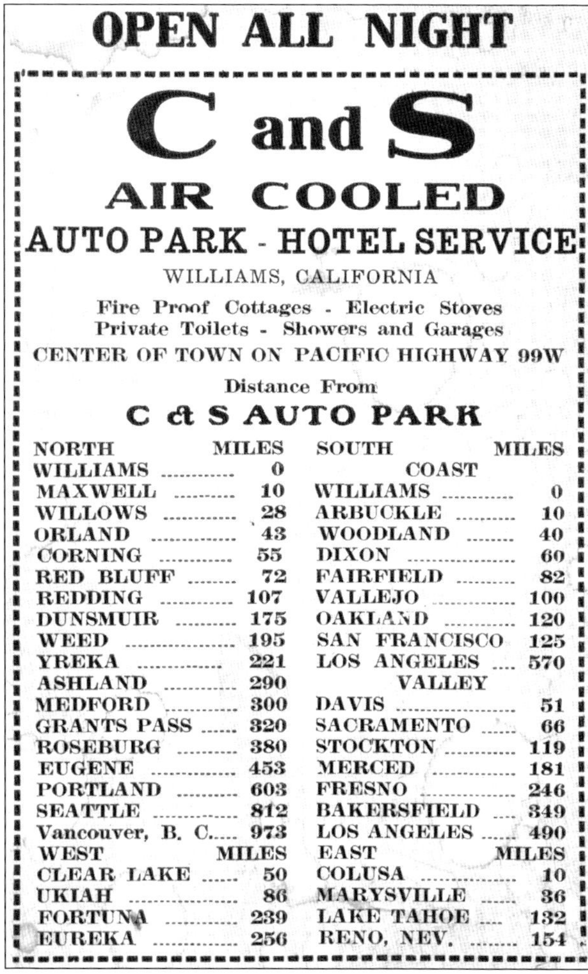

OPEN ALL NIGHT

C and S

AIR COOLED

AUTO PARK - HOTEL SERVICE

WILLIAMS, CALIFORNIA

Fire Proof Cottages - Electric Stoves
Private Toilets - Showers and Garages

CENTER OF TOWN ON PACIFIC HIGHWAY 99W

Distance From

C & S AUTO PARK

NORTH	MILES	SOUTH	MILES
		COAST	
WILLIAMS	0	WILLIAMS	0
MAXWELL	10	ARBUCKLE	10
WILLOWS	28	WOODLAND	40
ORLAND	43	DIXON	60
CORNING	55	FAIRFIELD	82
RED BLUFF	72	VALLEJO	100
REDDING	107	OAKLAND	120
DUNSMUIR	175	SAN FRANCISCO	125
WEED	195	LOS ANGELES	570
YREKA	221		
ASHLAND	290	VALLEY	
MEDFORD	300	DAVIS	51
GRANTS PASS	320	SACRAMENTO	66
ROSEBURG	380	STOCKTON	119
EUGENE	453	MERCED	181
PORTLAND	603	FRESNO	246
SEATTLE	812	BAKERSFIELD	349
Vancouver, B. C.	973	LOS ANGELES	490
WEST	MILES	EAST	MILES
CLEAR LAKE	50	COLUSA	10
UKIAH	86	MARYSVILLE	36
FORTUNA	239	LAKE TAHOE	132
EUREKA	256	RENO, NEV.	154

This street scene shows the front of the Williams Theatre. The building was three stories with a theater and a grocery store on the first floor, a card room on the second floor, and a dance hall on the third floor. The theater was located on the northwest corner of Seventh and F Streets and burned in 1958. (Jauregui family collection.)

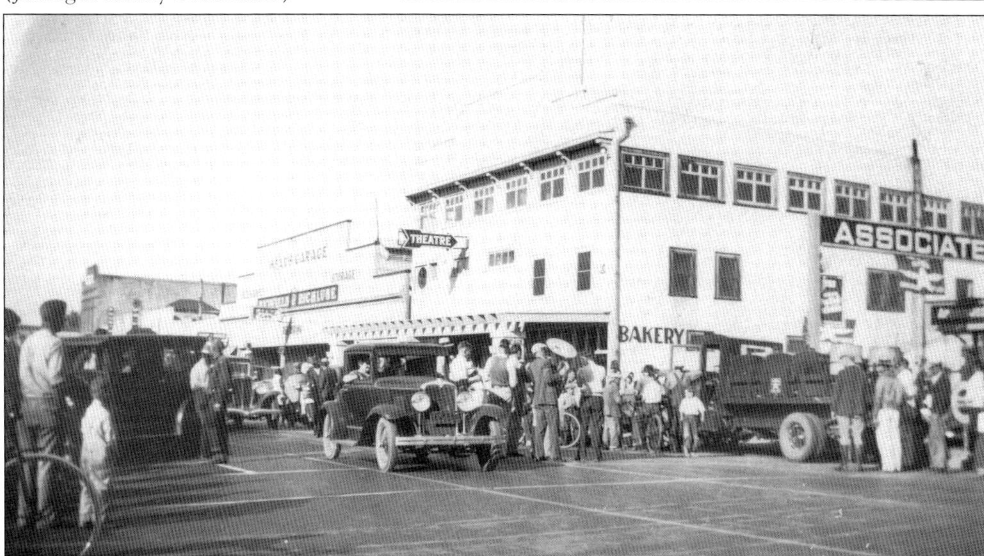

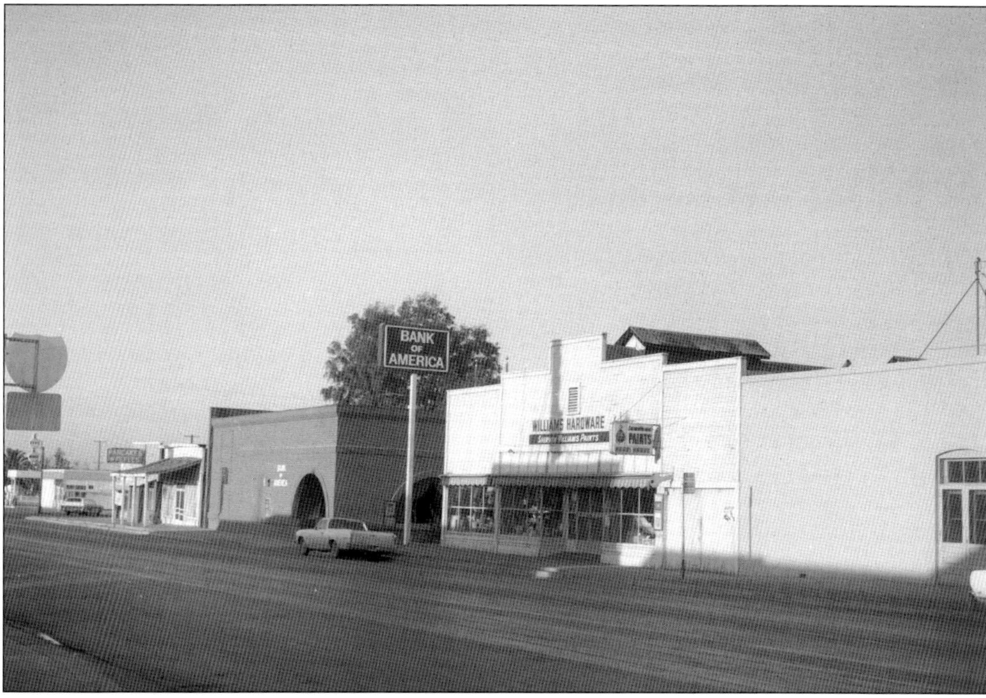

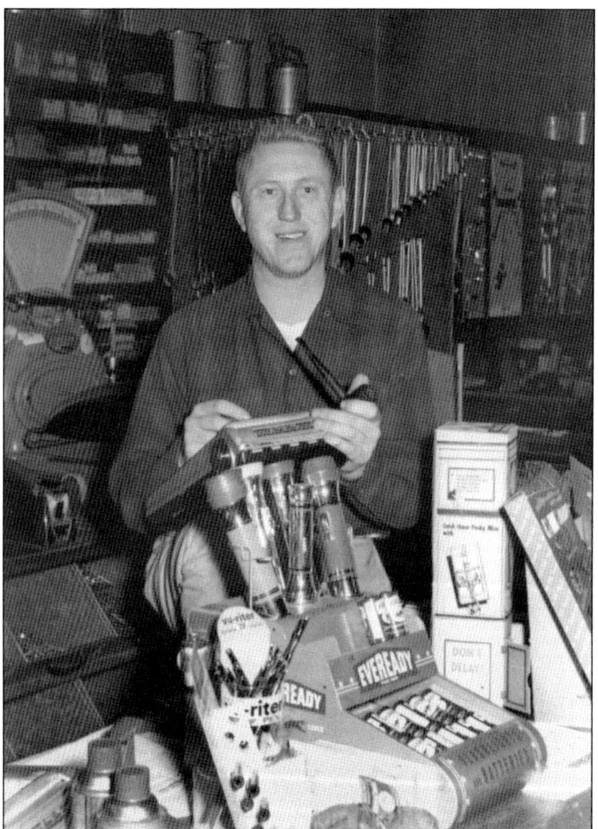

Williams Hardware has been in business for over 100 years and has changed hands several times. In June 1923, the store was operated under George Comstock until Elbert Brim and Frank Wallace purchased it, and the name changed to Williams Hardware. In 1946, Elbert Brim sold the business to Joe Azevedo and Hal Stober, both former employees of a hardware wholesale in Sacramento. Elbert Brim retained ownership of the building for a while, staying to help introduce the two new men to the community. Eventually, Azevedo left, and Hal and his wife, Rosalie, ran the store for over 40 years. "Happy Hal your Hardware Pal" made sure that if he did not have it in stock, he would "have it for you on Friday." The Stobers were supporters of the young people of Williams and employed many high school students throughout their ownership and were well thought of in the community. (Both, Henry W. Rhoades family.)

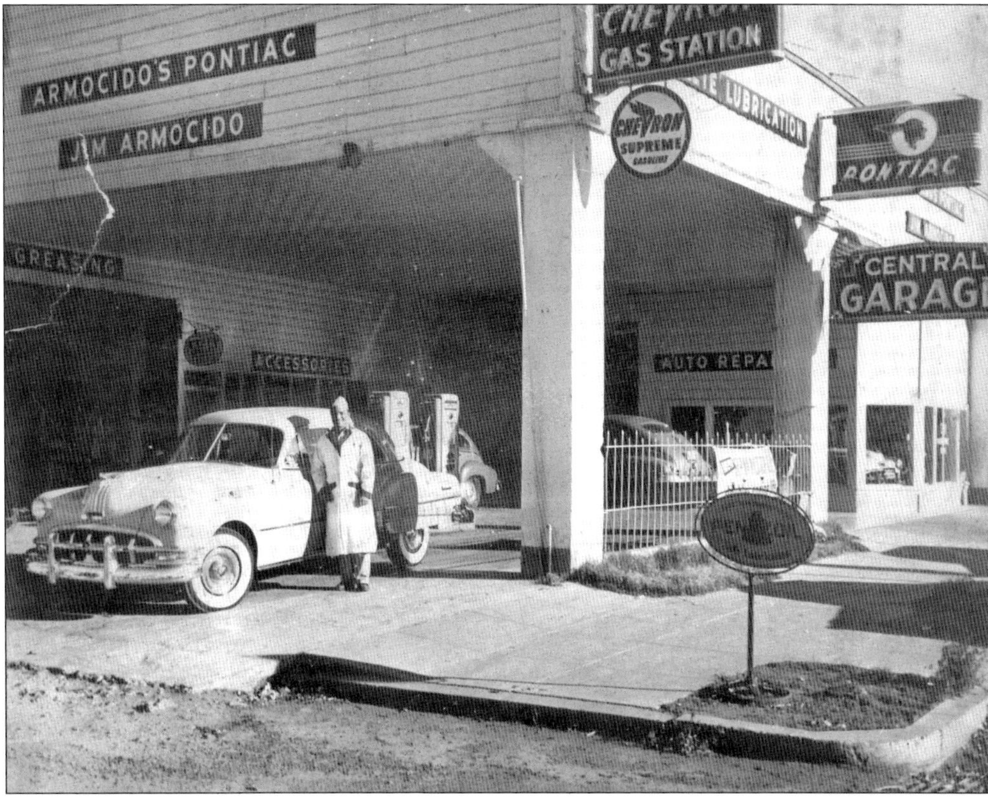

Armocido's Pontiac opened in 1947 and served people from Williams and throughout Northern California until 1969. Owners Jim Armocido and his wife, Joanne, were very active in the community and were diehard Giants fans. Jim sponsored bowling teams and managed baseball teams starting in 1950 and was a strong supporter of the Williams High School Yellow Jackets. Known to bend over backwards to help anyone, he was very proud to be a part of Williams. In 1958, he bought the Texaco Station across Highway 99 and could often be seen scurrying back and forth, dodging traffic to wait on customers at both businesses. (Above, Dick Armocido; right, Henry W. Rhoades family.)

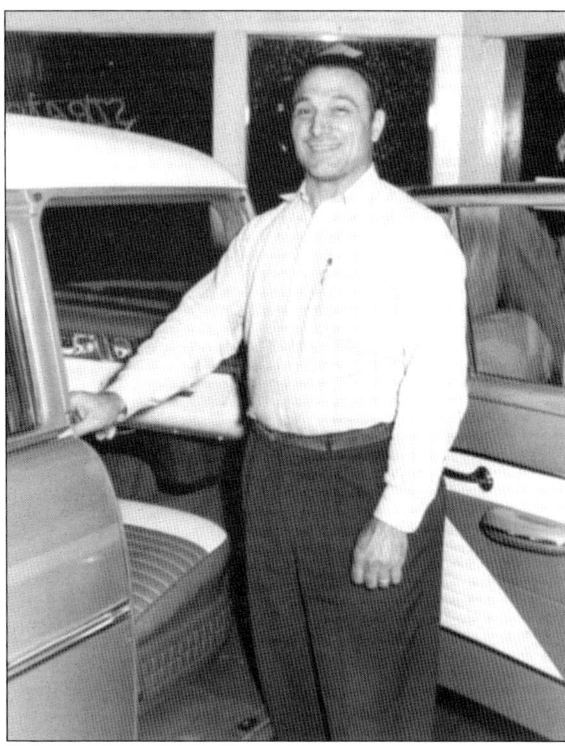

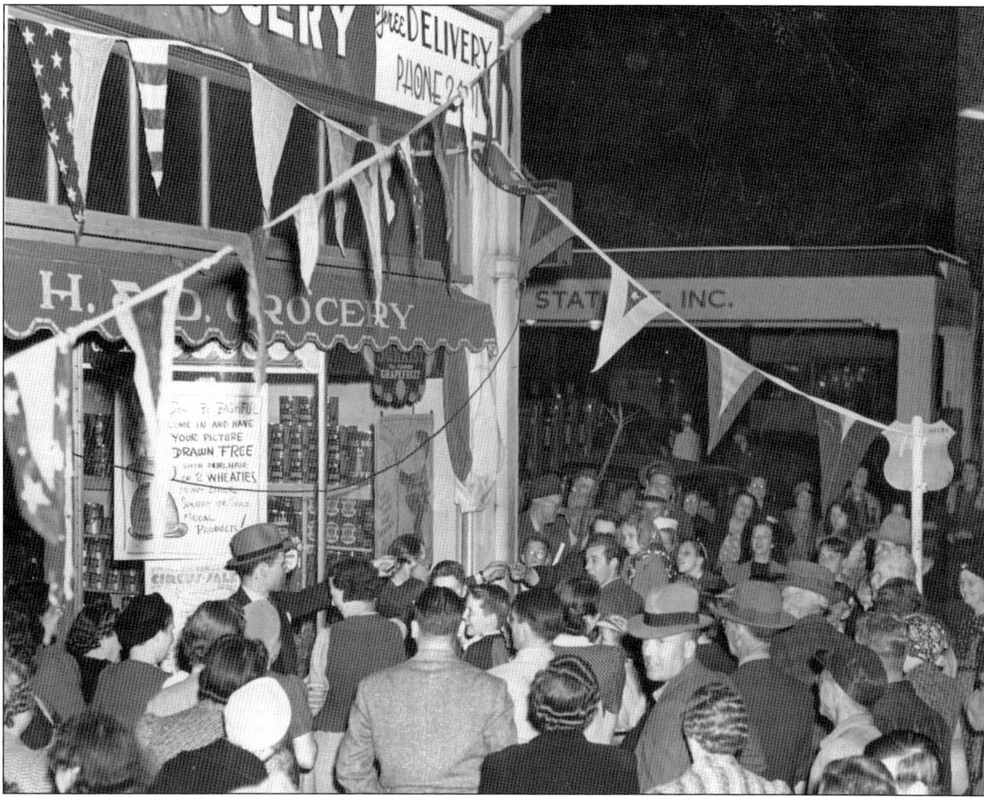

In 1936, a grand opening celebration was held for the new H&D Grocery Store in downtown Williams. Occupying the north corner of the Masonic Hall, the celebration lasted into the night. Owned by Donald M. Nason and Wayne F. Grishaber, the business eventually needed to expand. Before long, the storefront to the south of them became available, and the new and improved H&D was born. The interior of the store was well stocked and had the services of a full butcher shop. After Donald's death, his wife, Elza, continued with the business until the early 1960s, when she sold her interest to Wayne Grishaber. (Above, Wanda Bowen; below, Abernathy family collection.)

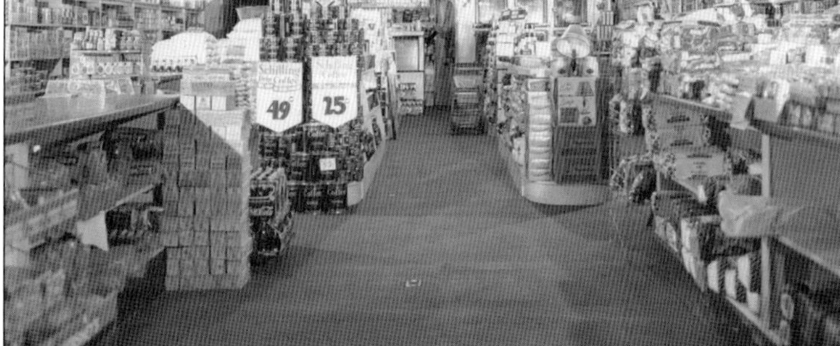

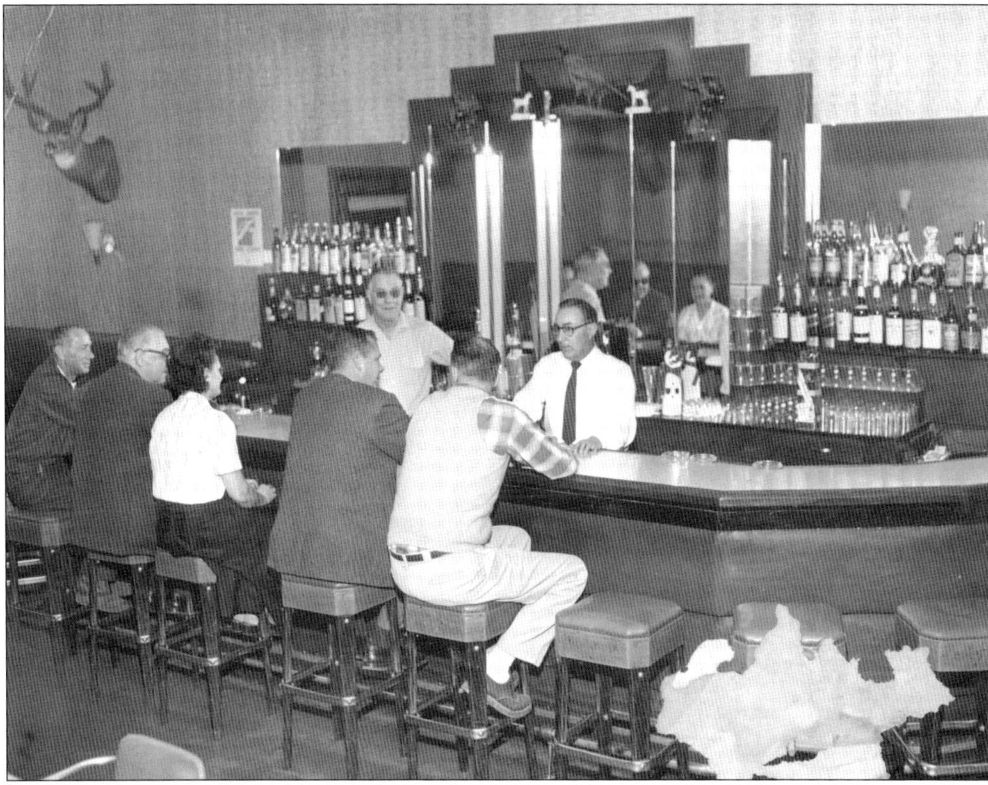

Louis Cairo's Restaurant, labeled the "Talk of the Valley," was founded in 1945. Louis, along with partner John Pitalo, bought Wilson's Bar. Under the law at the time, in order to get a liquor license, meals had to be served. In order to comply with the new law, the owners started serving dinners and then added lunches in response to demand. The business is still in operation today. Louis (in the white shirt and tie) is pictured doing what he did best: pouring the libation and chatting with customers. Louis was famous for remembering everyone's name once they met, the secret to his success. (Louis Cairo family.)

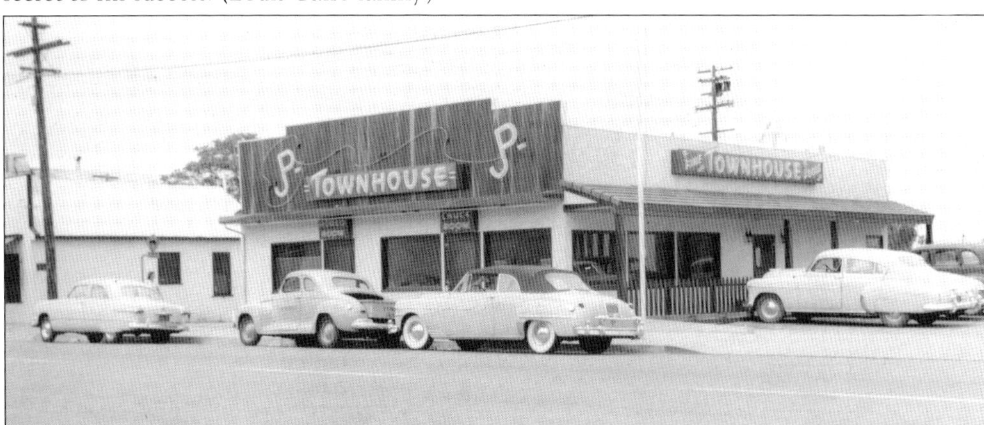

After dissolving the partnership with Louis Cairo in 1949, John Pitalo opened the Townhouse. The restaurant and bar had a Western theme and was designed by the owner. John's wife, "Babe," was in charge of the cocktail lounge. The business had its grand opening in May 1951 and entertained a packed house. (Diane Lucas.)

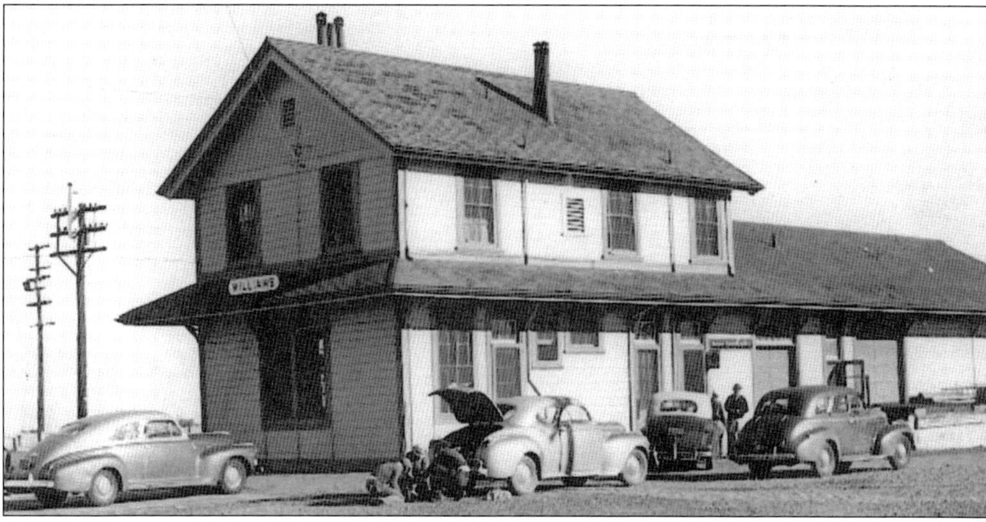

The Williams Depot was one of the busiest places in Northern California for many years. From August 1, 1926, to August 1, 1927, 1,540 carloads of freight were handled in Williams. Not including carloads, lots averaged 100–125 tons a month. The railroad deemed Williams's location ideal for receiving and shipping freight. The depot was also the receiving point for the cars sold at Armocido's Pontiac in Williams. Cars were off-loaded and then driven the one block to the dealership at the corner of Seventh and F Streets. (Dick Armocido.)

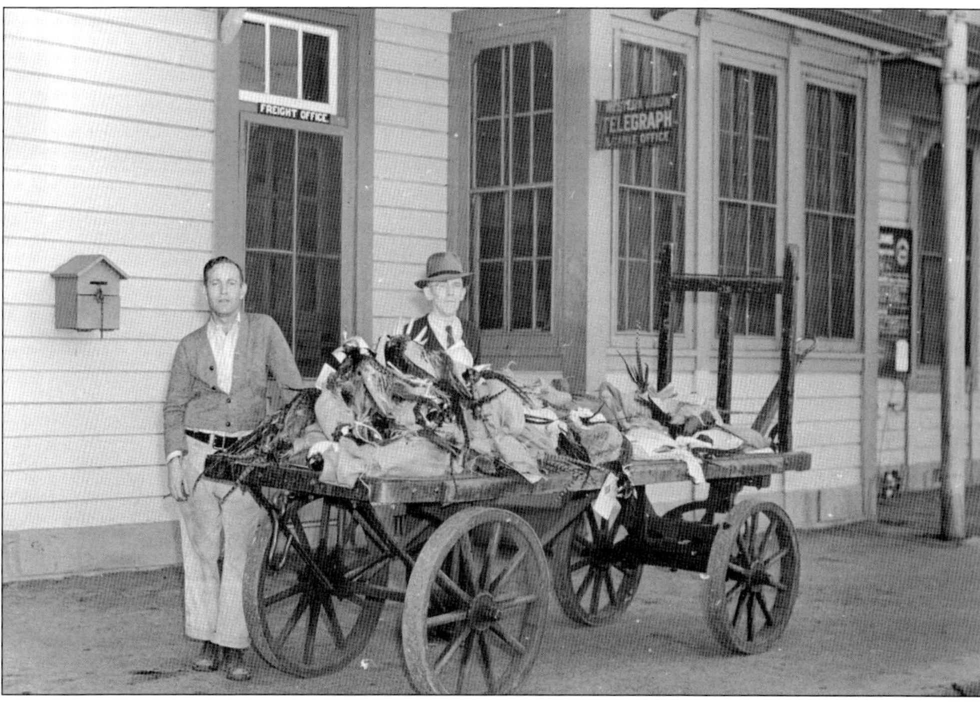

In one week in 1928, Williams handled 25 car lots, not including 28 cars of cantaloupes, four cars of lumber, three cars of cement, six cars of crushed rock and gravel, one car of structural steel used in constructing the Cache Creek Bridge, one carload of machinery for the Williams steam laundry, one car of Bartlett water leaving for San Francisco, two cars of grain, and seven cars of stock, including a car of mules bound for Hawaii. (Sacramento Valley Museum.)

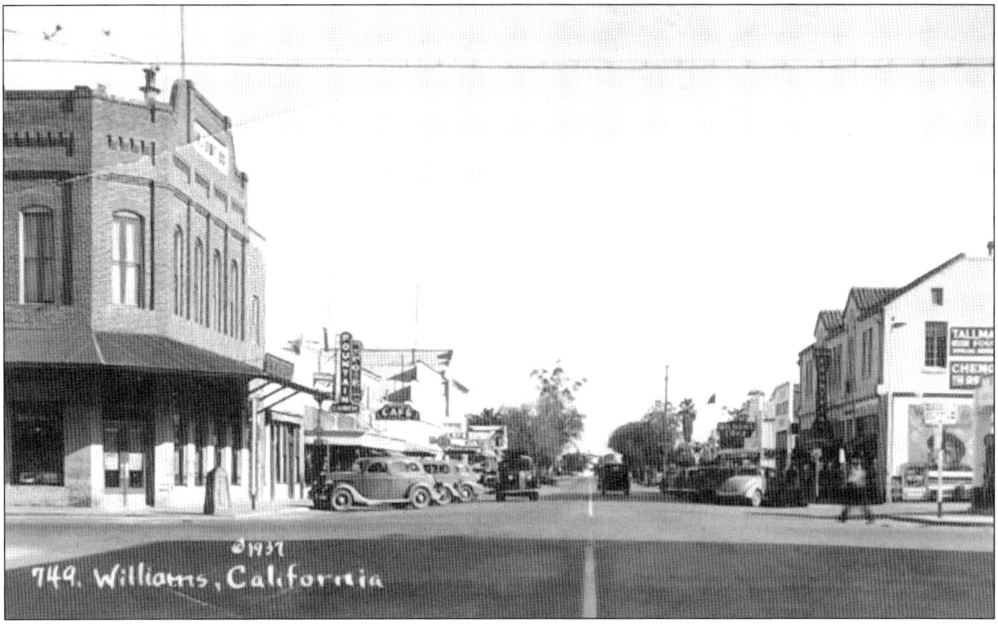

In this photograph, the parking is at a diagonal, and the Masonic Hall's bottom businesses are Chenoweth's Red and White Grocery at the north end and Irene Tallman's café on the south. The exact date of the photograph is unknown, but it is known that the parking was changed to parallel in 1939 by order of the California Highway Department. (Bill Barrett.)

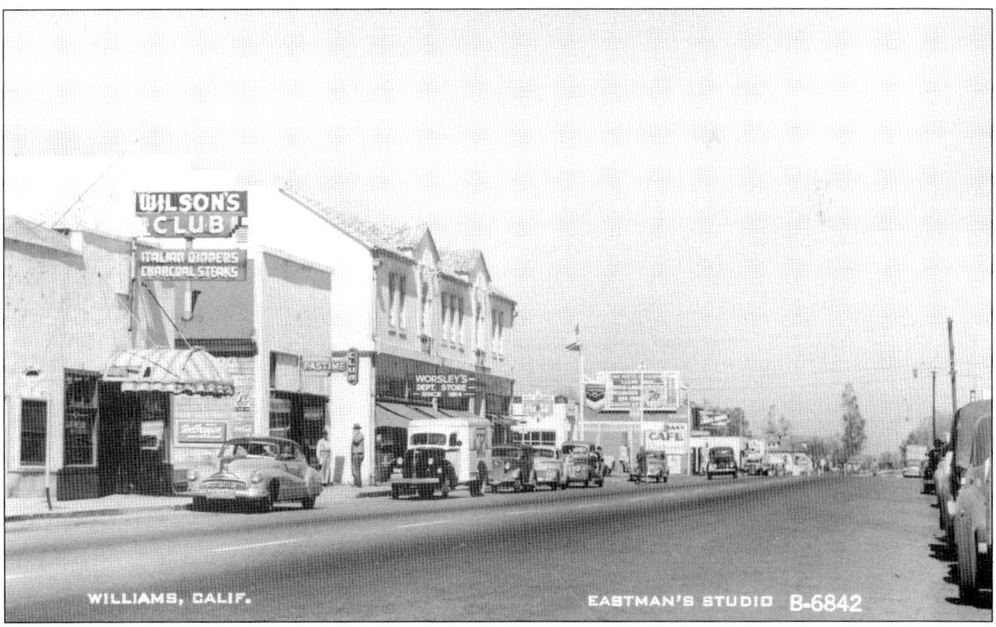

The business block on the west side of Seventh Street included Wilson's Club (Louis Cairo's), the Pastime Club, and Worsley's Department Store occupying the lower part of the Masonic Hall along with H&D Grocery. The Standard Station was on the corner. On the next block were the Union Station, Crossroads Bar, and C and S Tire Service with C and S Auto Park at the far end. (Mike Ferraiuolo.)

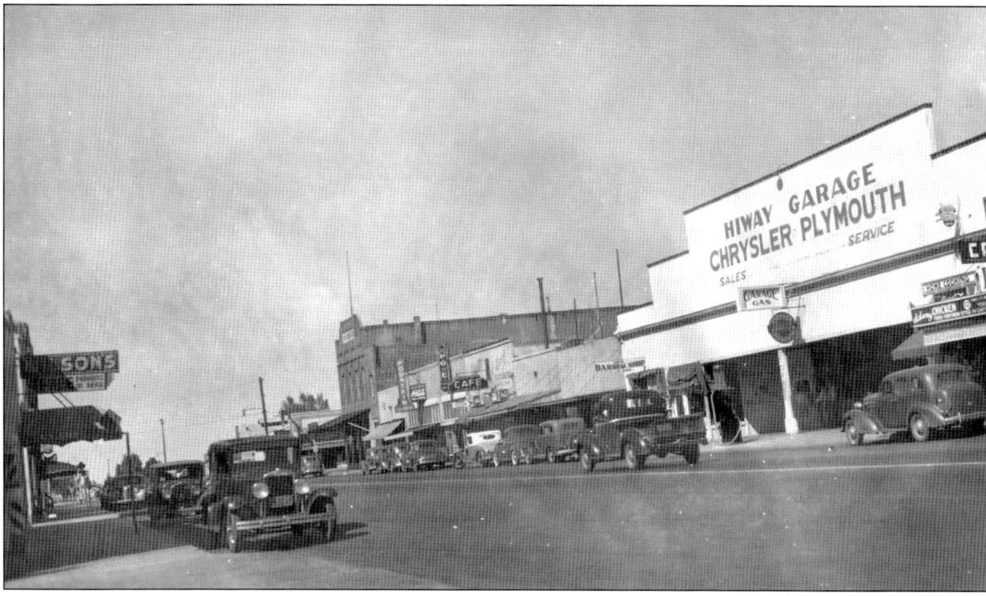

The east side of the street included a chicken restaurant, the Hiway Garage and car dealership, Barr's Barbershop, Atwood Insurance, Cannon's Café, the PG&E office, Elzey's Variety and Fountain, Dr. Keith's office, and the Odd Fellows Hall. (Diane Lucas.)

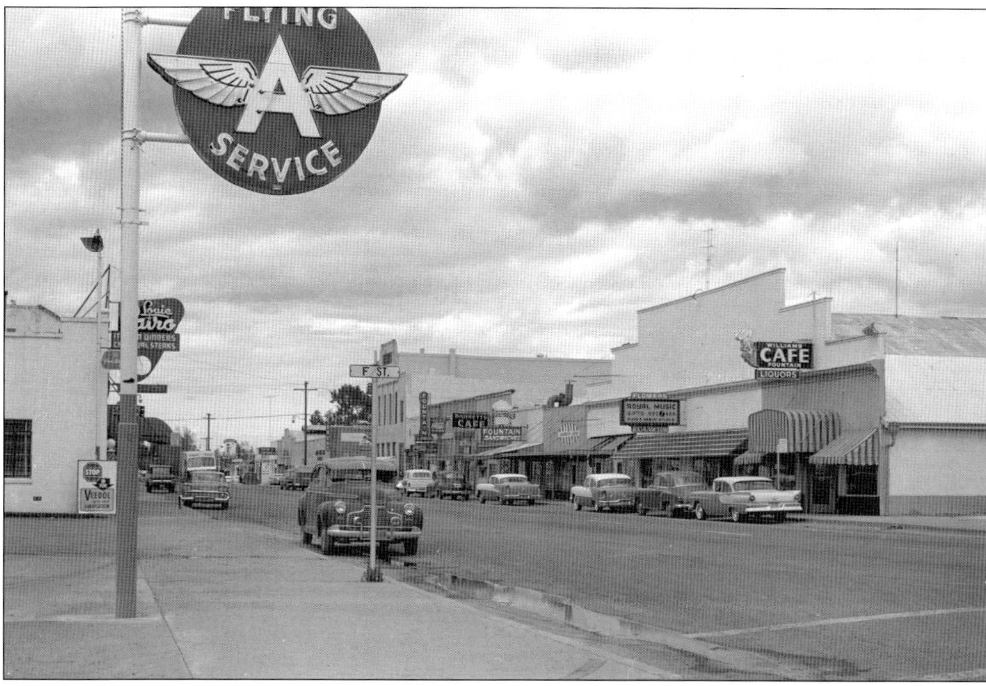

The east side of the block changes complexion, with Dart's car dealership being replaced by the Royal Music Shoppe, which was opened by Vivian Dalton and then later owned by Elaine Lausten. Besides having flowers and other gift items, piano and ballroom dance lessons, musical instruments, and sheet music were also available—not to mention the latest in 45 rpm records and albums. Further down are Meyer's Fountain, Barretts Café, and Laird's Café. (Henry W. Rhoades family.)

Three

Schools and Churches

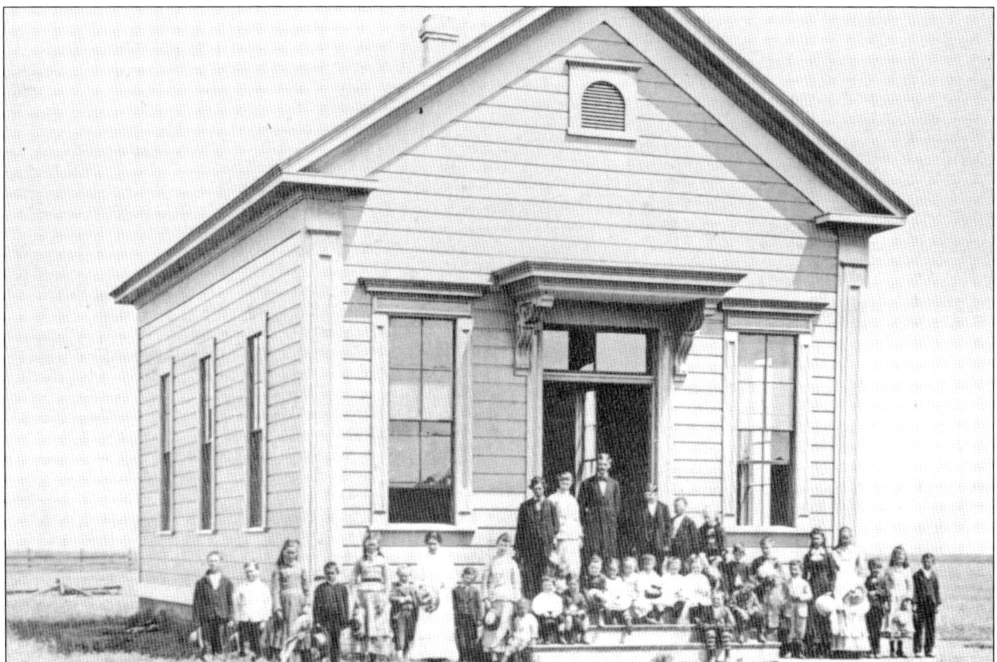

When Williams was established in 1876, it had no school. Students would travel south three miles to where the Central School was established in Central. The people of Williams called for an election, and when it was held in September 1877, it resulted in a tie, so the school was to remain in Central. A petition was sent to the board of supervisors, and a school was built in Williams that held 50 students. It was thought to have occupied Seventh Street between E and F Streets. (Marjorie Manor Marengo.)

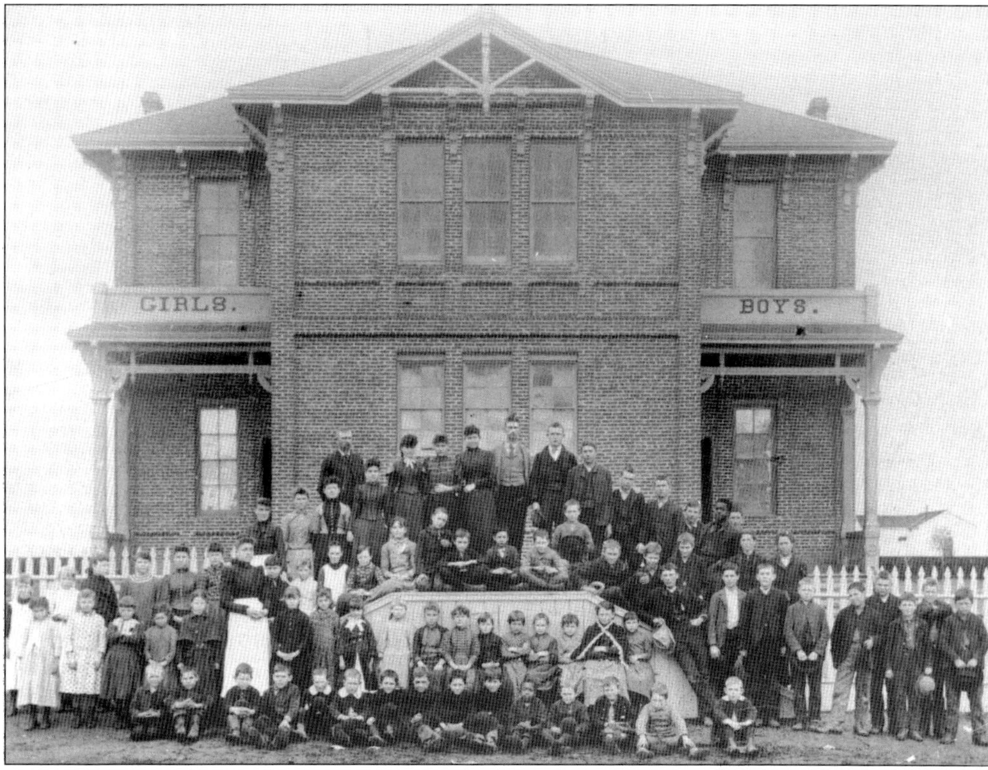

It did not take long to outgrow the first school in Williams. Photographed in 1889, this school was reported to have been between Eighth and Ninth Streets at C Street. In 1893, there were 106 pupils enrolled, with a principal and two teachers on board. (Marjorie Manor Marengo.)

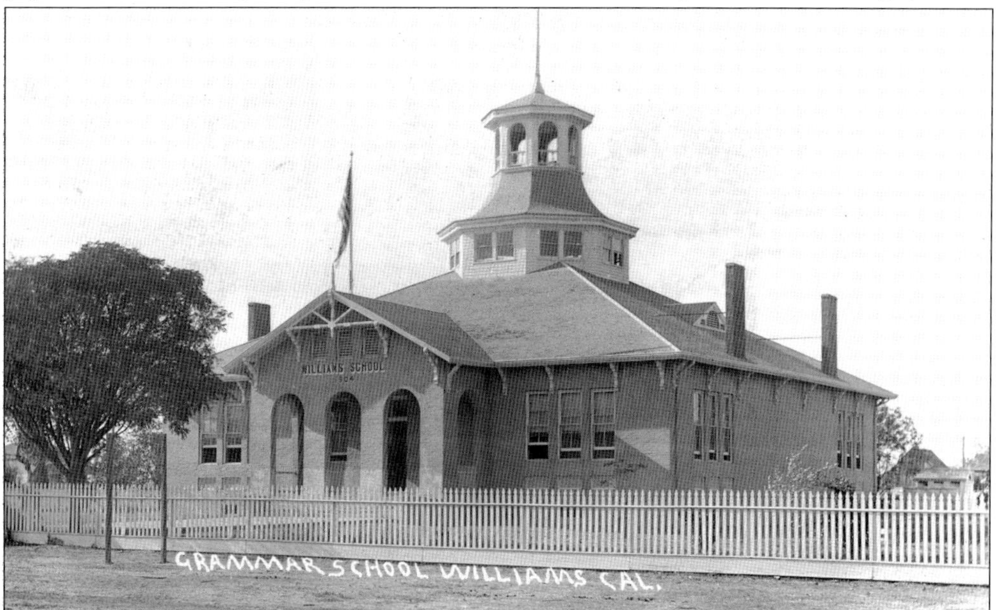

In 1904, another new school was built at the same location and served the community until it was outgrown once again. (Gilbert Allen family.)

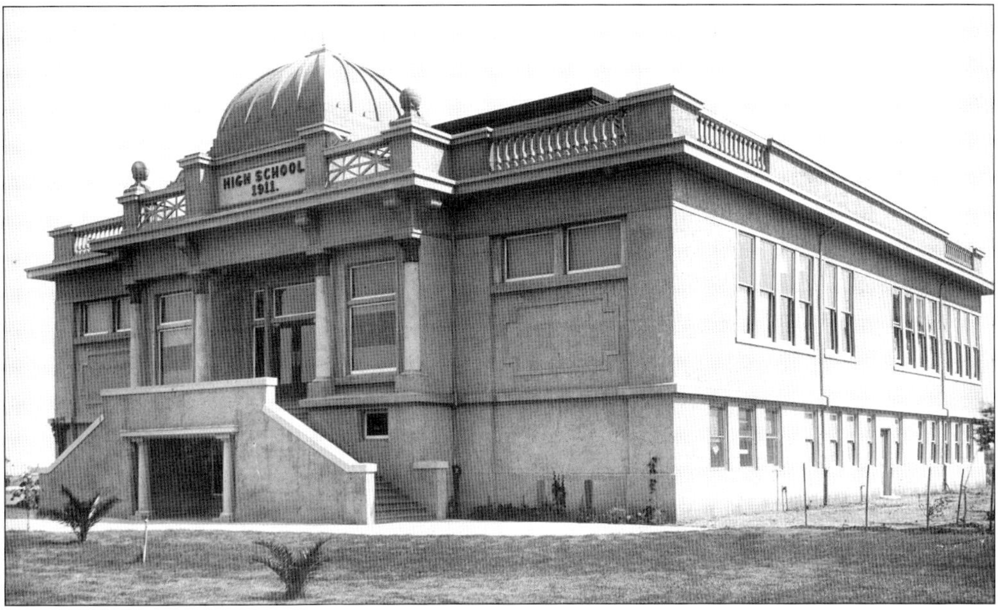

By 1909, it was obvious that a new high school was needed when the IOOF Hall was used to house classes. In 1911, a bond was passed, five acres were purchased, and the school was under construction by March and completed the following October at a cost of $25,000. It was heralded as an example for the rest of the state, and valuable collections were donated to the school. (Sacramento Valley Museum.)

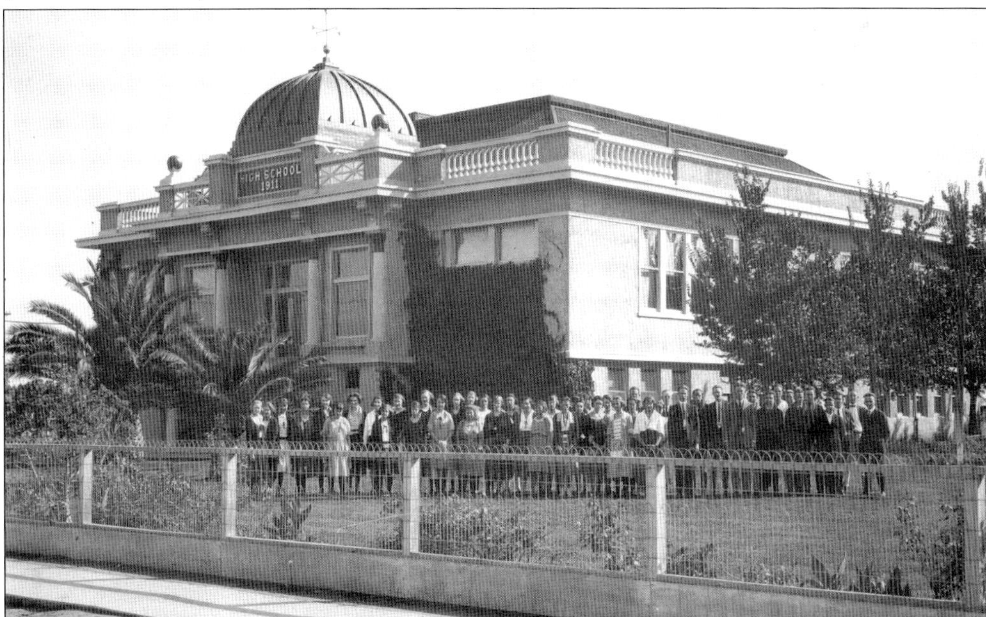

A more finished high school is seen here in the 1920s, showing off the classes and the completed landscaping. This school served the community until a new school was built in 1956. In 1912, the first graduating class had two students and a student body of 40. The first graduates from the new high school were Viola Forsythe, who was responsible for choosing the school colors of brown and gold, and Helen Ware. (Wanda Bowen.)

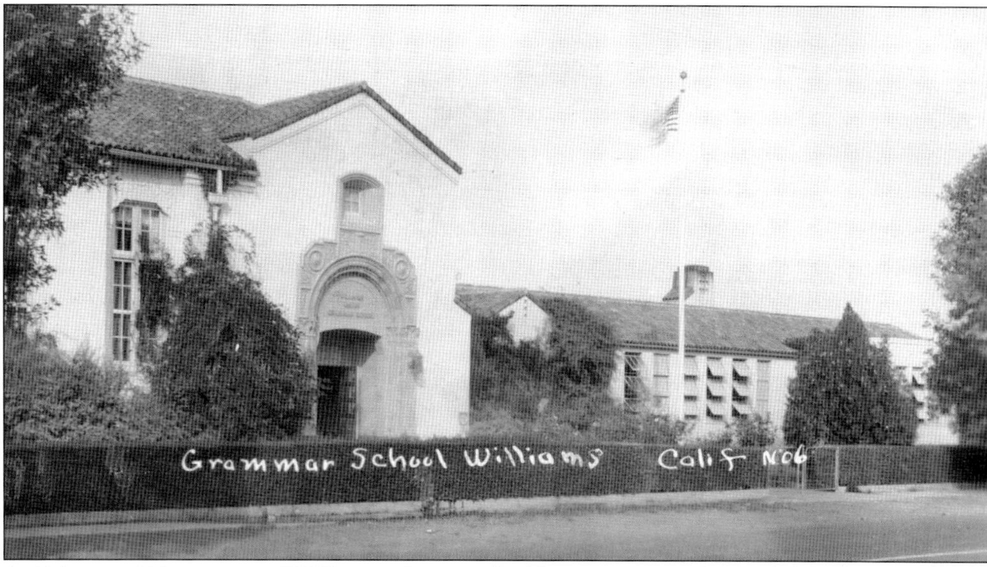

In February 1930, voters of Williams chose to build a new, up-to-date elementary school. The building was bid at $75,481 plus furnishings and was state-of-the-art. It had spacious classrooms, an auditorium with a stage, and a projection room. The school served the needs of the community until the board deemed it unsafe and not earthquake proof. It was then torn down, and the current school replaced it. (Mike Ferraiuolo.)

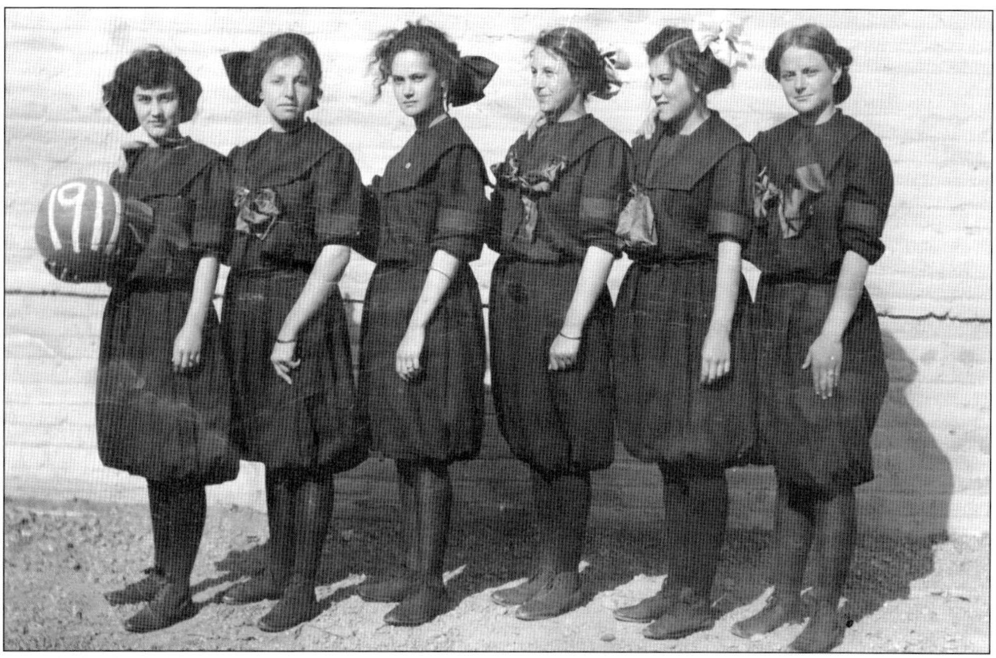

A girls' basketball team was organized while at the grade school, and when members reached high school, they were a favorite with the townspeople. Under the instruction of Ralph Camper, a rural supervisor from Glenn County, they were Viola Smith, Mrs. Otto Miller, Mrs. Harry Crutcher, Mrs. Charles Thode, Mrs. D.L. Linbaugh, and Mrs. Walter Lindersmith. The article, which was printed in 1936, gave only the women's married names, and it is unknown if the names are in order with the photograph. (Sacramento Valley Museum.)

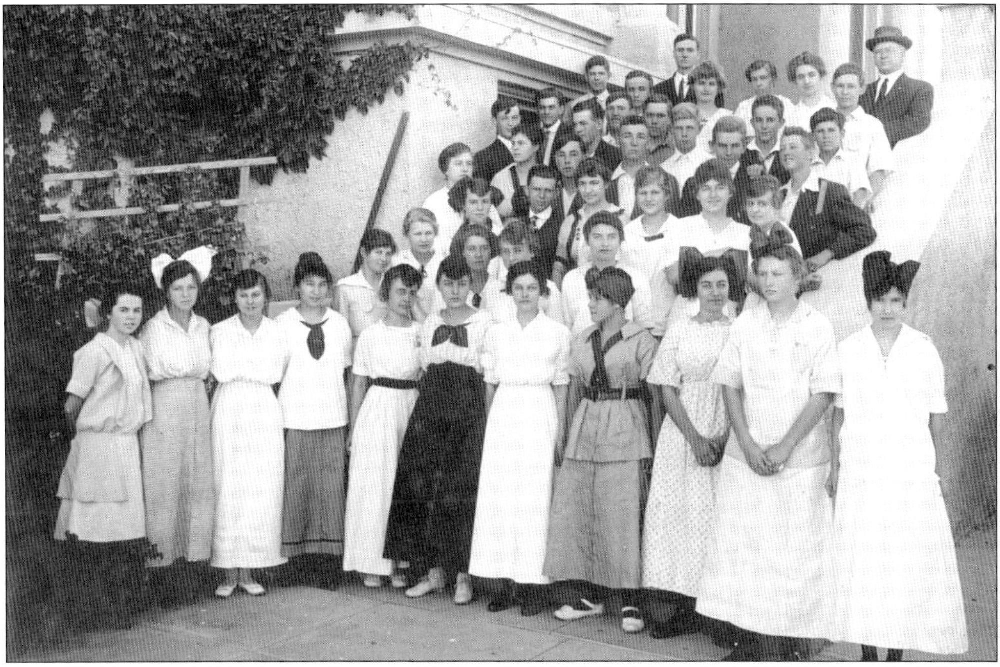

This early photograph of students and faculty at Williams High shows Oma Retterath Tuttle in the second row, far left, who was the first girl in history to attend the Northern California High School Athletic League as a delegate in 1915. Representing one of the smallest schools in the league, it was said that she did not fail to make her presence known, and the interests of Williams High School were well taken care of. (Jauregui family collection.)

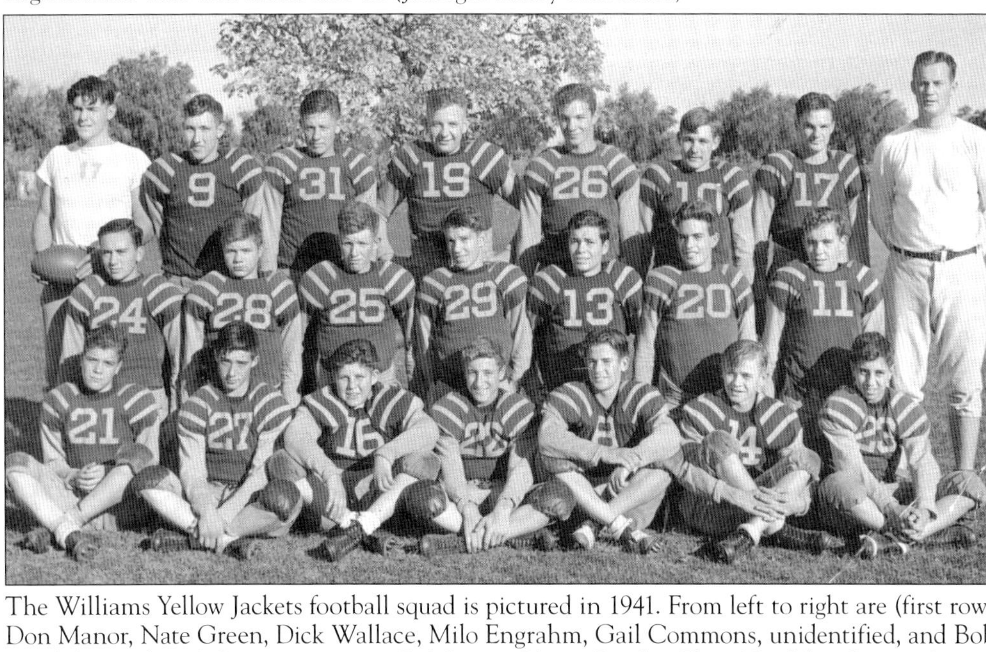

The Williams Yellow Jackets football squad is pictured in 1941. From left to right are (first row) Don Manor, Nate Green, Dick Wallace, Milo Engrahm, Gail Commons, unidentified, and Bob Dutil; (second row) George Marengo, Bob Lewis, Blaine Danley, Elmo Nordyke, George Green, and Warren Rathburn; (third row) Zane Marshall, Tommy Overholser, Frank "Sy" Kemp, Richard Jensen, Kenny Egbert, Keith Jenson, and coach Marty Mathison. (Diana Kemp Azevedo.)

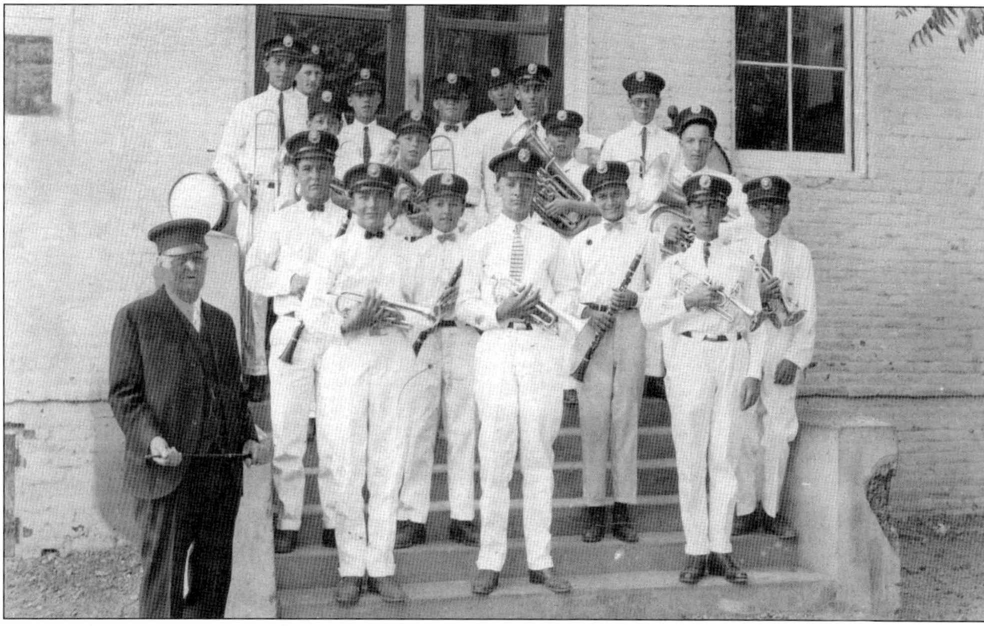

Pictured in 1924 is the Williams Elementary band with Erastus Kimball as director. From left to right are (first row) Leonard Beauchamp, Garland Bashore, and Junior Merle; (second row) Veryl Goodin, Max Forsythe, Joe Kintana, and Beverly Collin; (third row) Joe Lanoutte, Charles Schaad, unidentified, and Elbert Gassaway; (fourth row) Frank Wallace, Roland Sweet, Williams Carpenter, Hanline, and Fred Rippon; (fifth row) Marvin Davis and Eddie ?. Kimball chewed tobacco, and the students always tried to hit the right notes so he would not foul their mouthpieces. (Author's collection.)

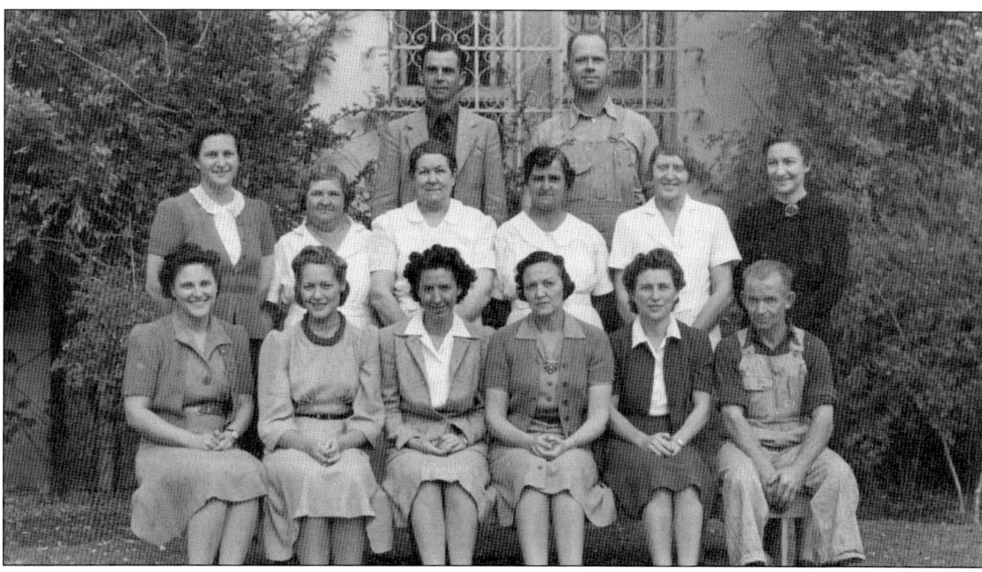

The elementary school staff members are, from left to right, (first row) Helen Cangiamila La Grande, two unidentified, Lucille Smith, unidentified, and Fred Nichols (custodian); (second row) unidentified; kitchen crew Myrtle Nordyke, Mrs. Platt, Mrs. Morris, and Stella Baker; and Elizabeth Comstock (teacher); (third row) Joe Mitchell (principal) and Bert McMartin (custodian). (Jauregui family collection.)

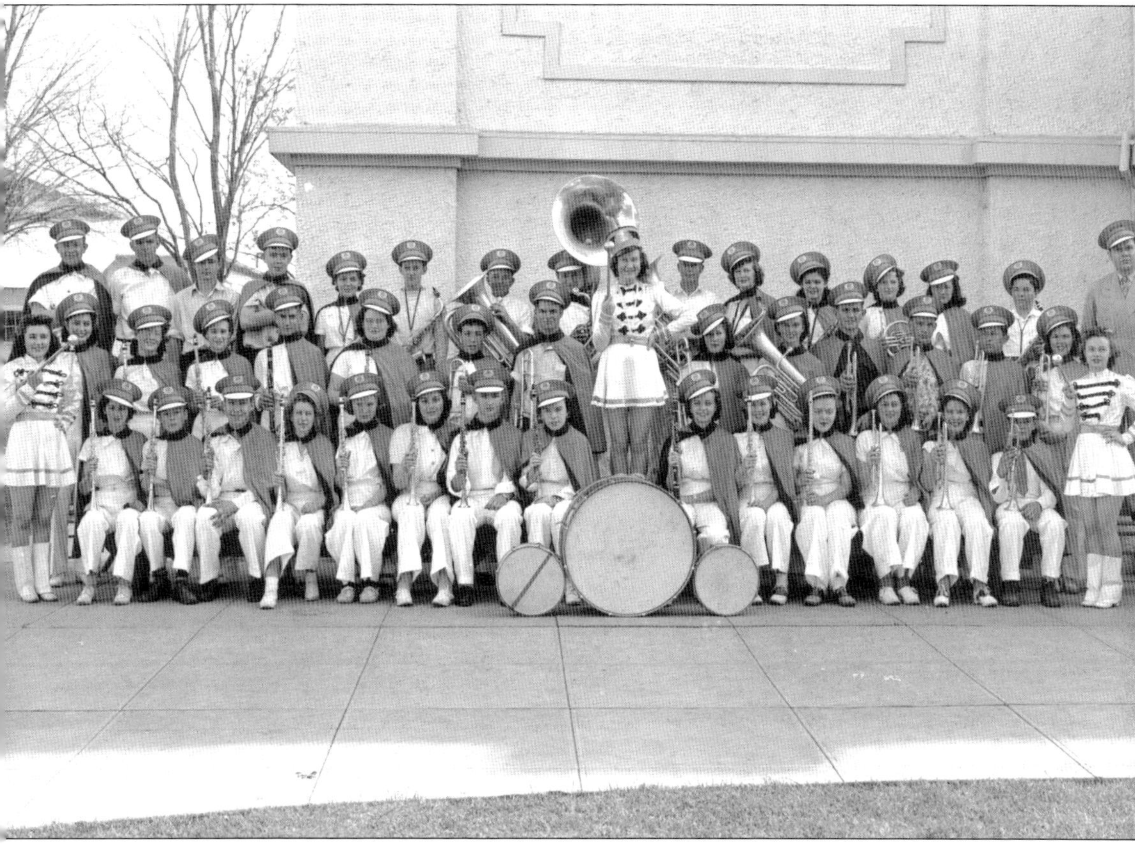

This 1940 photograph shows the Williams High School marching band. From left to right are (first row) Dorothy Kintana, Ray Higgins, Lemuel Schaad, Phyllis Matzka, Shirley Mathiesen, Lou Ellen Gray, Franklin Fouch, Alice Lee Griffin, June Franke, Patricia Allen, Colleen Hurt, Katheryn Apperson, Florence Bowen, Mary Louie Hall, and Donald Hall; (second row) Aura May Chatfield, Joene Lewis, Georgia Hall, Annette Bassetti, Harold La Grande, Marilyn Boyd, Wally Gray, Keith Jensen, Betty Rae McMullen, Betty Jane Casey, Harold Beauchamp, Elmo Nordyke, Richard Lee Mock, Ruby Locke, and Betty Schaad; (third row); Frank Kemp, Charles Manning, Kenneth Egbert, Warren Rathbun, Marjorie Manor, Raymond Schaad, Raymond Schaad, Wayne Morrow, Milo Engrahm, Floyd Murphy, Betty Cook, Jeanette Barker, Rita Keegan, Patsy Keith, Edwin Campbell, and Wesley Hull (director). (Henry W. Rhoades family.)

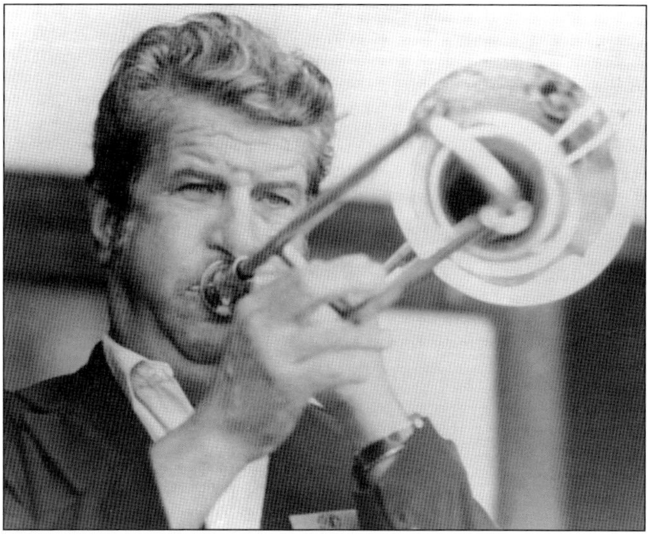

A well-known musician to graduate from Williams High School was the famed Melvin "The Terrible Turk" Murphy, who went on to own Earthquake Magoon's in San Francisco. Having played at Carnegie Hall a few months before his death, Turk, his famed trombone, and his signature song, "A Closer Walk with Thee," helped keep alive the old-time jazz born in the South. Turk died at the age of 71 in 1987. (Sacramento Valley Museum.)

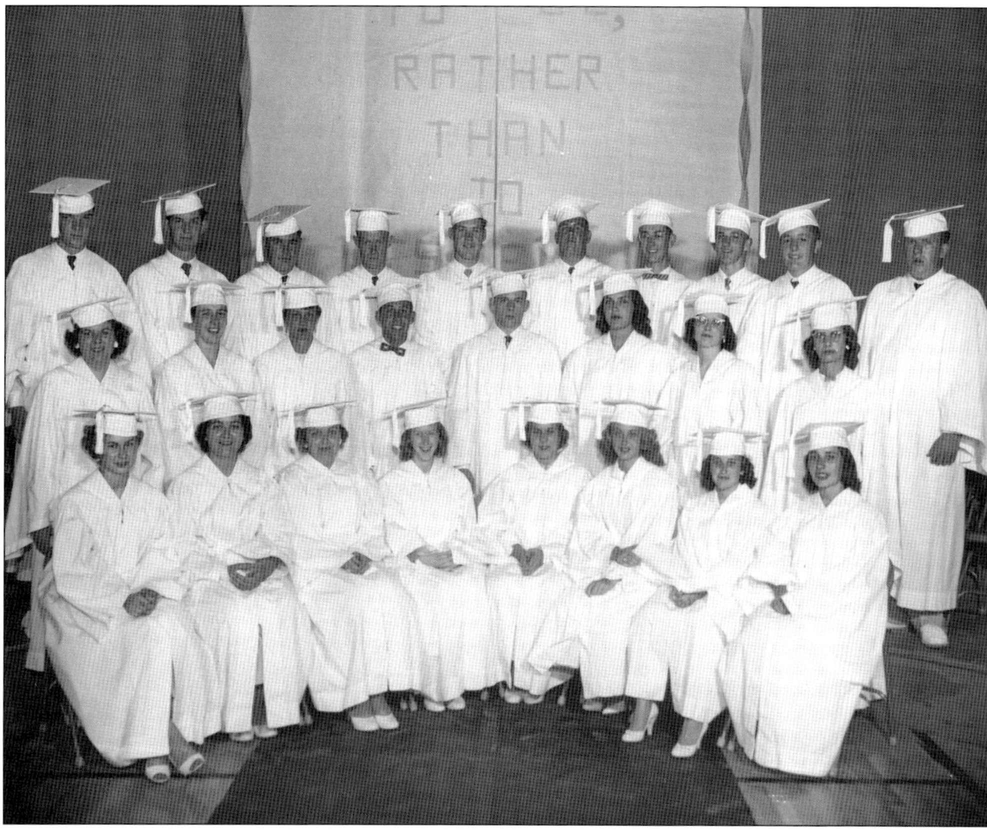

The current high school was dedicated on August 31, 1956, with the first graduating class in 1957. From left to right are (first row) Sue Jenkins, Josephine Bascochea, Shirley Mathews, Diane Nason, Florence Nissen, Kay Stores, and Linda Jewett; (second row) Jessie Irvin, Susan Rogers, Jone Smith, Ted Olds, Bill Hornbuckle, Linda King, Martha Clark, and Liz O'Bryant; (third row) Ed Gassaway, Ed Middlewick, Charles Bradshaw, Richard Reister, Wes Fry, Gene Mays, Danny La Grande, Everett Brainard, John Troughton, and John Snelgrove. (Sacramento Valley Museum.)

In 1898, there were 36 schools in Colusa County with most of them being one-room schoolhouses, located throughout the districts. Central School was originally about three miles south of Williams on Zumwalt Road. When Williams had its own school, Central School was then moved to Lone Star Road, where it stood well into the 1970s. (June Wallace O'Sullivan.)

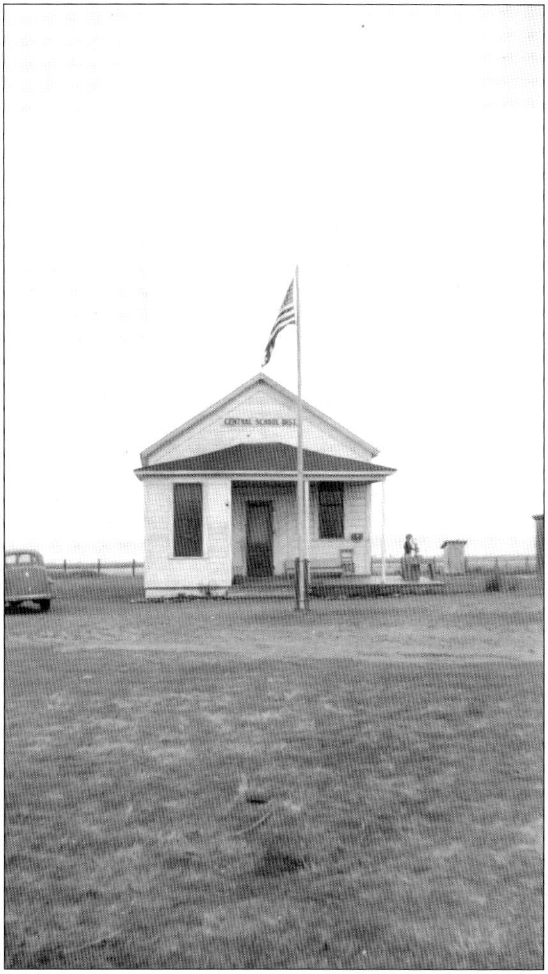

The Cortina School was located south of Williams. In 1942, the board of supervisors approved the merger of the Central and Cortina School District with the Williams Elementary School District on petitions presented to the board, and it was passed on a three-to-two vote. The Cortina School was moved to Williams and became part of the Veterans Hall. (Gilbert Allen family.)

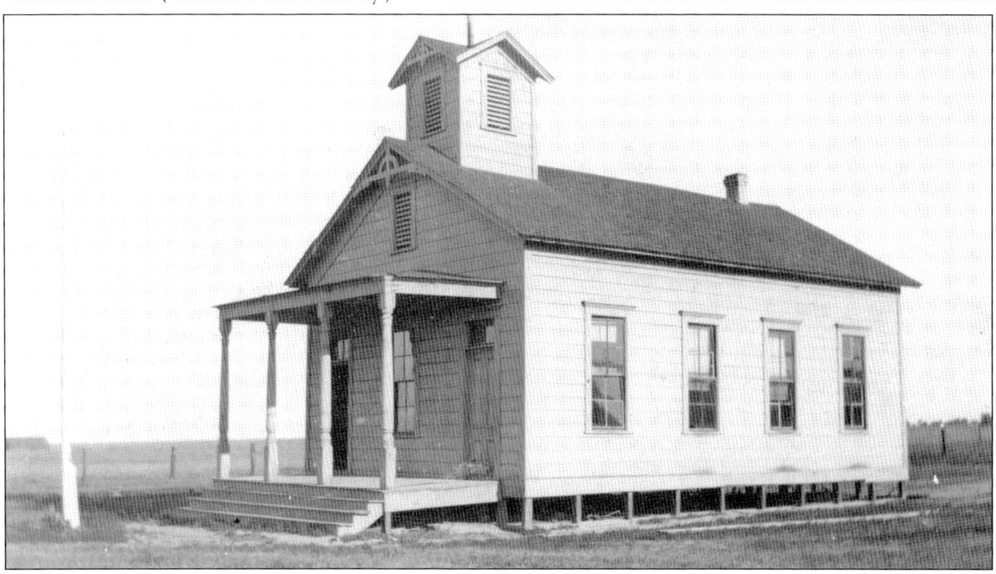

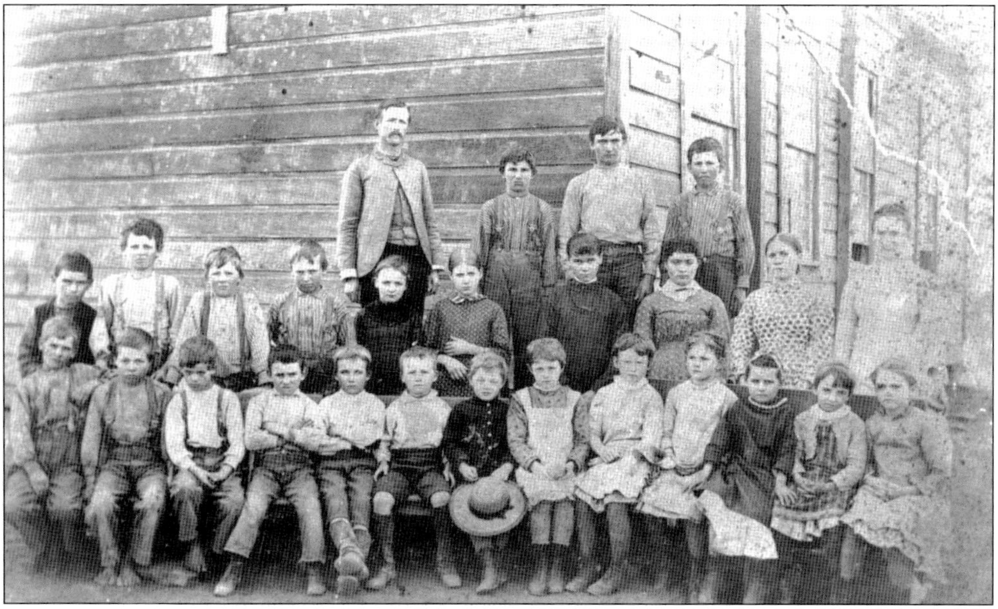

The Glenn Valley School was located northwest of Williams. In 1885, these students had John T. Washer as their teacher. From left to right are (first row) Charlie Gobel, John Vostinjer, Jim Gobel, John Otten, Will Thomas, Joe Harlan, Charles Robinson, Myra Robinson, Molly Paxton, Ida Paxton, Julia Richter, Katie Otten, and Birdie Gilliam; (second row) Adolph Richter, Arch Paxton, Pearl Gilliam, Will Harlan, Mattie Harlan, Lilly O' Neal, Lizzie Richter, Mollie Gilliam, Ella Gilliam, and Mrs. Hildram; (third row) John T. Washer, John Ochs, Ed O'Neal, and Helm Harlan. The school closed in 1939, and the building was moved to town in the 1940s and used as the Farm Bureau Hall, Girl Scout Cabin, and Rugby Clubhouse. It was most recently moved to the Sacramento Valley Museum, where it was renovated. (Above, Doug Gassaway; below, Sacramento Valley Museum.)

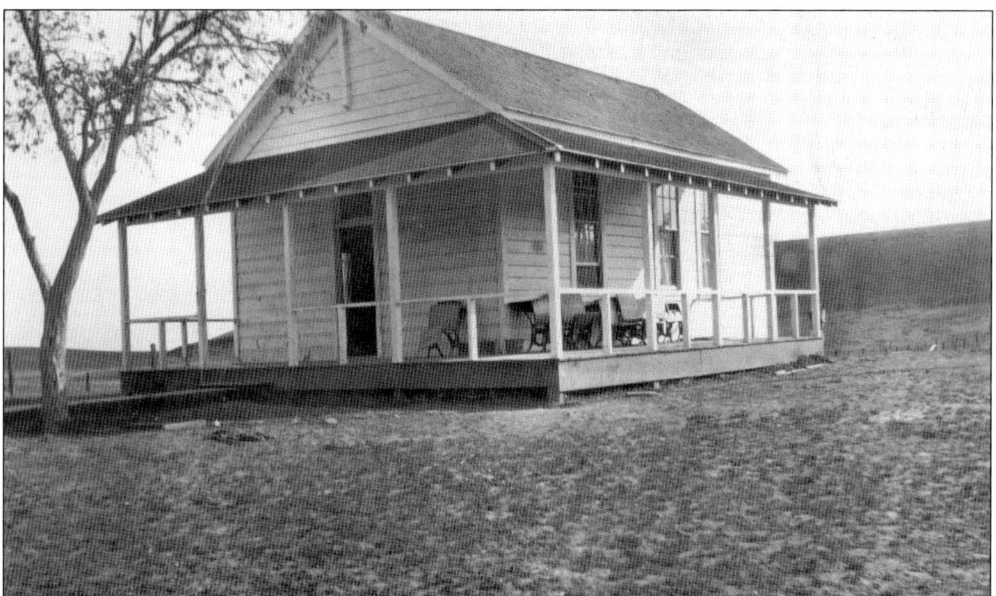

The average daily attendance record for the Freshwater School in 1920 is shown, and only two students, Rebecca Gibson and Avis Stovall, were present. Alta Lane, who taught in one-room schoolhouses as well as Williams schools for 41 years, signed it. J.L. Mendenhall verified the attendance record. (Author's collection.)

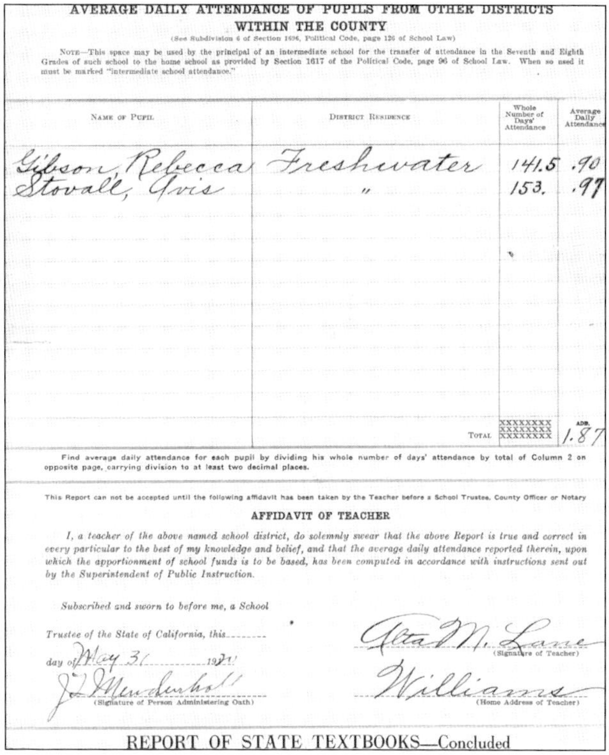

AVERAGE DAILY ATTENDANCE OF PUPILS FROM OTHER DISTRICTS WITHIN THE COUNTY

(See Subdivision 6 of Section 1696, Political Code, page 126 of School Law)

NOTE—This space may be used by the principal of an intermediate school for the transfer of attendance in the Seventh and Eighth Grades of such school to the home school as provided by Section 1617 of the Political Code, page 96 of School Law. When so used it must be marked "intermediate school attendance."

Name of Pupil	District Residence	Whole Number of Days' Attendance	Average Daily Attendance
Gibson, Rebecca	Freshwater	141.5	.90
Stovall, Avis	"	153.	.97
	Total	XXXXXXXX	ADA. 1.87

Find average daily attendance for each pupil by dividing his whole number of days' attendance by total of Column 2 on opposite page, carrying division to at least two decimal places.

This Report can not be accepted until the following affidavit has been taken by the Teacher before a School Trustee, County Officer or Notary

AFFIDAVIT OF TEACHER

I, a teacher of the above named school district, do solemnly swear that the above Report is true and correct in every particular to the best of my knowledge and belief, and that the average daily attendance reported therein, upon which the apportionment of school funds is to be based, has been computed in accordance with instructions sent out by the Superintendent of Public Instruction.

Subscribed and sworn to before me, a School Trustee of the State of California, this .... *day of* May 31 1921

J. L. Mendenhall
(Signature of Person Administering Oath)

Alta M. Lane
(Signature of Teacher)

Williams
(Home Address of Teacher)

REPORT OF STATE TEXTBOOKS—Concluded

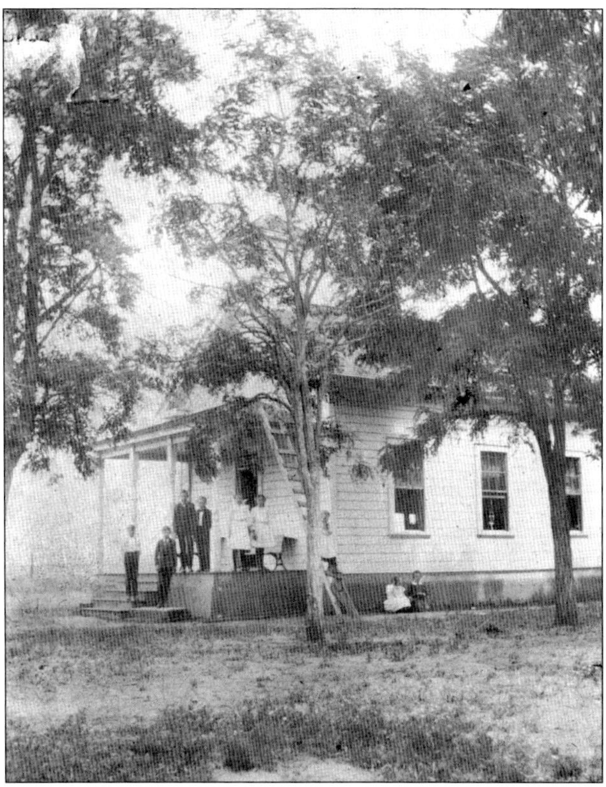

The Freshwater School was built on the land of John F. Abel, located northwest of Williams. Abel donated the land and was the school director from 1869 to 1903. In 1930, the building was sold at auction, and the records show that for 61 years, it operated at the wrong site due to either an error in wording of the document or the recording description. (Annette Abel La Grande.)

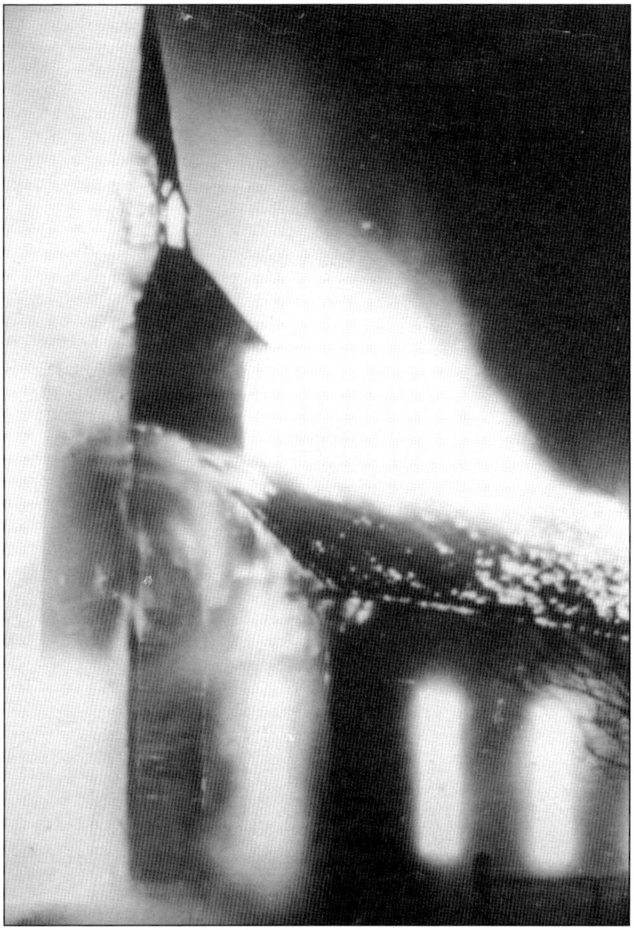

In 1877, Prof. J.C. Keith, president of the Pierce Christian College in College City, founded the Christian Church in Williams. In 1881, the articles of incorporation were filed, and through the efforts of Mr. Williams, the church was able to buy three lots at the cost of $55. Charles Crocker of San Francisco delivered the deed for the purchase, and when it was completed in 1881, Mr. Williams donated a new organ. On February 4, 1916, the church burned to the ground, and everything was lost. They vowed to rebuild, and within nine months, the new church was built and was dedicated on November 5, 1916. On Easter Sunday 1922, the First Christian Church became known as the Williams Community Church. Over the years, the church has undergone several remodels; the photograph below shows how it looked in 1958. (Schaad-Fouch family collection.)

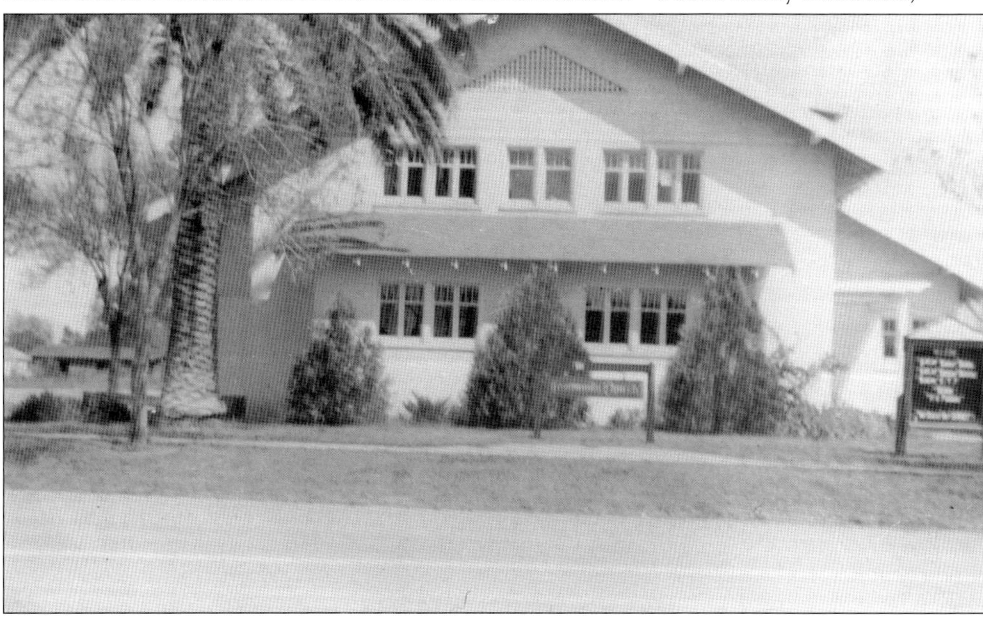

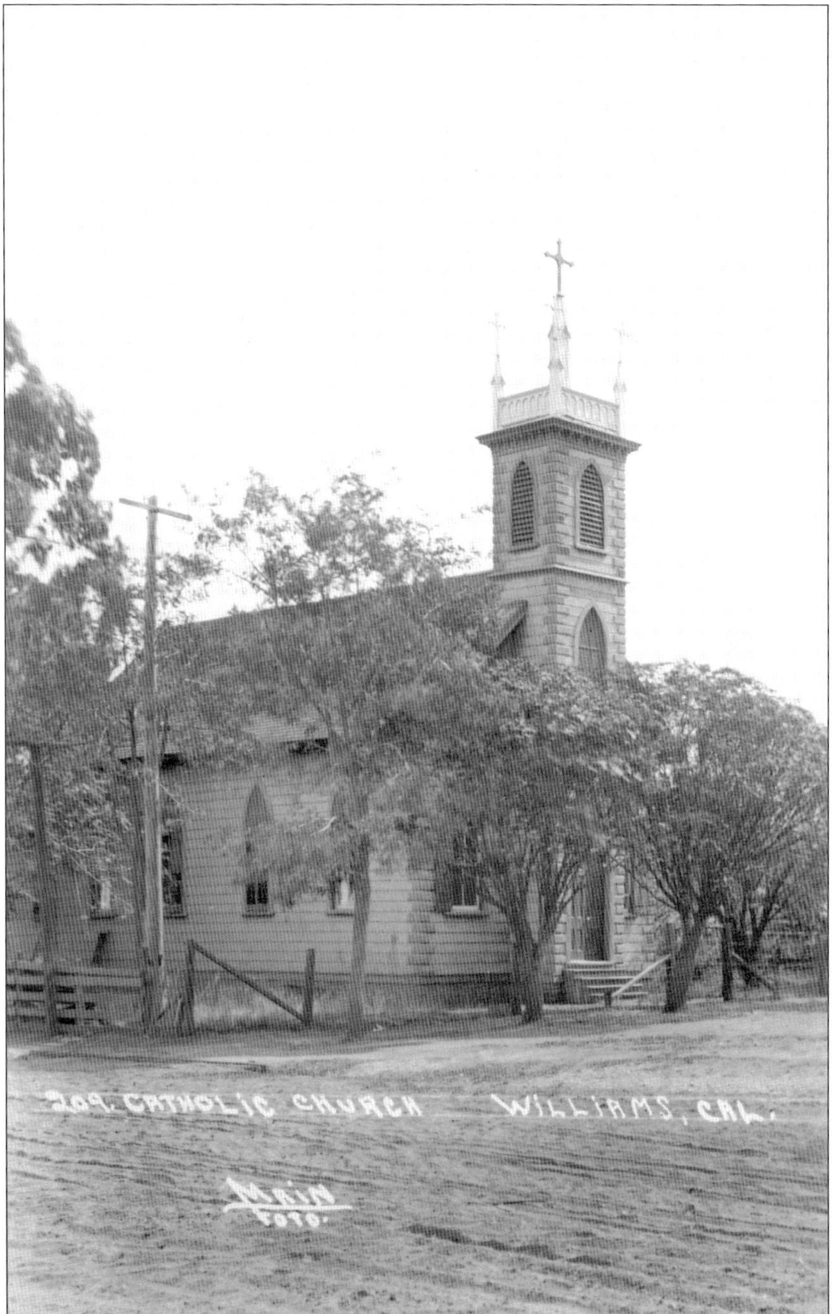

The Williams Catholic Church was brought from Marysville around 1890 and placed on land donated by J.O. Zumwalt, where it stood at the corner of Eighth and F Streets until the current church was built in 1977. There is a difference of opinion as to how it arrived in Williams. Some say the church was cut in half and hauled in by wagon, and others say that it arrived by train. The original church was almost lost in 1923 when the Williams Hotel burned, sending embers onto its roof. It was through the diligence of citizens helping to fight the fire that the church was saved. (Gayle Vaughn.)

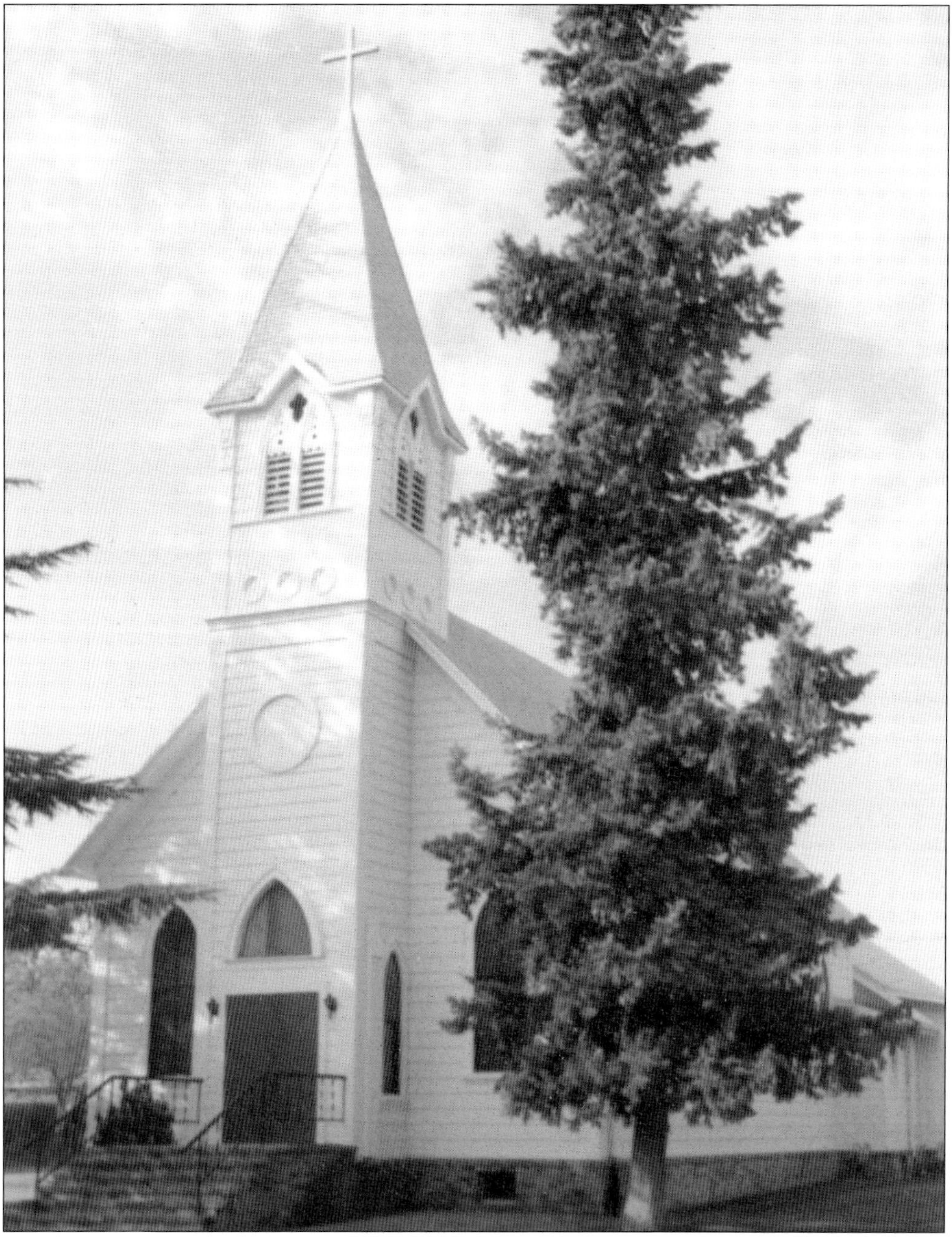

The Williams Methodist Church still stands at the corner of Ninth and G Streets on land also donated by J.O Zumwalt. It is the only church still in operation today in its original form. (Diane Lucas.)

Four

Doing Our Part

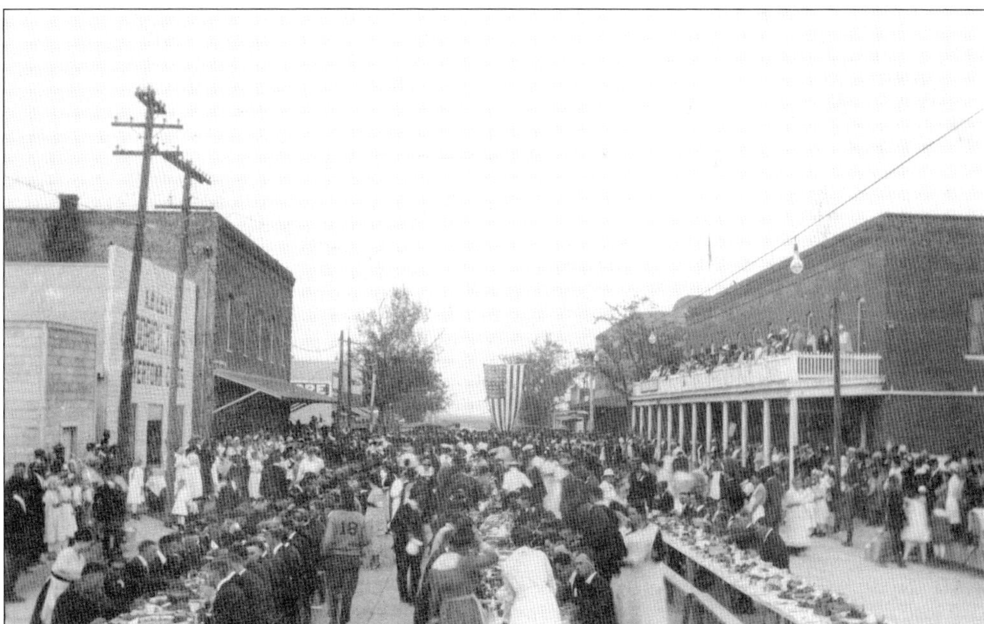

During World War I, trains loaded with men on their way to American Lake, Washington, would pass through Williams. The Red Cross made arrangements for the people of Williams to feed them, but little did they realize that they would be feeding 2,000 men before they were through. The train stopped on three different occasions, and the whole town turned out with food and volunteers to serve before the men boarded back onto the train. (Sacramento Valley Museum.)

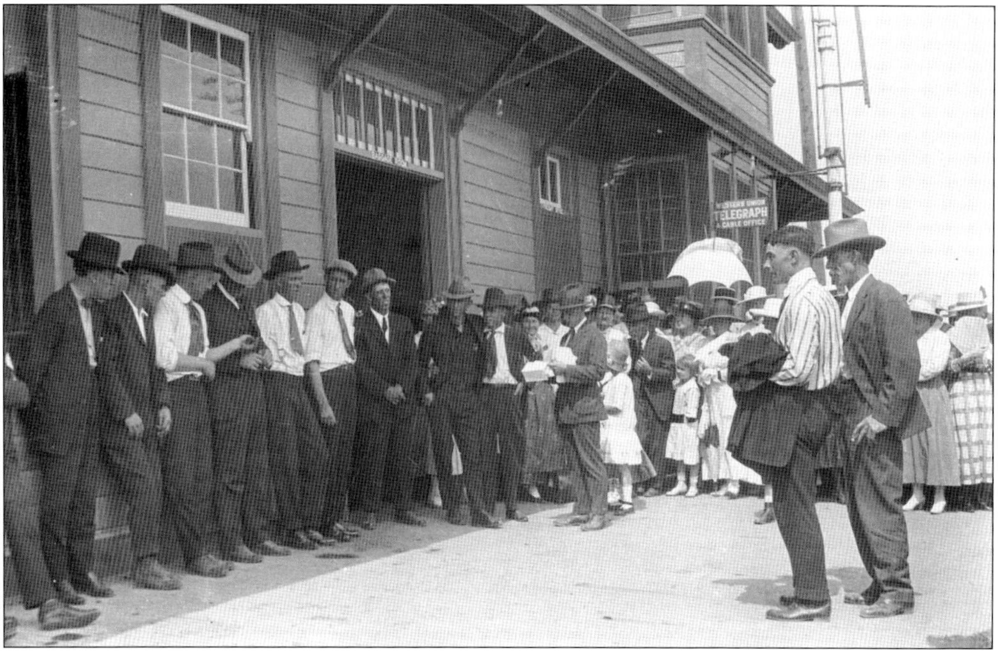

During the World War I ceremonies at the Williams Depot, the Colusa County men's names were read, and then they boarded the train. Many of the area's men volunteered for service and went to great lengths to get to the depot in time to go. Although these men are nameless in the photograph, the author thought it was important to include them. They were indeed a very important part of our history. Shown below, Judge Weyand is to the far right during the induction ceremonies at Williams. (Gibson family collection.)

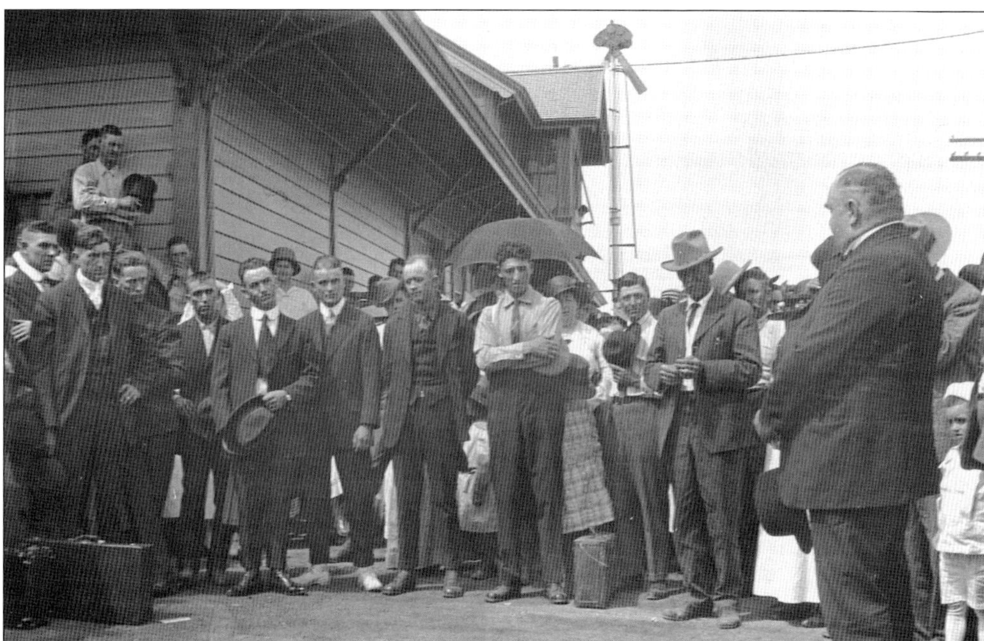

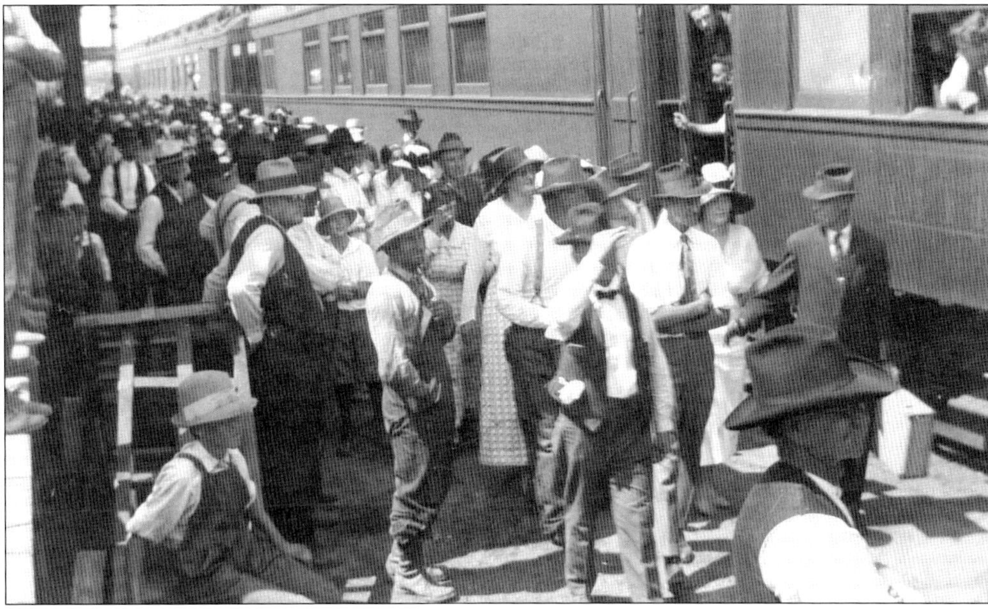

Large crowds gathered at the depot in Williams for the roll call of local boys being called into service. As their names were called, the men boarded the trains. The whole county turned out to see the men off to Fort Lewis for training. (Gilbert Allen family.)

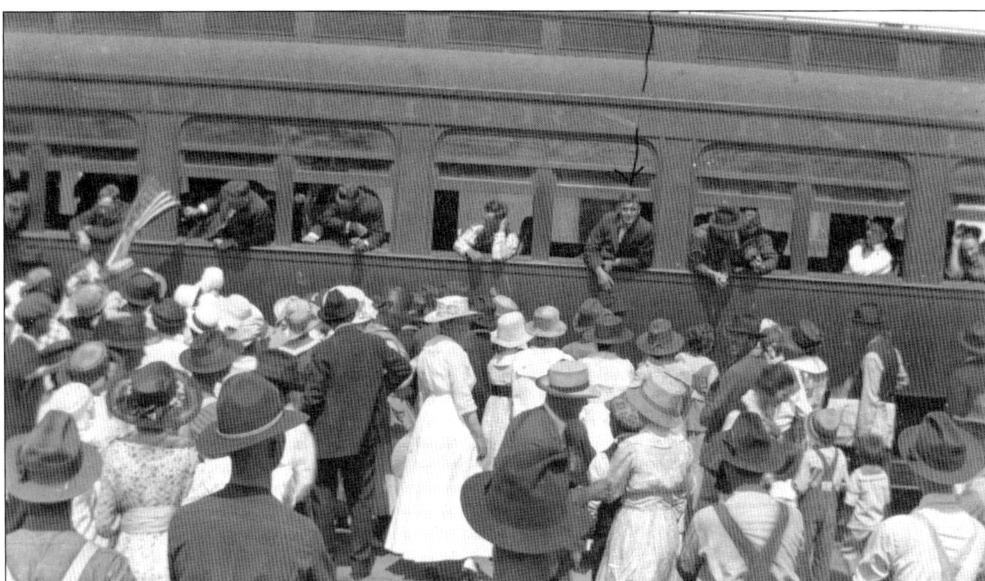

Men boarded the train and said their goodbyes as onlookers cheered them on. The woman looking back toward the camera is Alta Lane of Williams, and the young man looking from the train into the camera is Vernie Engrahm of Williams. (Gilbert Allen family.)

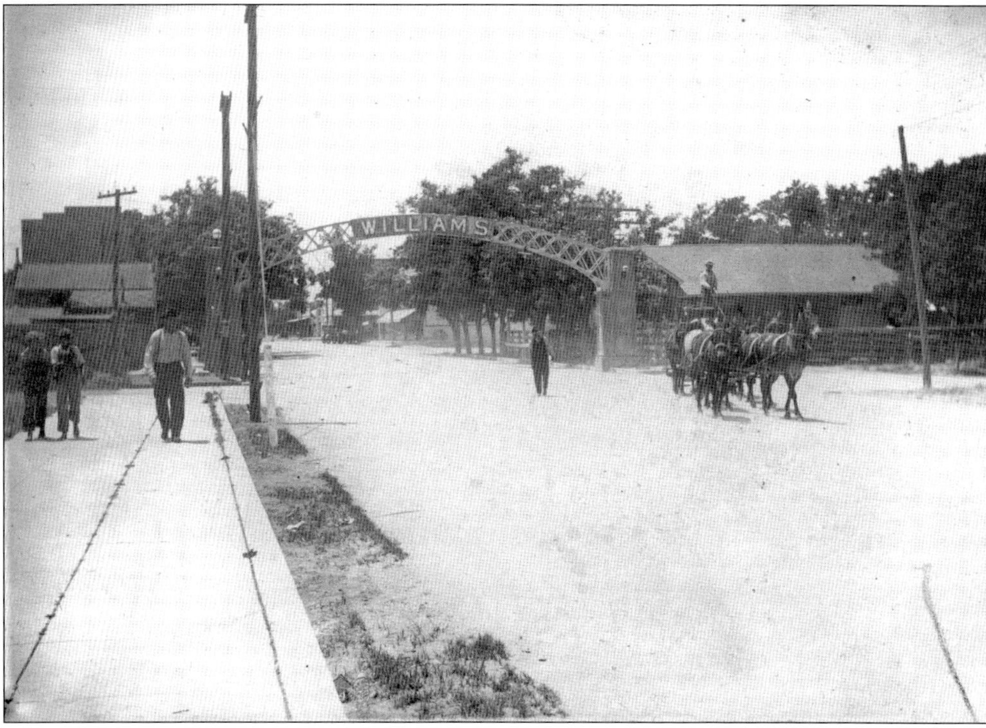

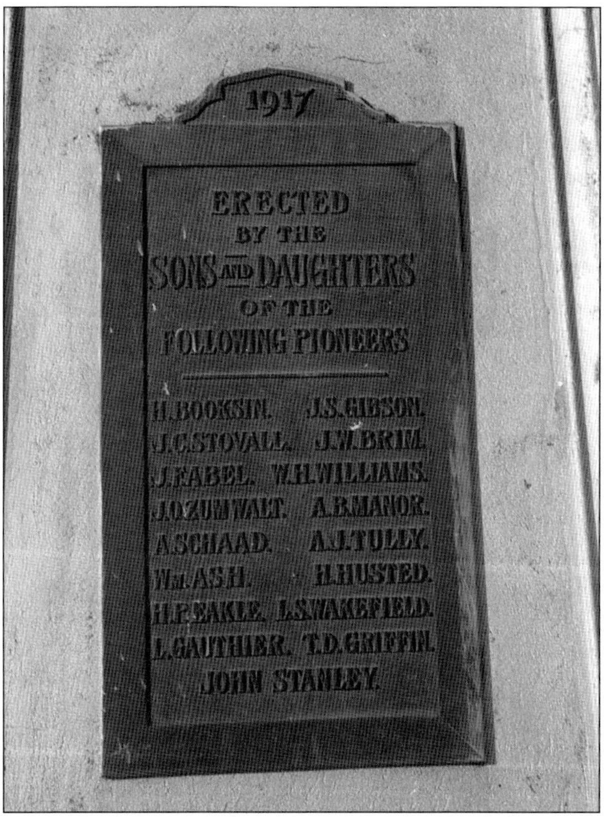

On February 2, 1917, blueprints for a proposed arch over E Street at Sixth Street were revealed by Molly Tedford, who originated the idea. Built of concrete and steel, it would be a tribute to the pioneering families. A committee of E.A. Brim, L.M. Zumwalt, J.F. Abel, H.W. Manor, and G.W. Gibson appeared before the supervisors to obtain a permit. Originally thought to cost $1,000, it proved to be much more. Due to World War I and the resulting lack of steel and labor, the project was put off until 1918. Families donated in memory of their pioneer ancestors, but due to the $150 charge, many families were not—or could not—be represented. As Frank Schuckman once said, "I know where I live, why do I have to pay to tell other people where I live?" (Above, Sacramento Valley Museum; left, Henry W. Rhoades family.)

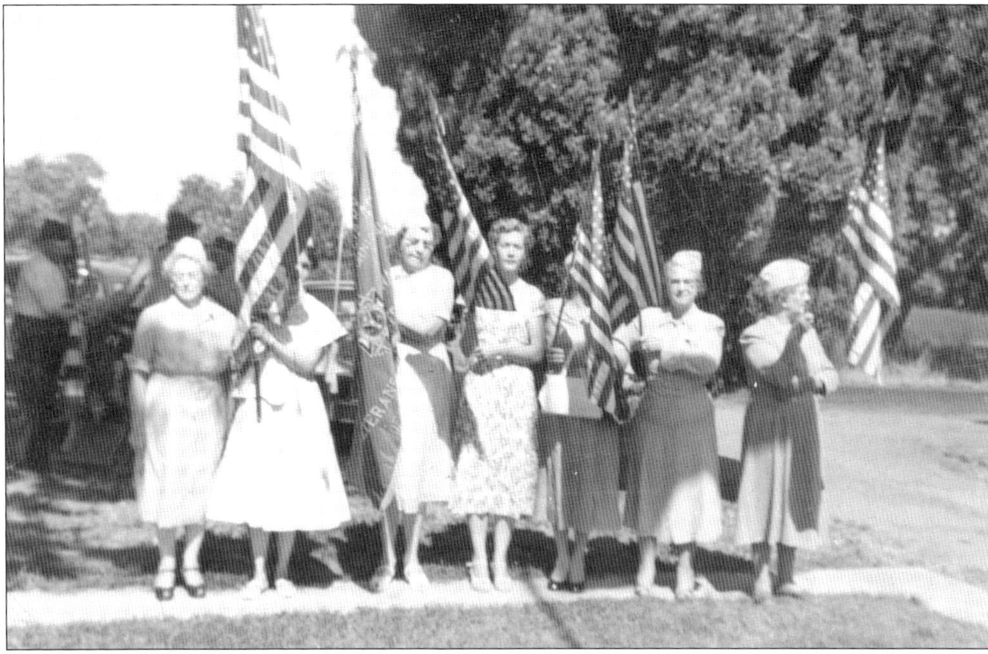

The women of Williams were very much involved in supporting the American Legion and later the VFW. These ladies were the flag bearers for a Memorial Day service. From left to right are Irene Haller, Faye Turner, Violet Smith, Claire Dutil, unidentified, Mary Vann, and Mary Manor. (Author's collection.)

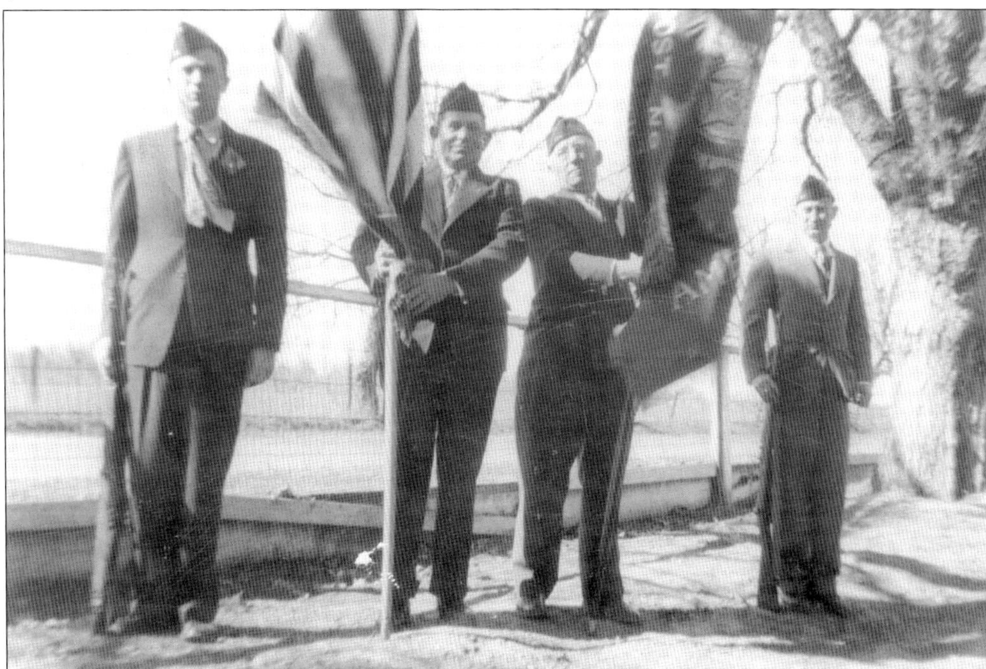

The color guard in this photograph spans from World War I to World War II. From left to right are Bill Keegan (World War II veteran), Mahlon "Bunk" Wallace and Daryl Carpenter (World War I veterans), and Jay West (World War II veteran). (June Wallace O'Sullivan.)

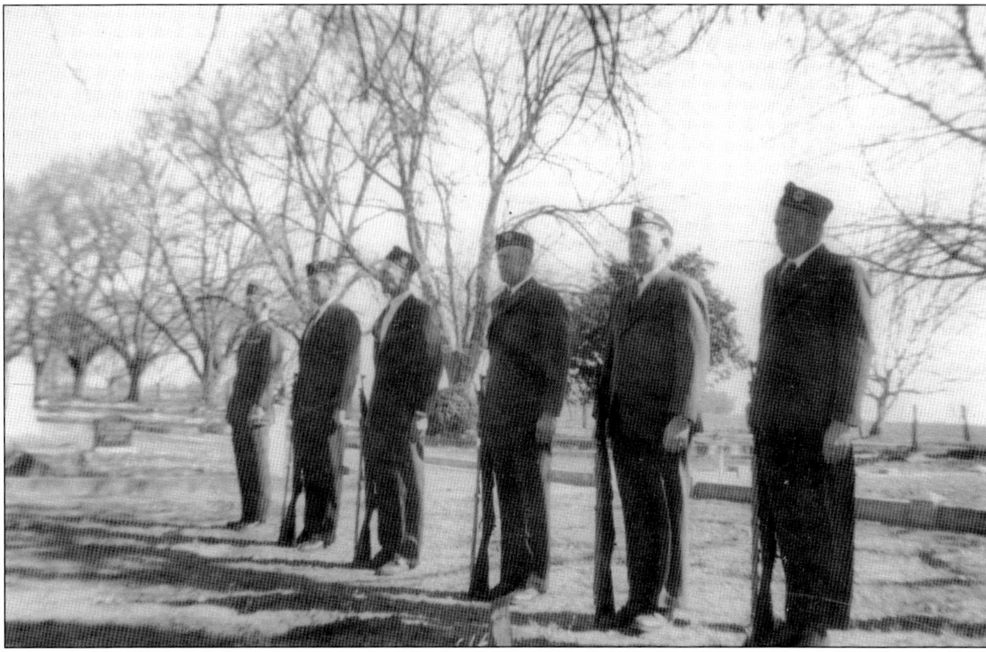

At military funeral services, veterans provided the honor guard. Leaving their businesses, they would honor those who served by giving the last 21-gun salute to the fallen heroes. Pictured from left to right are Franklin Fouch, Alva Lane, Gilbert Davis, Charles Davis, Hal Stober, and Macy Morrow. (June Wallace O'Sullivan.)

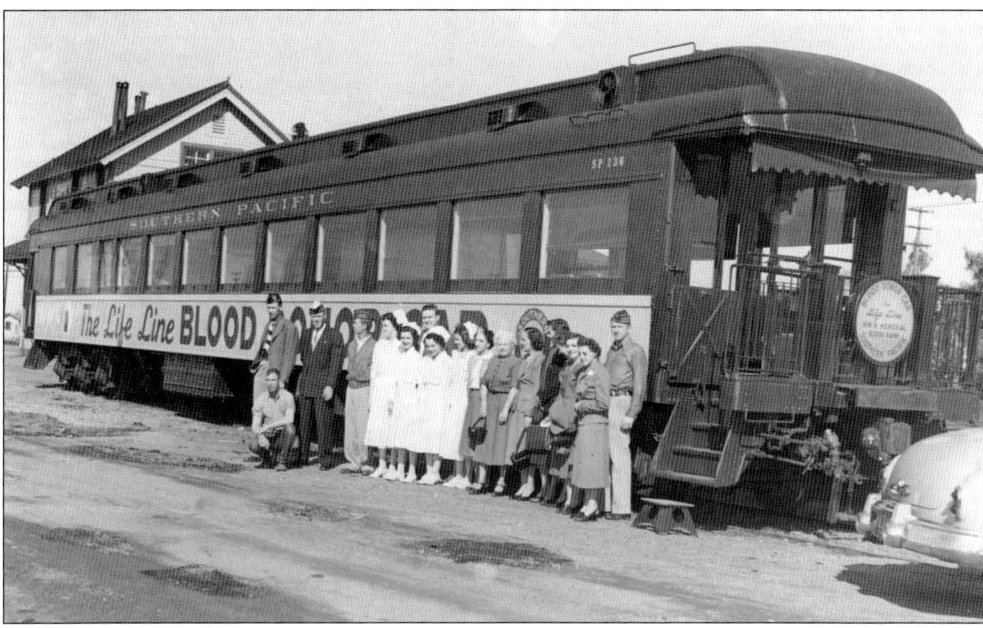

A blood drive with World War II veterans was held in a Southern Pacific railroad car at the depot. From left to right, the veterans are Ernie La Grande, Alva Lane, Roy Kitts, and Dr. Van De Pol and his staff members Ivor Lausten, Mrs. Jacobsen, Mrs. Welch, Mrs. Johnson, Mary Manor, Mrs. Charles Stone, Mrs. Babcock, and Bill Keegan. Kneeling in front is the first person to arrive at the blood drive that happened to be driving by the railroad car. (Sacramento Valley Museum.)

From 1913 to 1956, Williams had a "swim tank" at the Almond Grove Auto Court, owned by Daddy Byrnes. The tank was filled weekly, allowing people to swim, and was then released into Byrne's almond orchard, alfalfa, and gardens. The tank was scrubbed every week, and dressing rooms were built. The pool closed in 1956 after the Williams Community Recreation Project built a community pool. (Sacramento Valley Museum.)

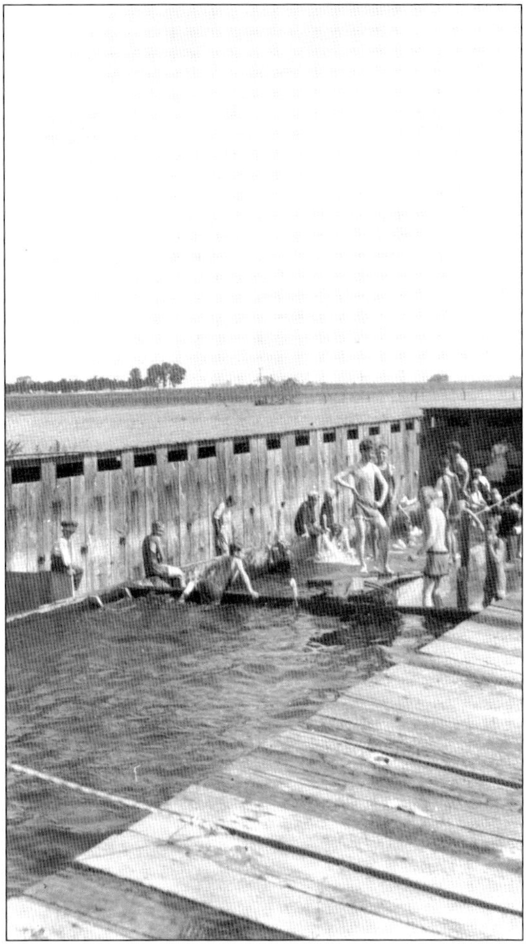

In 1954, the Williams Community Recreation Project (WCRP) was founded, and volunteers took on the mammoth project of providing a safe place for children to swim. This publicity photograph was taken on donated property that belonged to Belle Williams Moore. From left to right are Pauline Lynch, Mary Vann, unidentified, Thelma Fry, Reg Cheney, Pres. Bill Keegan, Trent King, Ronald Abernathy, Charles Stone, bank manager Mr. Ritter, and dragline operator Jack Goforth. (Sacramento Valley Museum.)

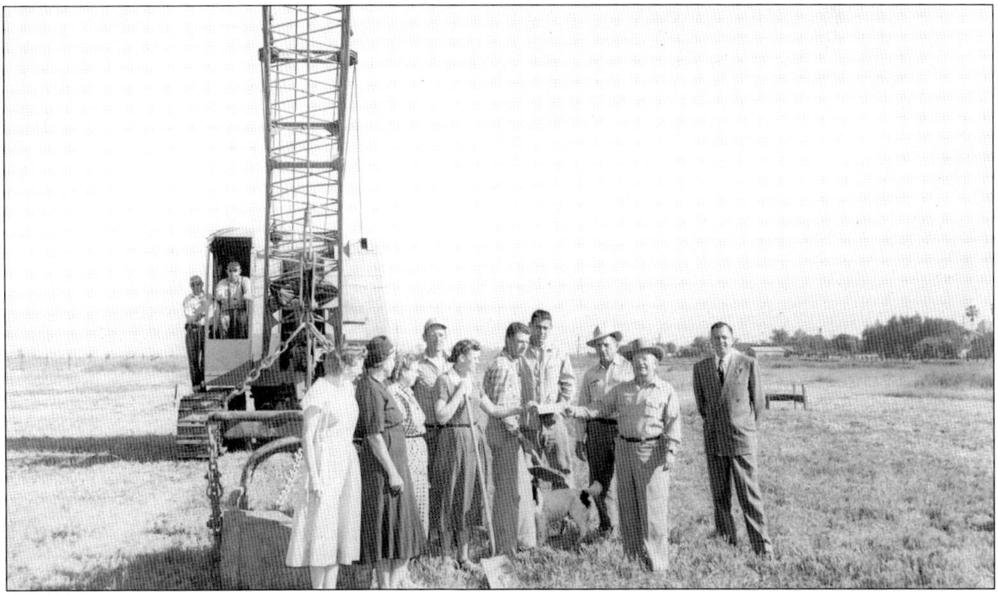

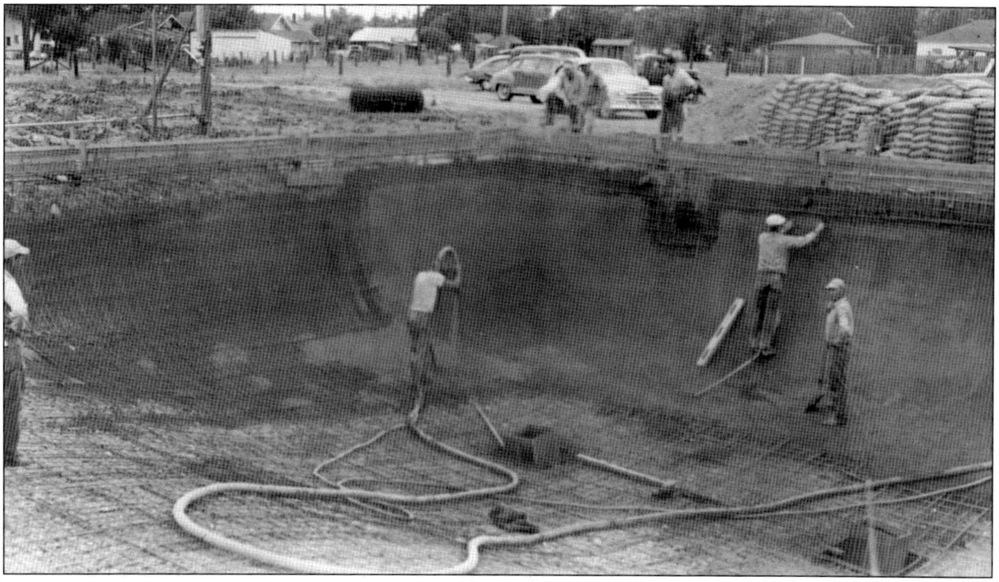

Work on the pool was done for the most part by volunteer labor, and materials were either donated or offered at a reduced price. The WCRP held fundraisers, such as pheasant hunts on lands donated by the farmers. A community festival was also held every year at the Sacramento Valley Milling Company with activities for children as well as adults, and a dance was held afterwards. (Sacramento Valley Museum.)

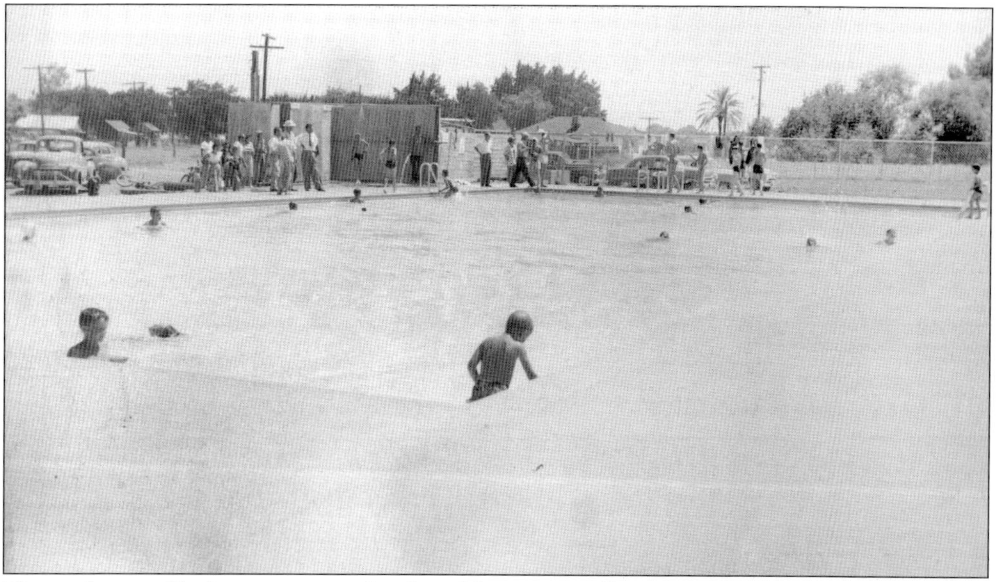

The pool opened before it was completed, and for years, Williams High School teacher and coach John Pappa organized and offered free Red Cross swimming lessons to everyone. It was John's goal and dream to have everyone able to at least swim the length of the pool before they graduated. John enlisted adults as volunteer instructors and young people as aides, and having 250 to 300 children enlist for classes was not unusual. (Sacramento Valley Museum.)

Five

PROFESSIONALS AND PROFESSIONAL VOLUNTEERS

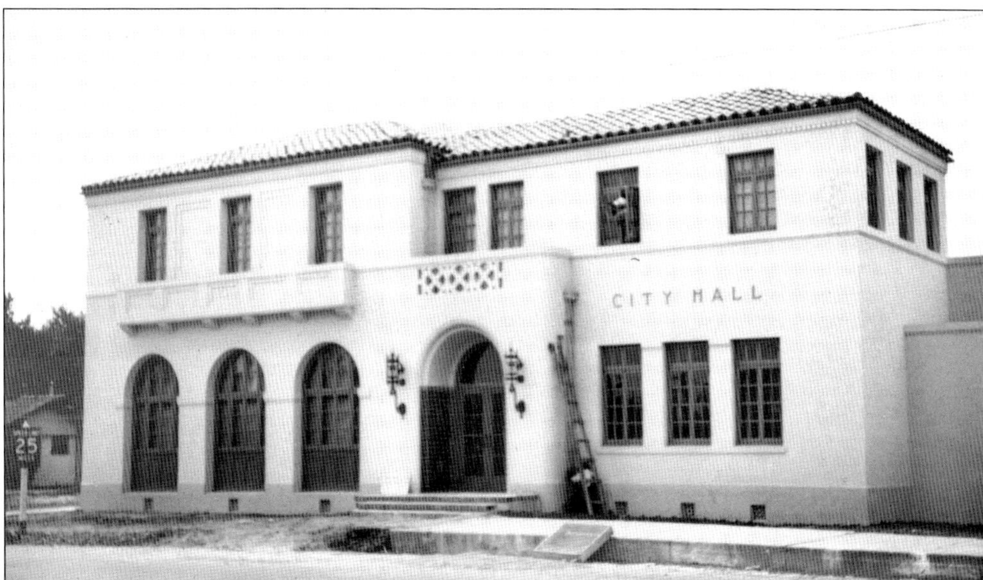

Williams City Hall was built in part with Public Works Administration funds from the federal government in 1937. The funds were part of the recovery act after the Depression. The plans were for a city hall and a jail facility on the first floor and a home for the Williams Fire Department. The upstairs was provided for the fire department with a donation of funds for its furniture from the Colusa County Board of Supervisors. The first story was poured on February 2, 1938, and an open house was held June 25, 1938. (Darolyn Marshall Mason.)

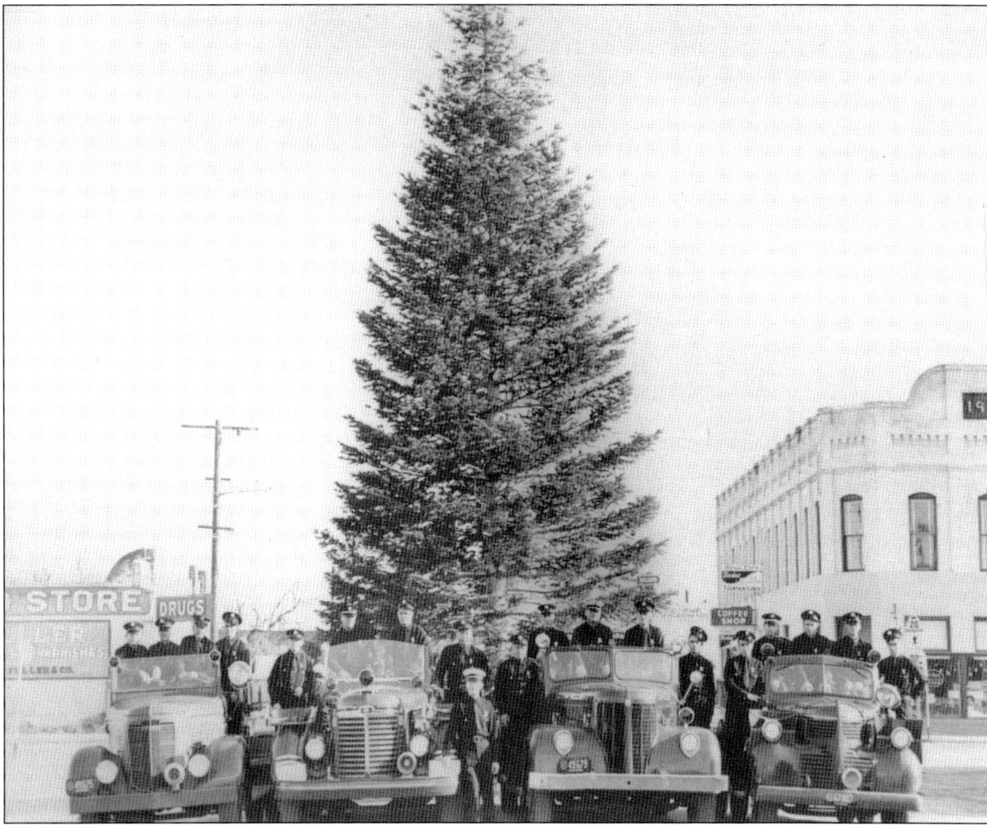

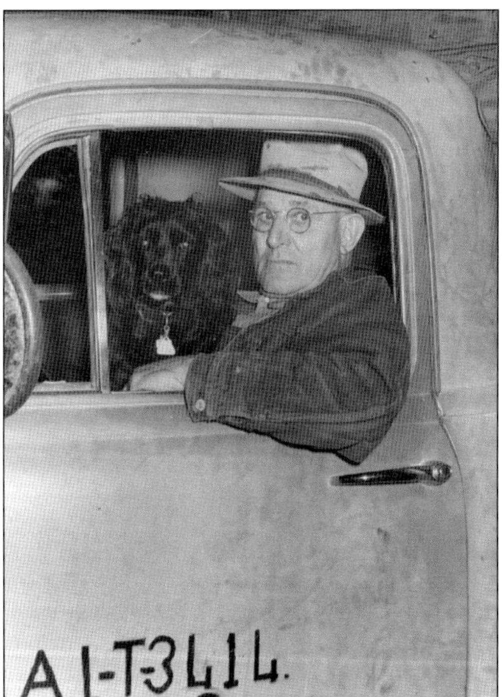

The Williams Volunteer Fire Department has always been the epitome of the word "volunteer" in the community. Since the mid-1920s, there has been a town tree, which the firemen secured, hauled, and put up in the middle of town, pictured here at the intersection of Seventh and E Streets. This photograph shows, from left to right, C. Schaad, Mel Fry, Bodie Bashore, F.B. Smith, Cliff Griffin, John McMartin, Bob Bowen, J. Laird, Otto Miller, D. Myers, J. Sutton (assistant chief), Jim Marshall, Glen Manor, Wally Gray, George Clifford (captain), Charlie Davis, Everett Brainard Sr., Ellis Rogers, and in front is Chief Don Nason. One fireman not shown in the group is Grover Wallace, shown left, who seldom failed to respond to an alarm. While he was a member, he never missed the rugged trip to secure the town tree for the community. (Above, author's collection; left, Henry W. Rhoades family.)

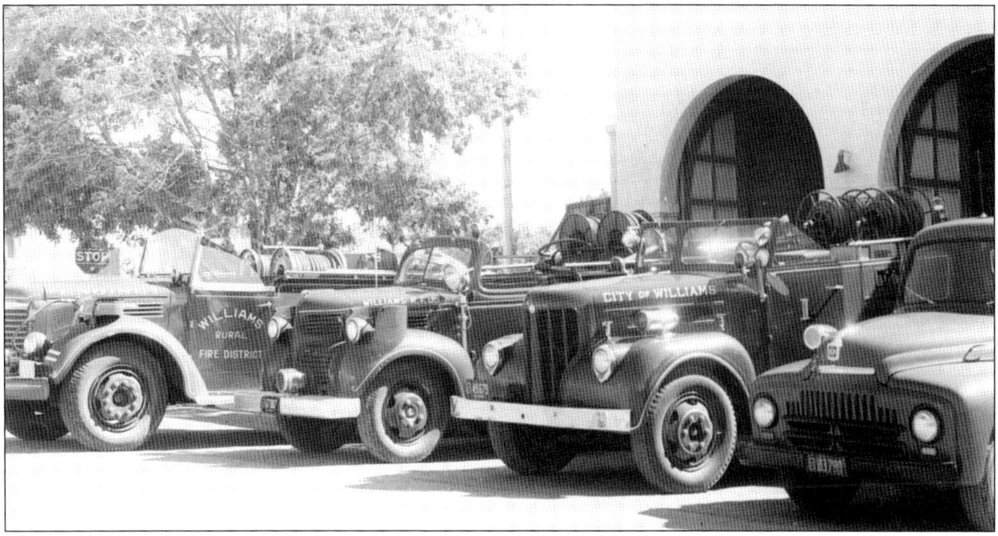

This is a publicity shot taken in 1949 for the local newspaper, the *Williams Farmer*, and shows off the fire department's trucks in front of the fire hall. The photograph below is of Jim Armocido, the Williams GMC dealer, presenting a new fire truck to the department. From left to right are Garr Rourke; Ken Flagor, city councilman; Jim Armocido; Charles Davis, Williams fire chief; and unidentified. (Above, Wanda Bowen; below, Dick Armocido.)

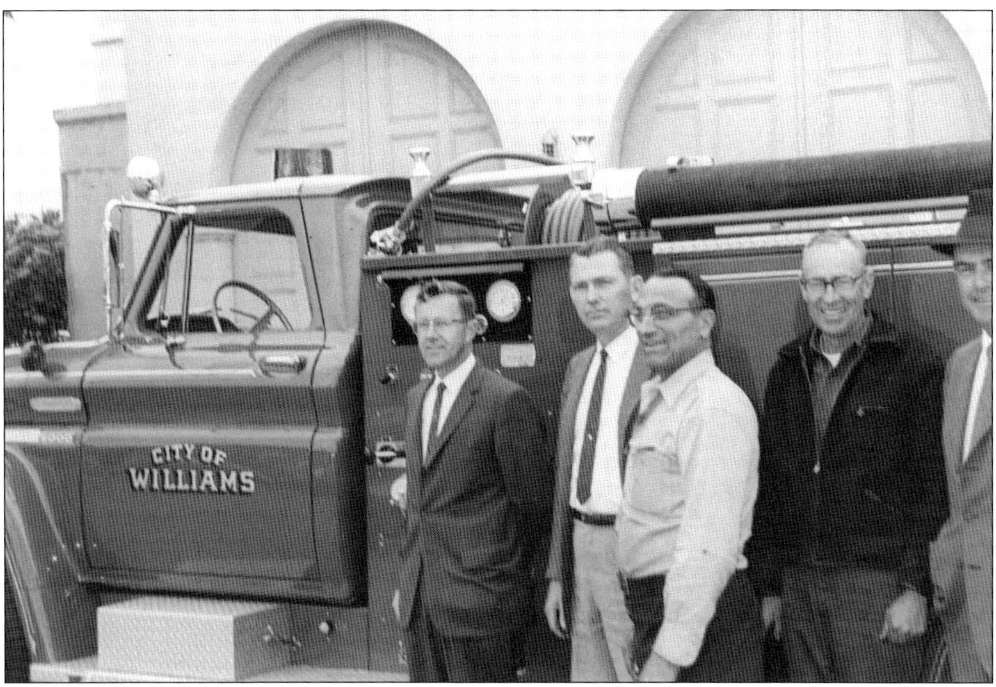

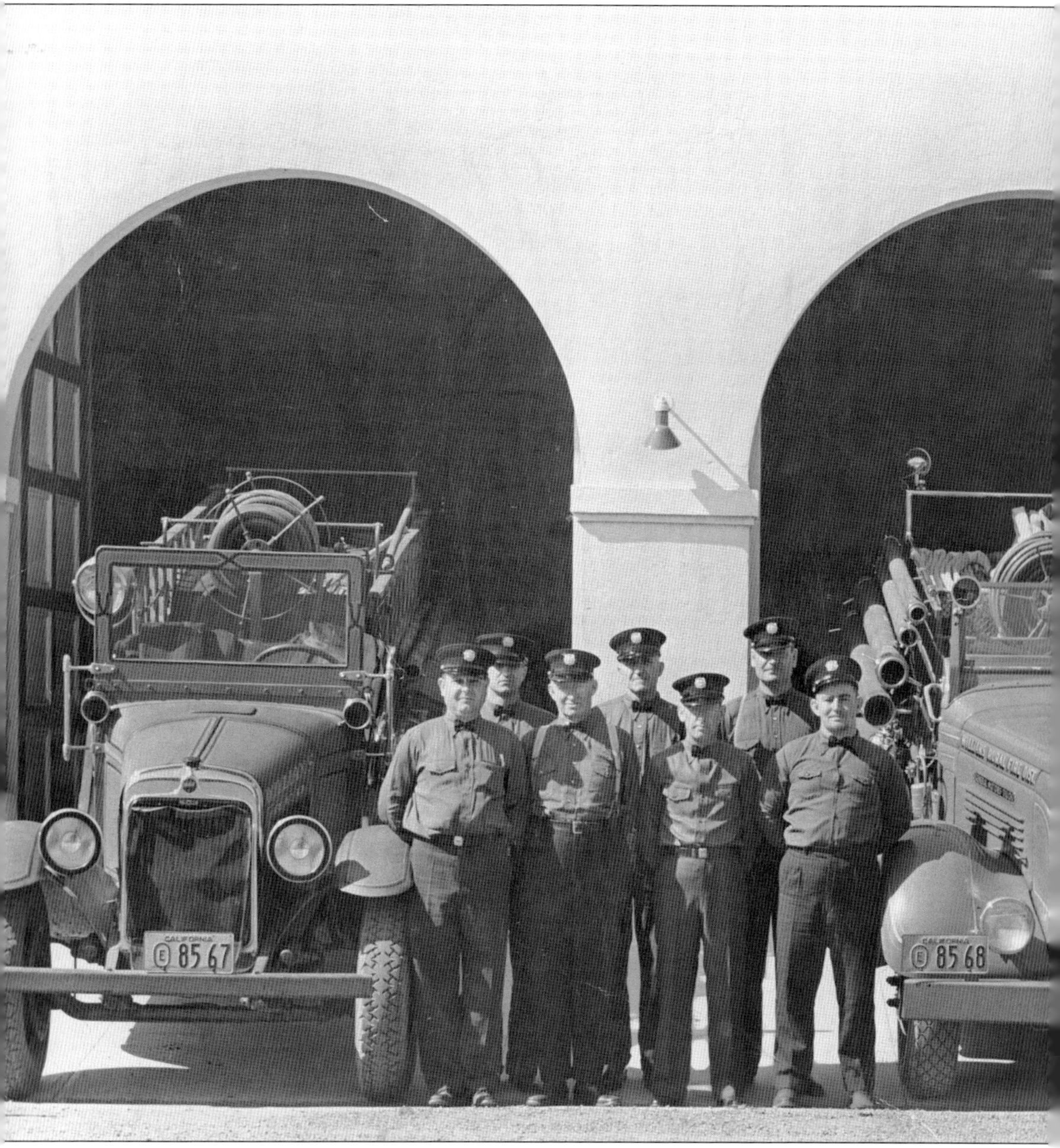

On August 24, 1906, a committee of men met to discuss the formation of a fire department for Williams. At that meeting, bylaws were established, and five trustees, officers of the department, and the first fire chief were appointed. A.E. Kidd was named chairman with John Fouch, W.H. Williams, J.L. Mendenhall, J.M. Stovall, and E.L. Christopher named as trustees and H.H. Retterath named as fire chief. By October 27, 1906, a building was being constructed to house the new chemical fire engine that was being shipped from St. Louis, Missouri. The building still stands today at the alley between Seventh and Eighth Streets and is now a retail space. The first fire bell was purchased in 1909 and stands at the corner of the Eighth and E Streets as a monument to all firefighters. In the early days, firemen had no meeting place, so they met at the Odd Fellows Hall, the justice court, and later at the legion hall above Miller's pool hall. With

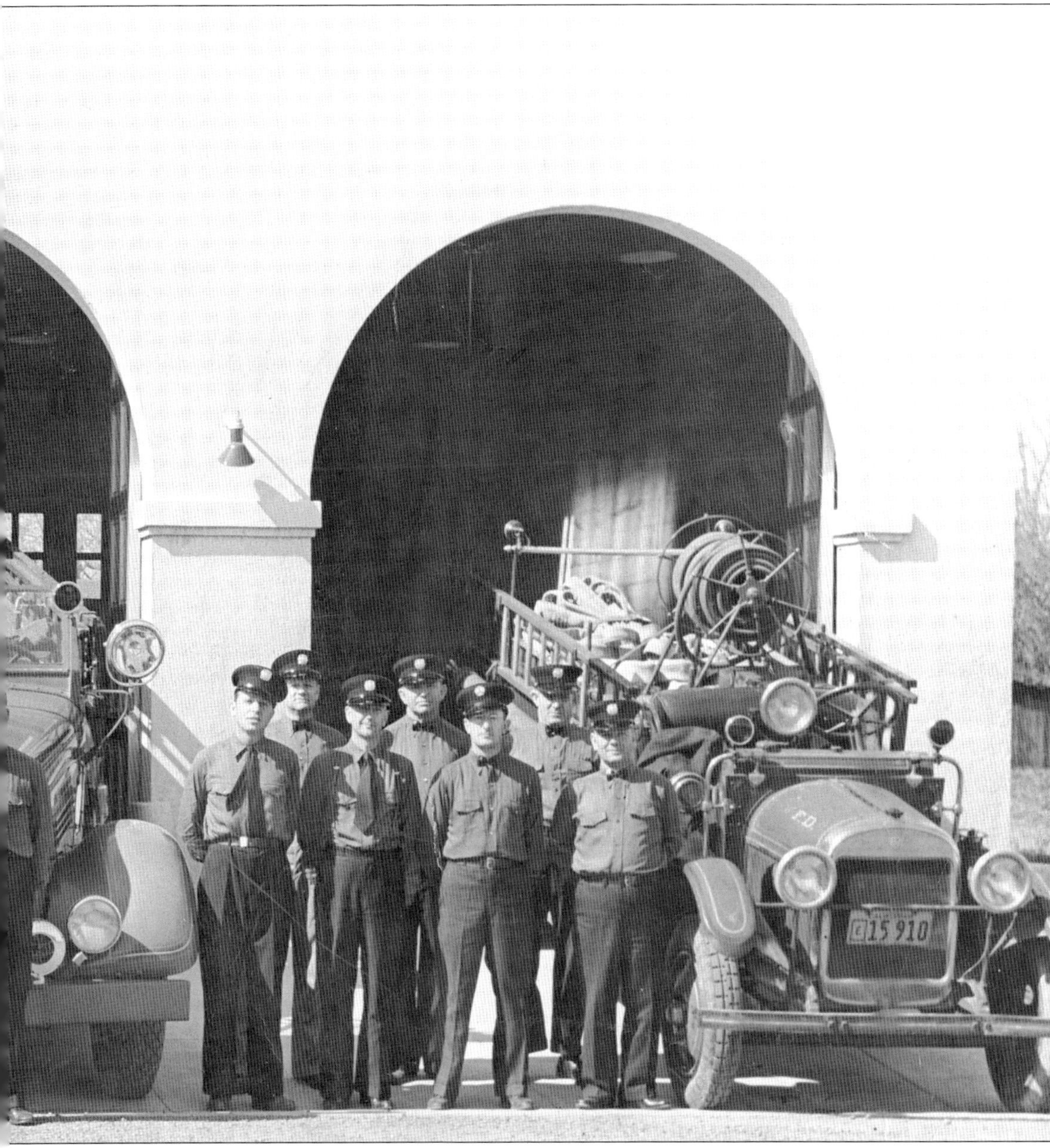

the construction of the city hall in 1937, a home was provided for the department, and with the anticipation of having a 24-hour staff at some point, an upstairs was provided. From those humble beginnings, the department has grown and progressed into a department "professionally staffed by volunteers." Over the years, the department has volunteered millions of hours of training and proudly serves its community. This 1939 photograph on the left shows, from left to right, (first row) Herb Christy, Jack Forsythe, Onlow Burrows, and Juney Davis; (second row) Ben Peters, Glen Foster, and Jim Sutton. In the center is fire chief Otto Miller, who served as chief from 1928 to 1942. Pictured on the right side are, from left to right, (first row) Charley Schaad, Soapy Abel, Don Nason, and Warren "Stub" Tallman; (second row) Harry Smith, Cliff Griffin, and Grover Wallace. (Jauregui family collection.)

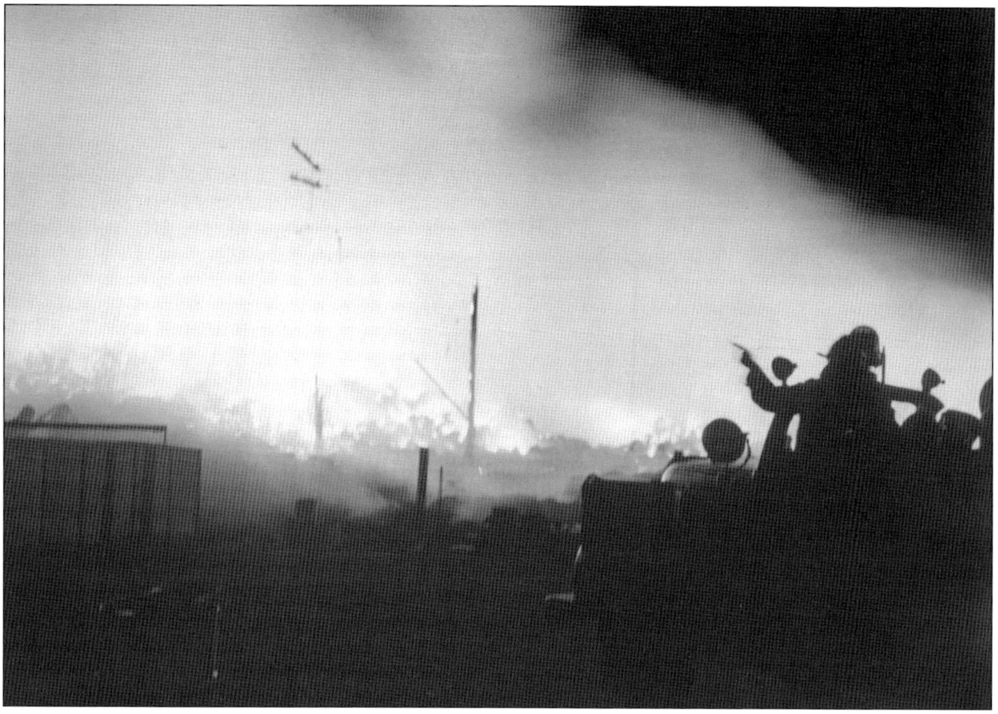

In recent years, one of the largest fires in Williams occurred on June 4, 1961, at Endeman Feed and Pellet, the company that occupied the old brick warehouse built by W.H. Williams. Endeman had a large pole barn with hay storage that caught fire the evening of June 4. All available men turned out with mutual aid from Arbuckle, Maxwell, and Colusa responding. The fire was contained miraculously to the property and did not spread to nearby houses. The fire continued to smolder for days, and the magnitude of the fire is captured by Henry Rhoades in these photographs. (Both, Henry W. Rhoades family.)

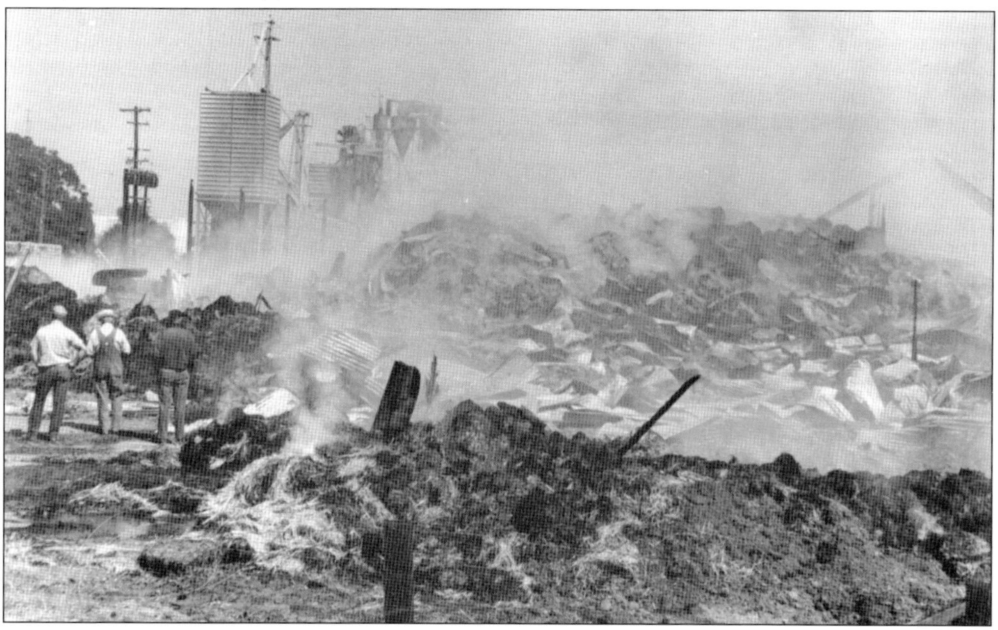

Men were called by the "plectron," a radio device that each fireman had in their home. When the fire phone was answered at the station, the details of the fire were sent to all firemen. Many showed up this night ready to fight the fire with just their street clothes on, and many bystanders were pulled into service as well. In the photograph below, kneeling with the hose in fireman turnouts is Jim Manor, other Williams firemen George Marengo and Parker Wallace, and Maxwell fireman Butch Martinez in the rear. Shown at right, Jim Manor is standing while Frank Kintana looks on. (Both, Henry W. Rhoades family.)

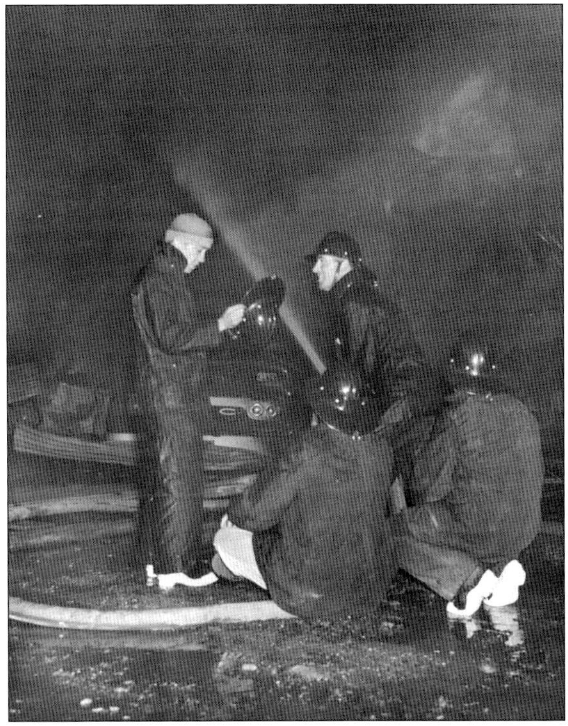

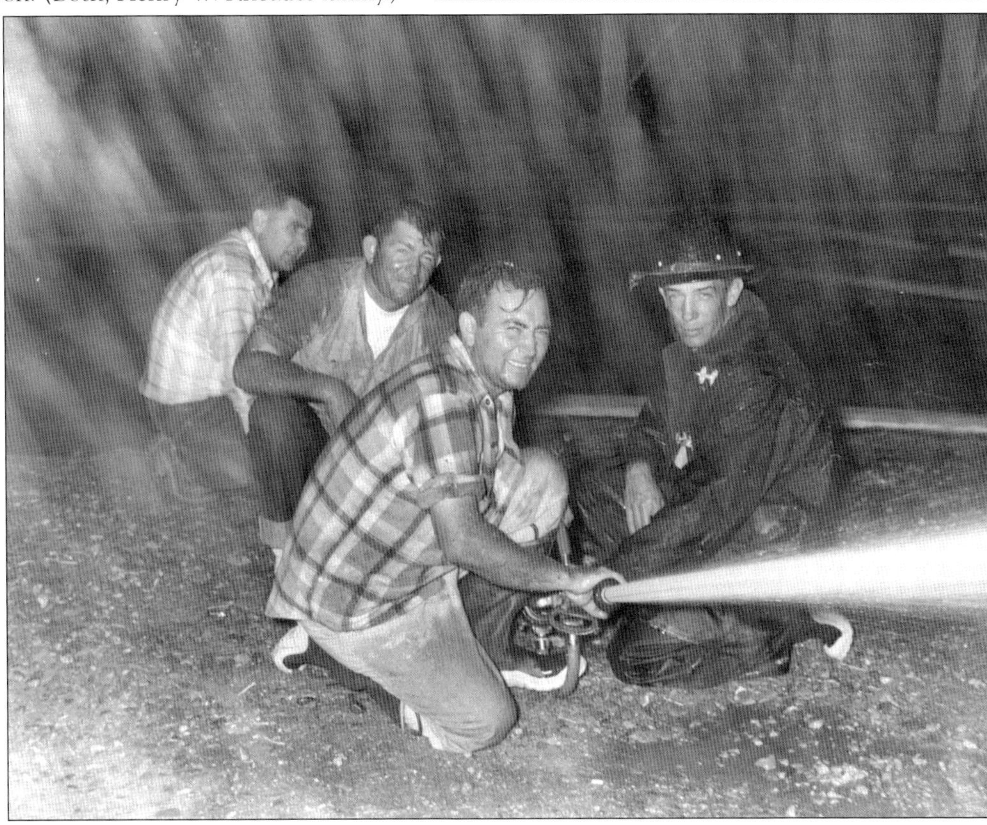

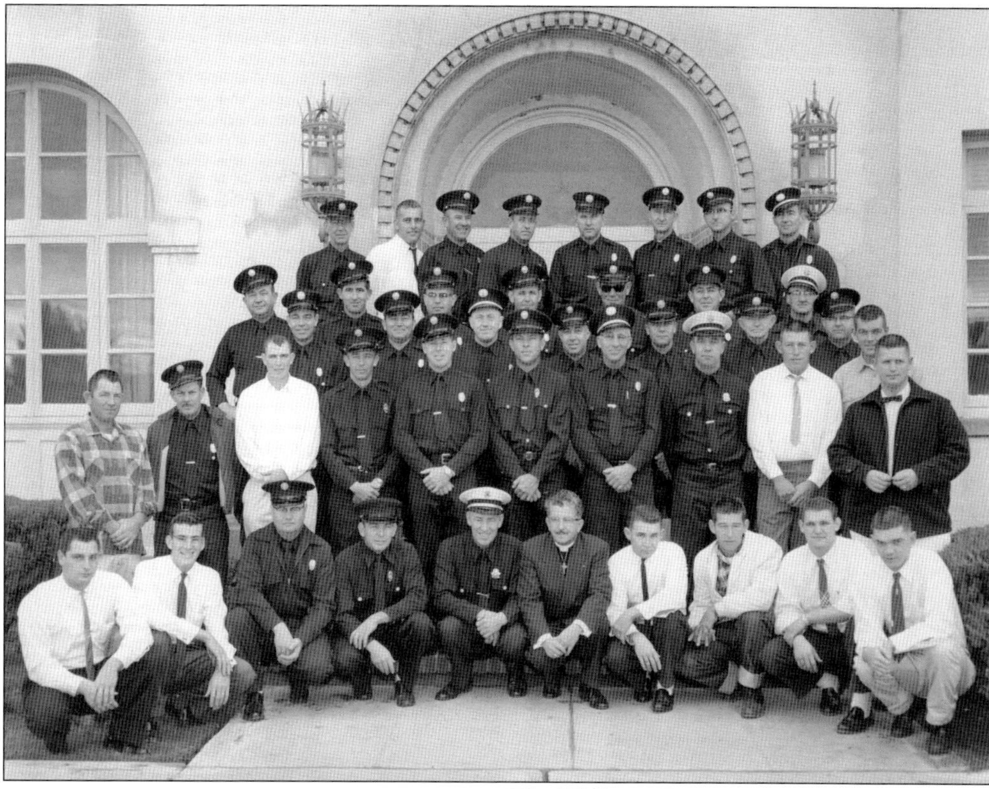

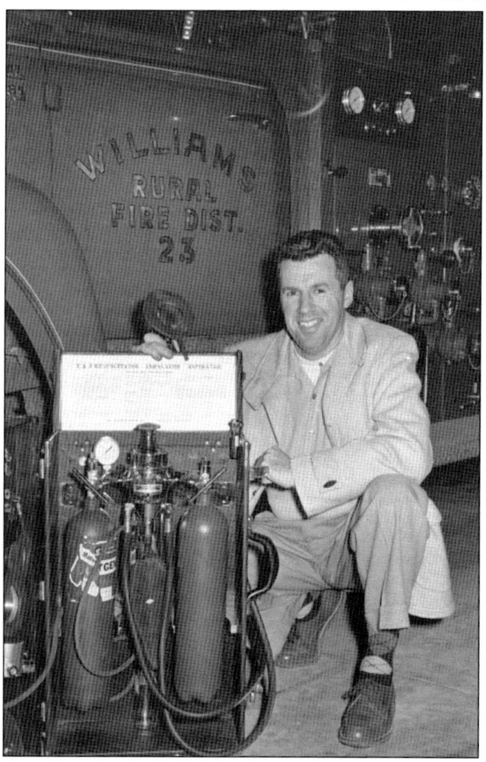

The Williams Fire Department is shown above with new inductees around 1961. From left to right are (first row) Marty Marengo, Dave Goforth, Jim Bowen, Milt Bruhn, Chief Charlie Davis, Doctor Hurtt, Roy Goforth, Harry Hunt, Wes Caudill, and Ed Gassaway; (second row) Parker Wallace, Bob Roof, Gary Fouch, Jim Manor, Milt Gentry, Bill Grussenmeyer, Elmer Goforth, assistant chief Glenn Manor, Russell Keffer, Russ Ohlsen, and Vern Swanson; (third row) Bob Roper, George Marengo, Hal Stober, Matt Jauregui, Don Manor, Cliff Griffin, and Jack Rice; (fourth row) Frank "Sy" Kemp, Frank Kintana, Bob Bowen, Holly Smith, Charlie Myers, Everett Kraft, and assistant chief Everett Brainard Sr.; (fifth row) Bryant Mendenhall, Larry Davis, Garland "Bodie" Bashore, Gene Arambel, Bill Boyes, Byron "Slim" Caldwell, Ray Weston, and Ellis Rogers. Also a member of the department was Al Waring (left), who brought the first resuscitator to the department. This photograph at left was taken January 1958. (Above, author's collection; left, Henry W. Rhoades family.)

Al and Annette Fouch Waring are pictured at the Sacramento Valley Museum with the display of the generations of doctors, pharmacists, and nurses from Annette's family. Annette was a pharmacist for over 68 years while Al, her husband of 70 years, obtained his pharmacist's license while in the service during World War II. (Henry W. Rhoades family.)

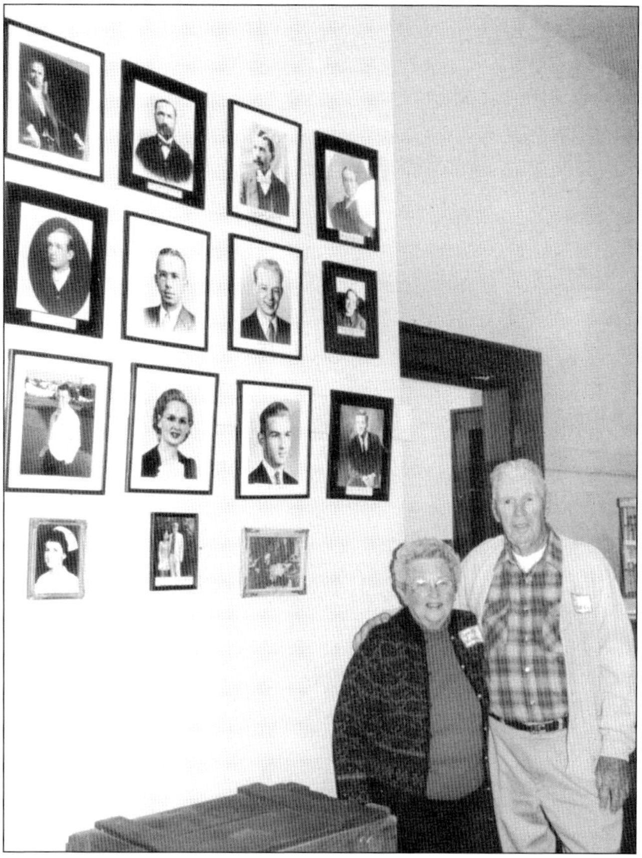

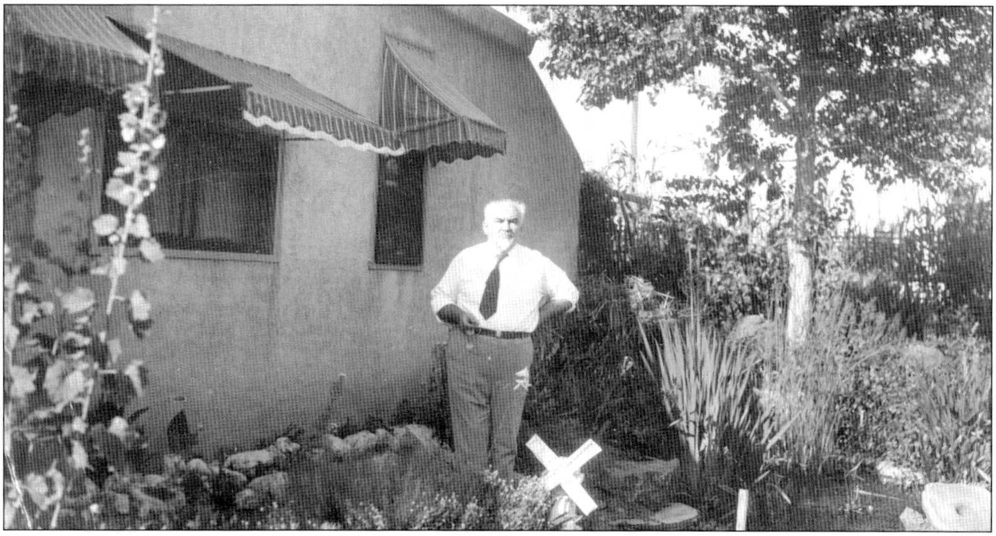

Dr. Ney Salter arrived in Williams on Christmas Eve 1911 and began his practice. During World War I, he enlisted in the medical corps of the US Army as a lieutenant. When he returned in June 1919, he opened a 10-bed hospital in Williams. Active in the Masons, Boy Scouts, Odd Fellows lodge, and a commander of American Legion Post No. 214, he left a grieving community and county at his passing in 1940. (Annette Abel La Grande.)

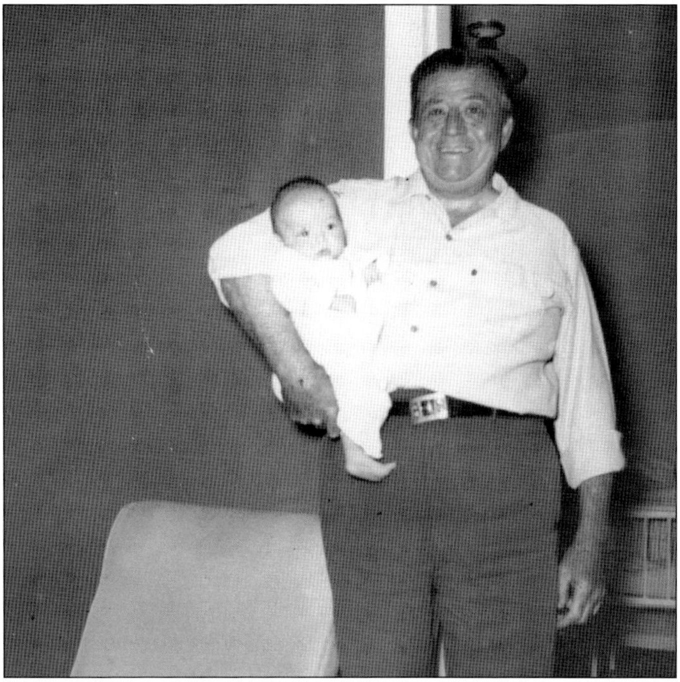

Dr. Charles Keith, another long-practicing physician of Williams, was the epitome of the country doctor. House calls were common, and payment was sometimes a home-baked pie or a chicken. Before the ambulance was available, Doctor Keith transported patients to the hospital himself. He was a member of the American Legion football team that was organized after World War I and was also an active member of the Shriners and the Kiwanis. (Susan Leardini.)

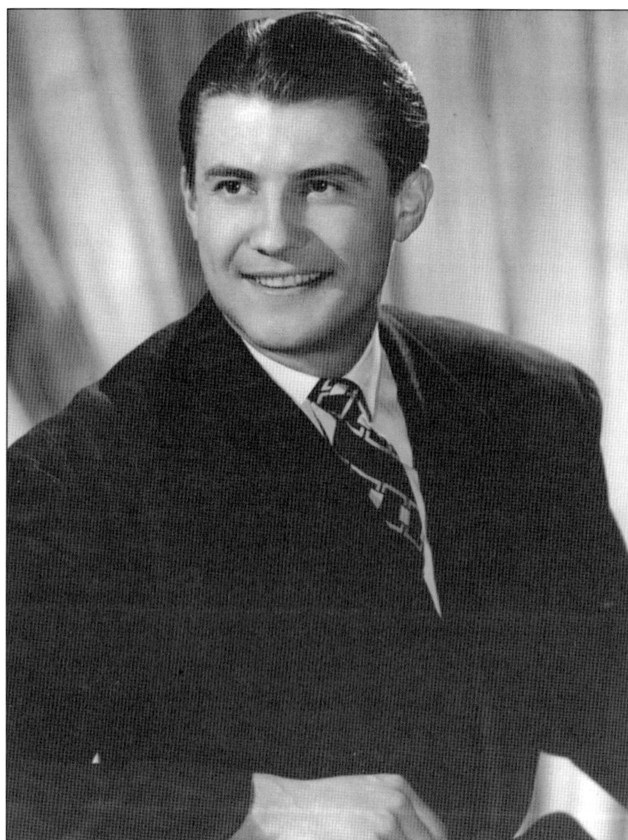

Filling in for two weeks in 1949, Dr. Charles E. McCarl ended up practicing for 62 years in Williams, delivering thousands of babies, helping to build a convalescent hospital, mentoring young people, serving on the Williams Union School Board, and acting as the Williams Yellow Jackets team physician for 58 years, and in 2010 the Williams High School football field was named McCarl Field in his honor. He was also active in Kiwanis and was never known to have an unkind word. He retired in November 2011. (McCarl family.)

Anson Crutcher, son of Harry and Fern Crutcher, was born in 1913, raised in Williams, and was a graduate of the Williams School system. He went on to become the first chief of the California State Police in 1933. He passed in 1970 at the age of 57. (Sacramento Valley Museum.)

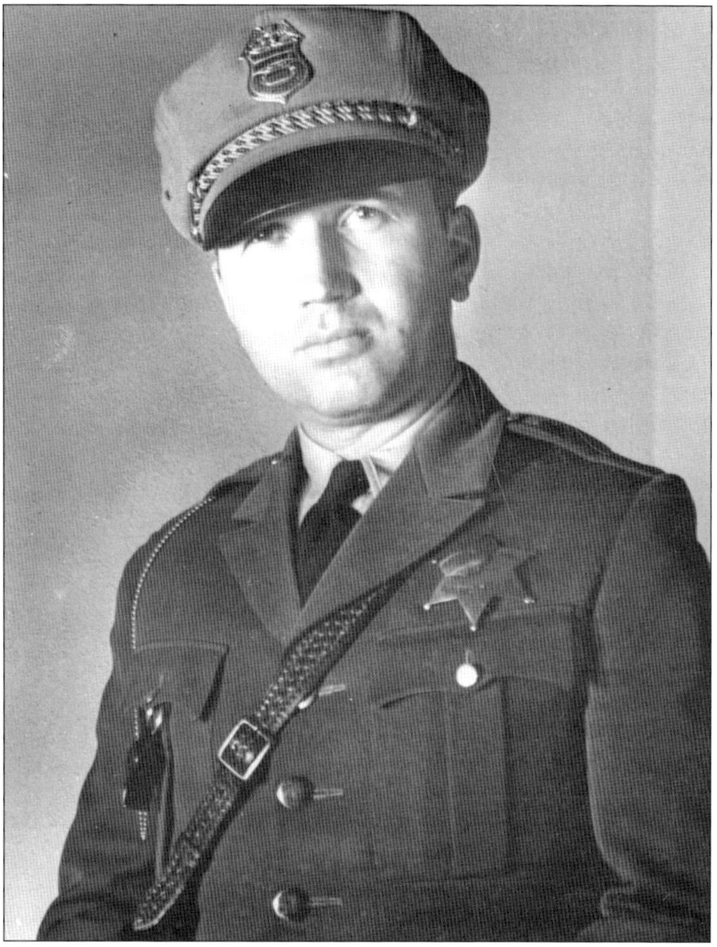

The California Highway Patrol has had an office in Williams for many years. This 1958 photograph shows the Williams squad, including the Willows substation, from left to right, Inspector Murray and Officers Costa, Robert "Bob" Swallow, Ewing, Flanagan, and Mitchell, Captain Bradley, Lieutenant Pierano, and Officer Pitter. (Bob Swallow family.)

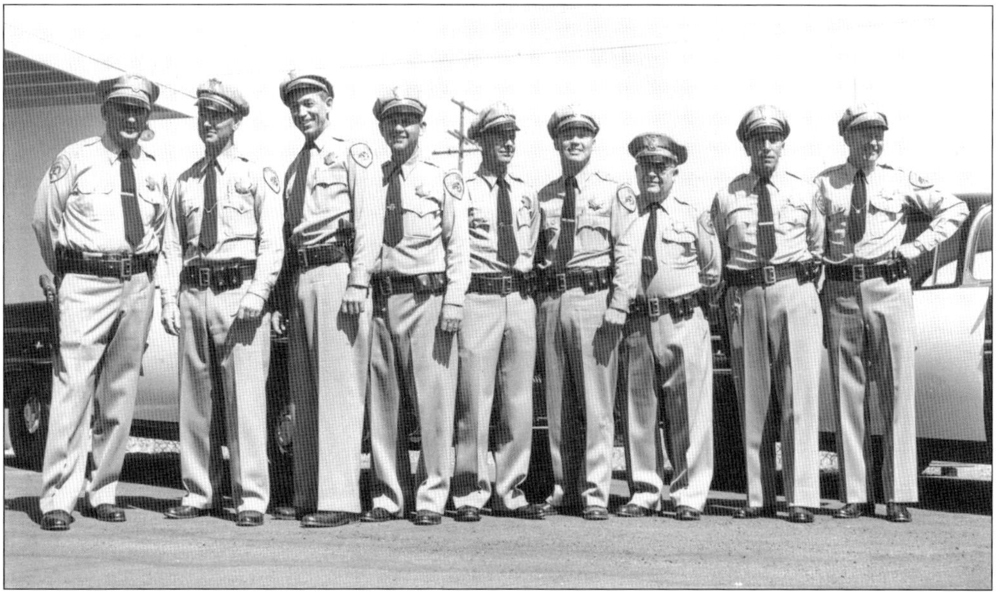

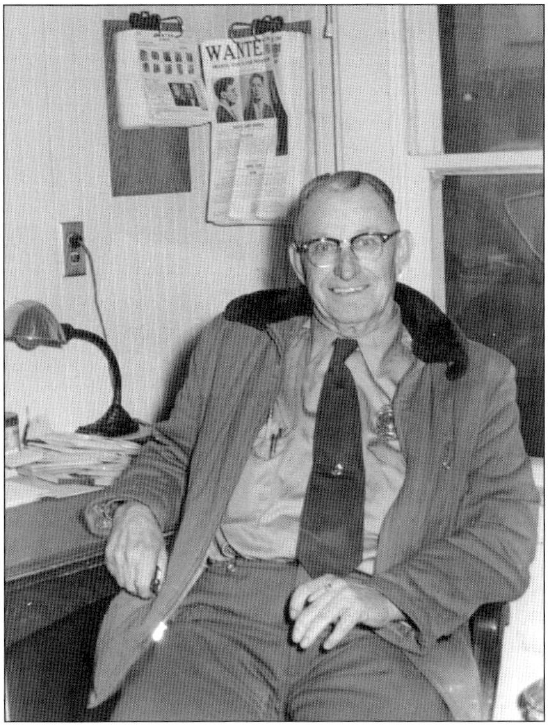

Before the days of a police force, a constable and chief of police protected the town. Shown in his office in 1956 is World War I veteran Jack Forsythe as constable. Below, Arch Matzka (police chief) at left is shown chatting with town mayor Ralph Fouch at his place of business, Fouch's Drugstore. Long before using the radio, these men were often seen around town visiting with the locals, and at night were known to walk the downtown business district rattling doors to doing security checks. Arch was a World War I veteran, joined the Williams Fire Department in 1924, and played on the American Legion football team made up of World War I veterans. (Both, Henry W. Rhoades family.)

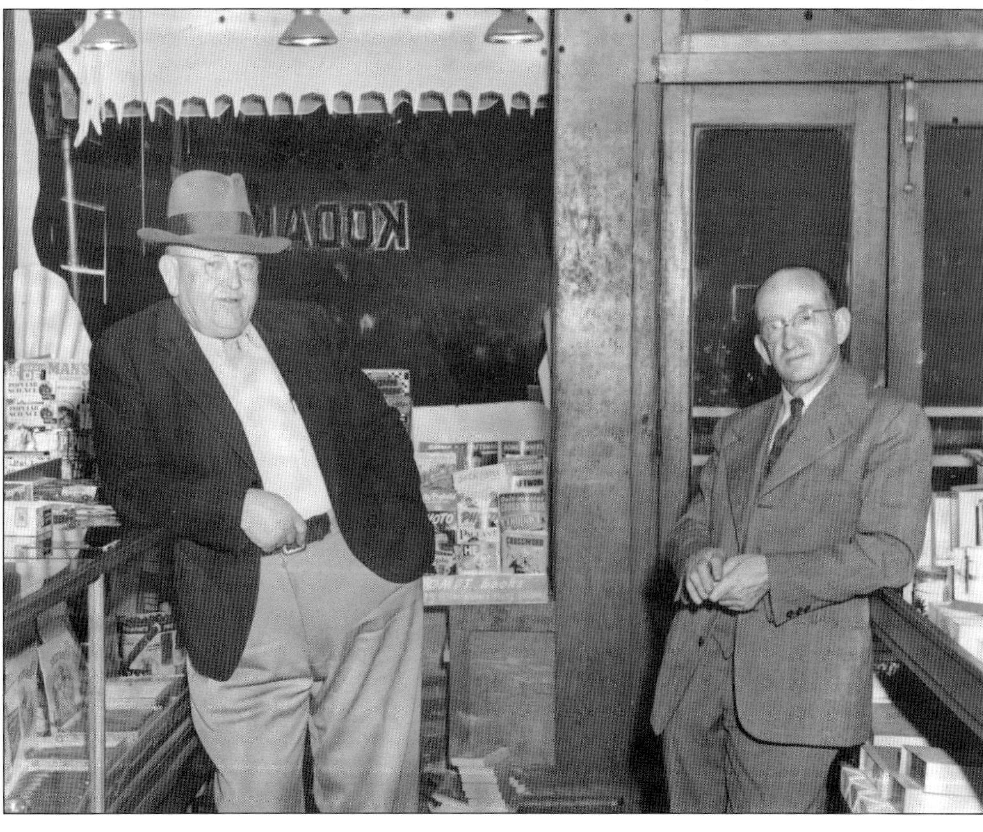

Six

THE MOUNTAIN HOUSE, SPRINGS, AND QUARRIES

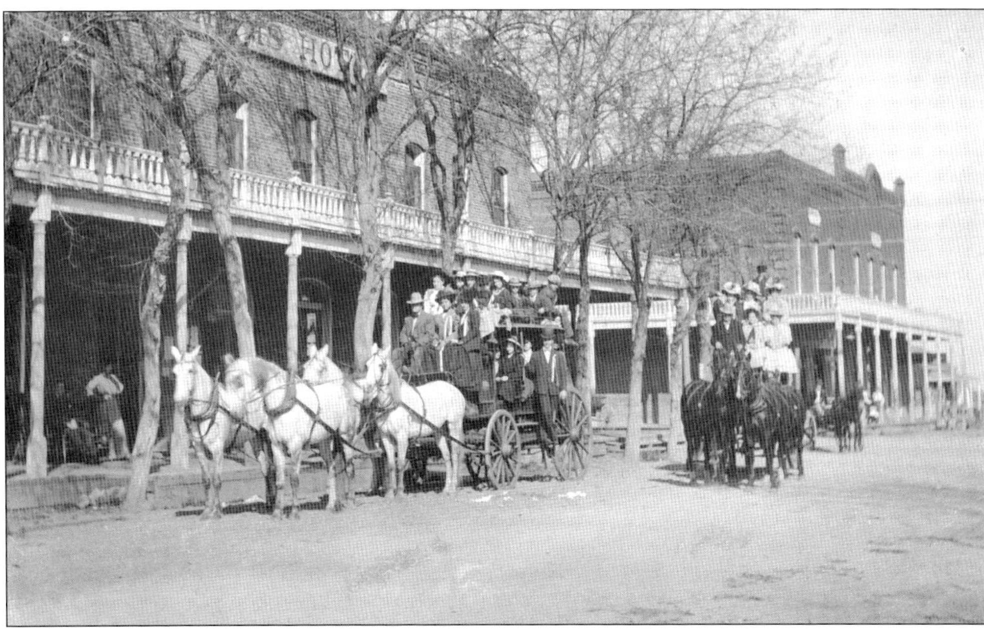

These two stages in front of the Williams Hotel are set for the springs. The mineral baths were a real asset to the economy of Williams. People would stay at the hotel and rest up after the long train trip and then proceed to any one of the health springs in western Colusa and Lake Counties. (Sacramento Valley Museum.)

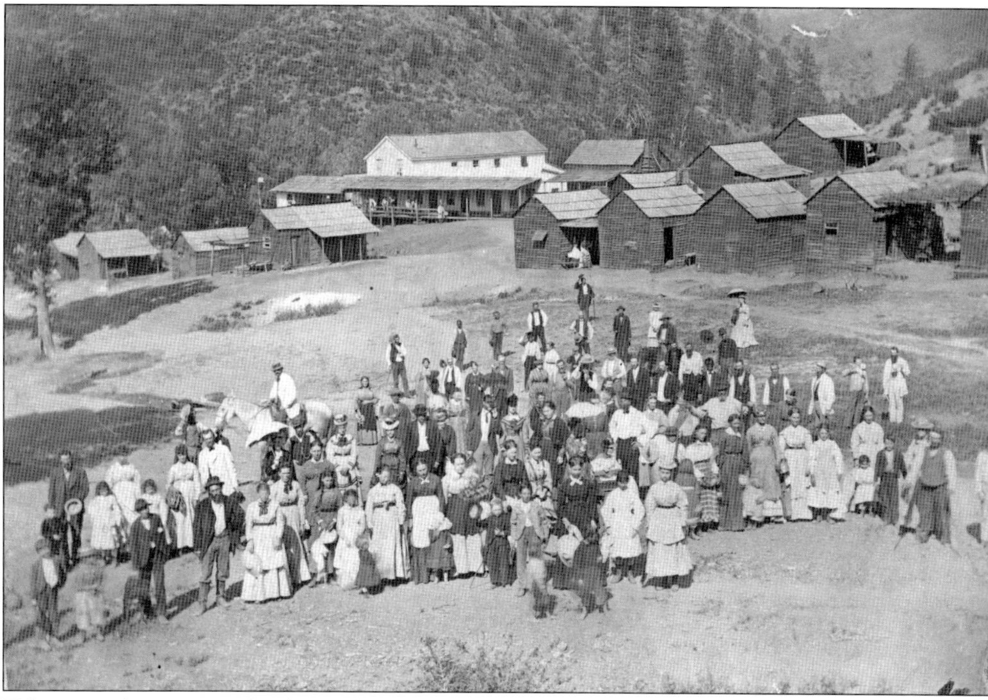

Taken just three years after being discovered by Green Bartlett in 1873, this is one of the earliest photographs found of Bartlett Springs. Already, buildings have sprung up, and an obvious showing of people has arrived to take advantage of the healing waters. (Doug Gassaway.)

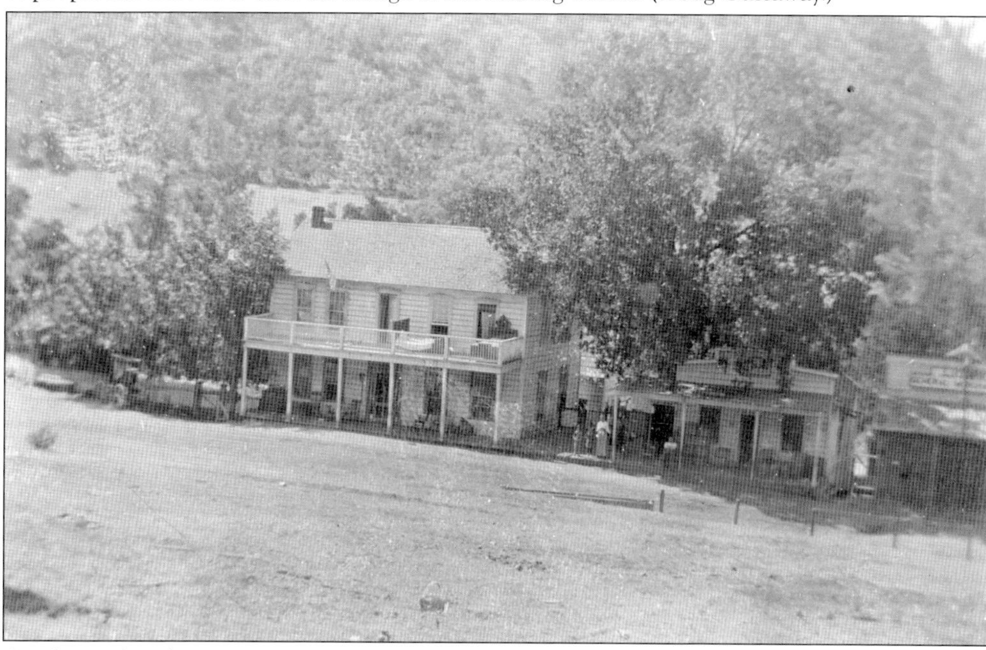

On the road to the springs was Leesville, a small village at the head of Bear Valley. Built by Peter S. Perdue in 1878, it consisted of 290 acres. He developed the business into a much-desired place to stay. Along with the hotel were a post office, express office, a general store, a large livery stable, and other shops. The hotel is still standing. (Jean Terkildsen.)

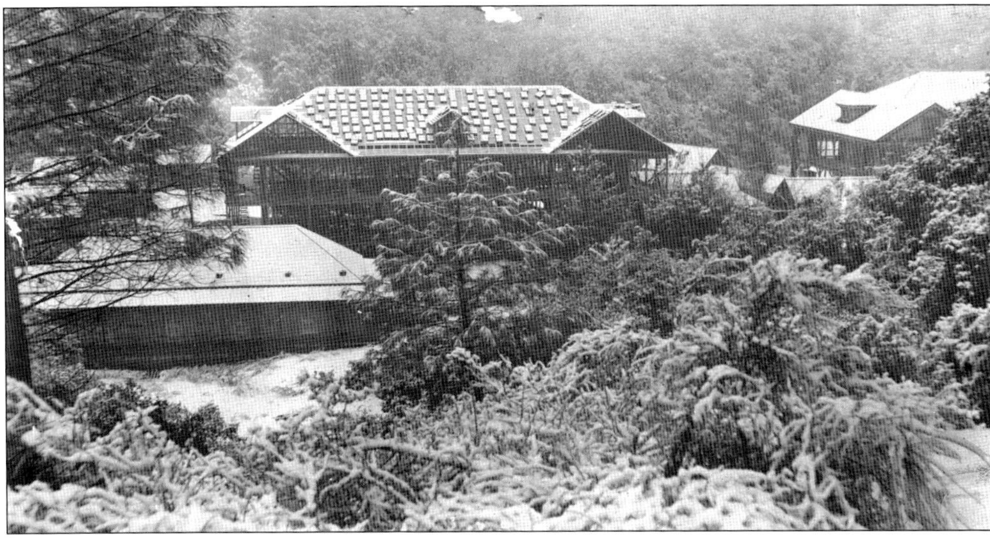

Around 1863, Reed Bartlett happened upon a mineral spring when stricken by rheumatism while hunting. Just over the Colusa County border, Bartlett Springs developed into a regular community with shopping and a school. In the early 1900s, it was not unusual to see 1,500 people in attendance. Many families spent the whole summer there, and when the more affluent would reject riding the stage, they would rent their own teams and buggies from the Williams livery stables. Many of the clientele were from San Francisco. These photographs, taken in 1907, show the new building that was going on after one of the many fires swept though the foothills. Built by Victor Weber, these photographs show the magnitude of the business. (Both, Sacramento Valley Museum.)

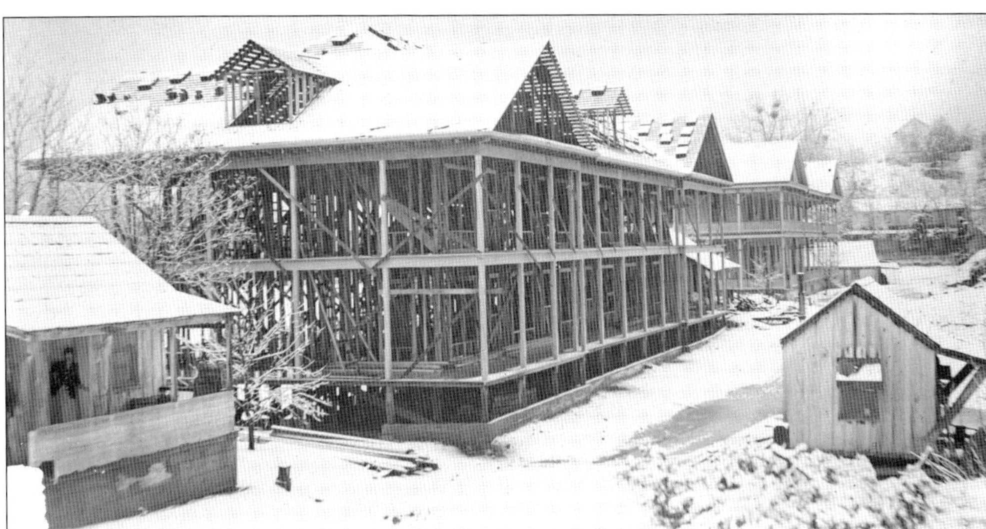

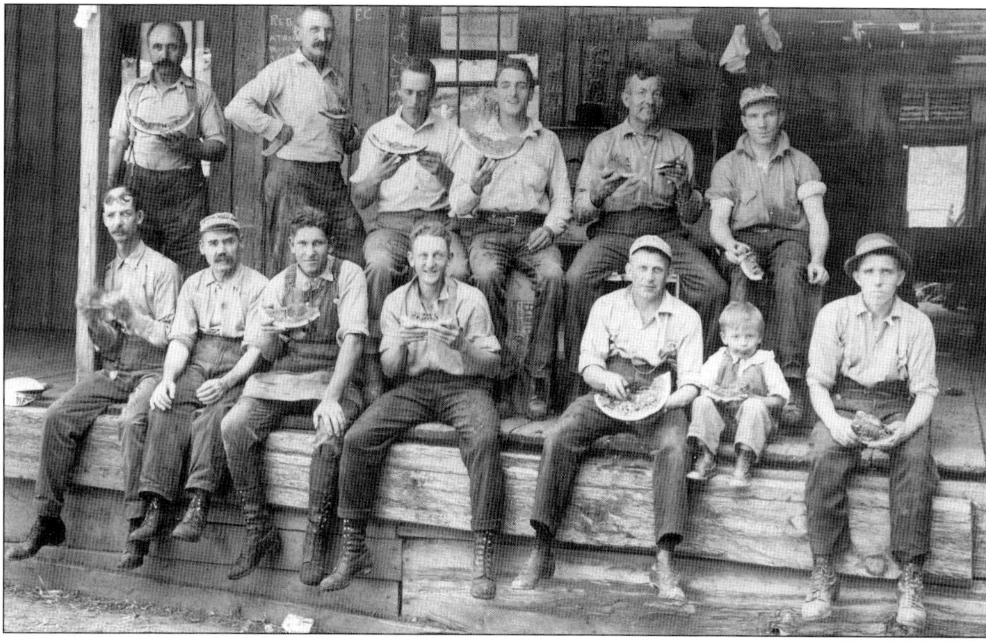

In 1893, Williams was made the central distributing point for Bartlett water, and before long, the town had 10,000 bottles stored in a warehouse and four freight teams hauling water regularly. The water was bottled from underground without exposure to air. This photograph shows the bottling crew taking a break and enjoying watermelon. In 1906, there were 35,000 cases of water, or 1,000,750 bottles, shipped that year alone, providing Williams with a huge contribution to the railroad freight lines. (Ash family collection.)

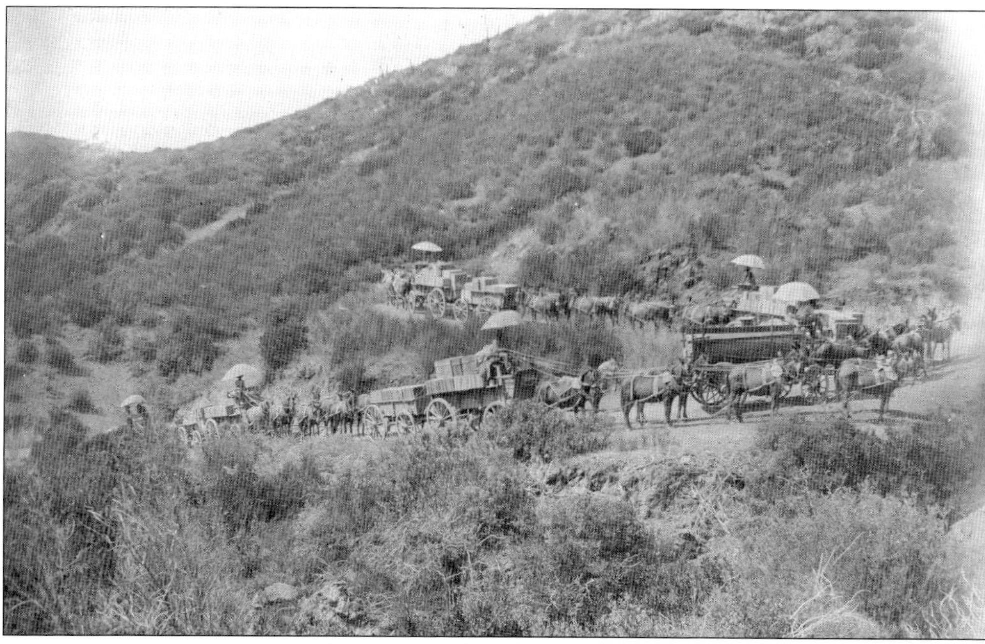

It was sometimes a long, slow, dusty trip with only a small umbrella for shade up and over the mountains, especially when teams were backed up. Nate Crawford is shown with his team and wagons, the next to the last in the train. (Jean Terkildsen.)

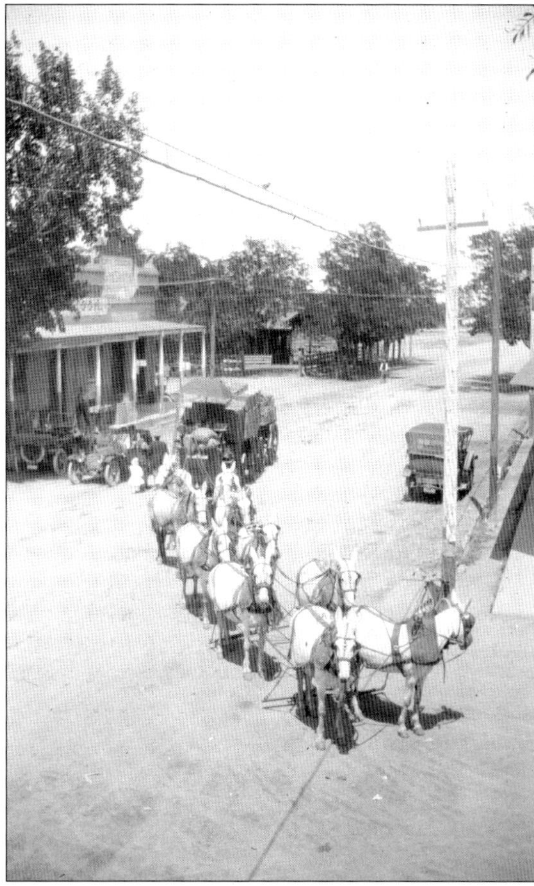

Wagons of water left Bartlett Springs on a regular basis. Leaving Williams, the teamsters would load the double sets of wagons with supplies bound for the springs, and then once unloaded, would load the wagons with water and return. The trips took an average of three days, stopping for sets of fresh mules at places along the way. Leaving Williams is Arch Paxton and his prized matched white mules, with another photograph of Arch leaving the springs with added mules for the long haul. Each mule was fitted with his own rigging made just to fit that particular animal. Arch was said to be the mule skinner extraordinaire of Colusa County. (Right, Gibson family collection; below, author's collection.)

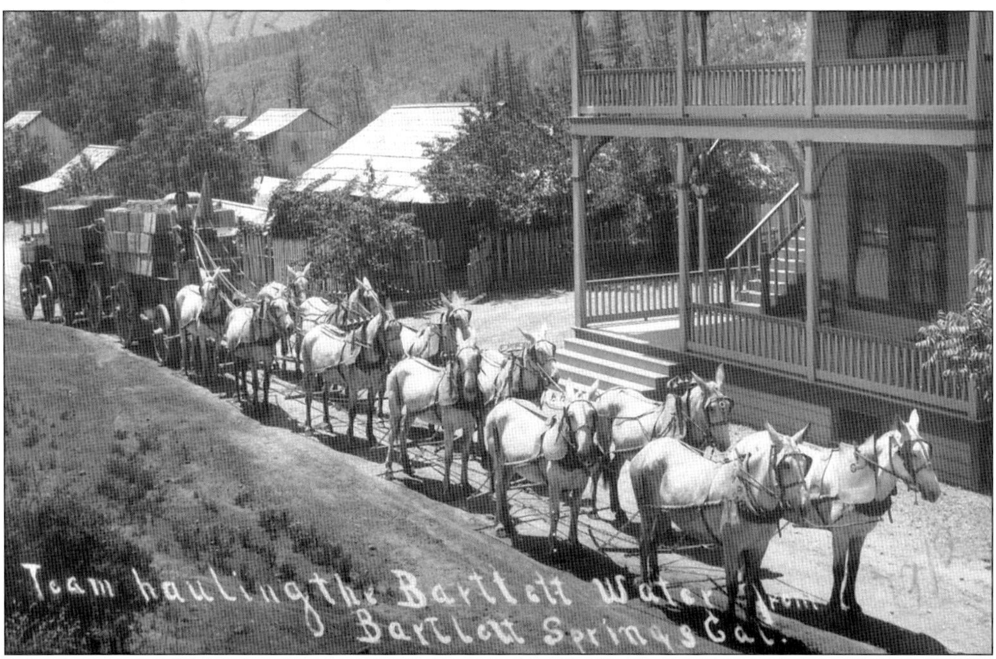

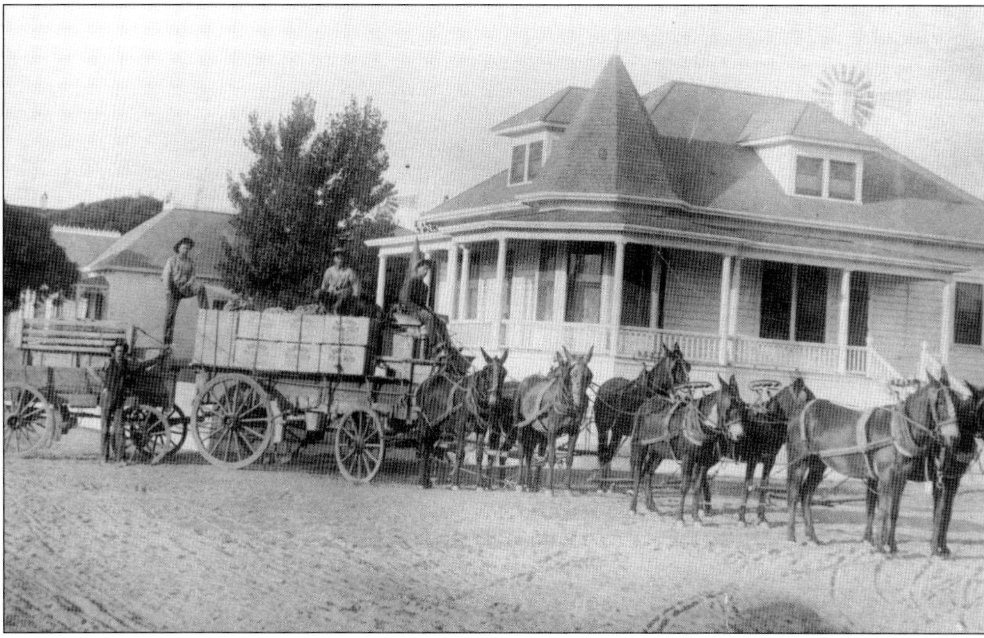

The Gassaway Bros. also had a freight line. They serviced all the springs of Colusa County and into Lake County. They are pictured in front of the Stovall house before 1904 with boxes marked Bartlett Springs. Below, they are seen coming out of Bartlett with water. The mules were furnished with bells so they could be heard coming around curves and at night. The mules knew what was expected of them, especially on the mountain grades. Six or seven miles an hour was considered making good time. The two back mules, known as wheelers, were larger than the two front ones, known as leaders. On sharp turns, the skinner gave rein, and the mules did the rest. The leaders picked up speed, swung to the outside of the grade, started to turn, and the wheelers held back just enough to stabilize the rest. (Both, Gassaway family collection.)

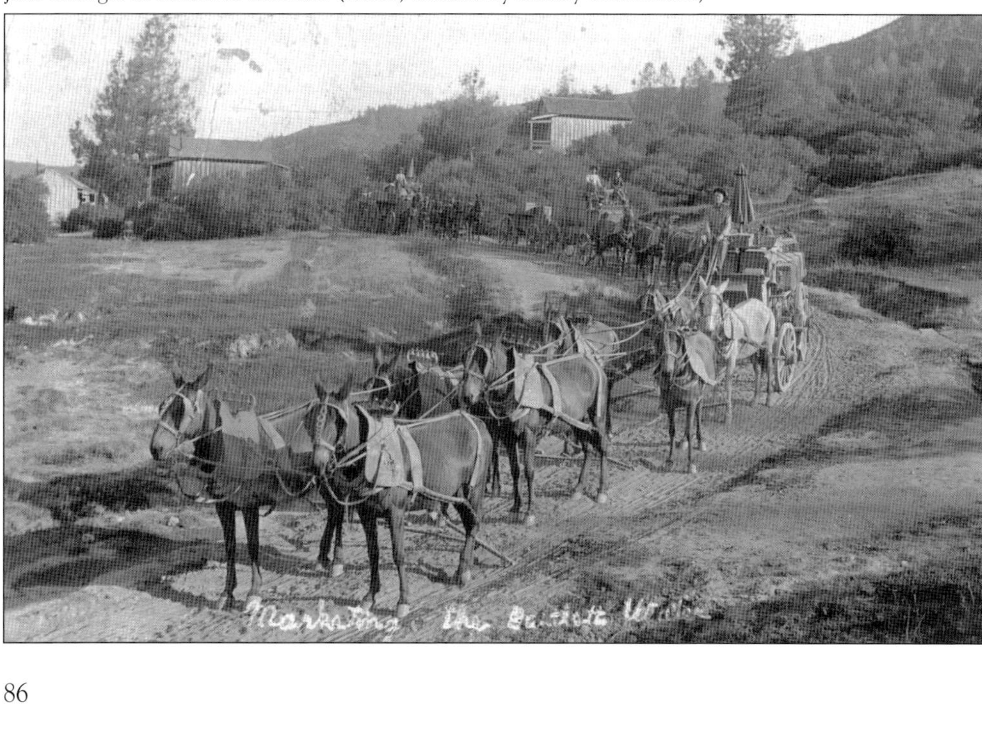

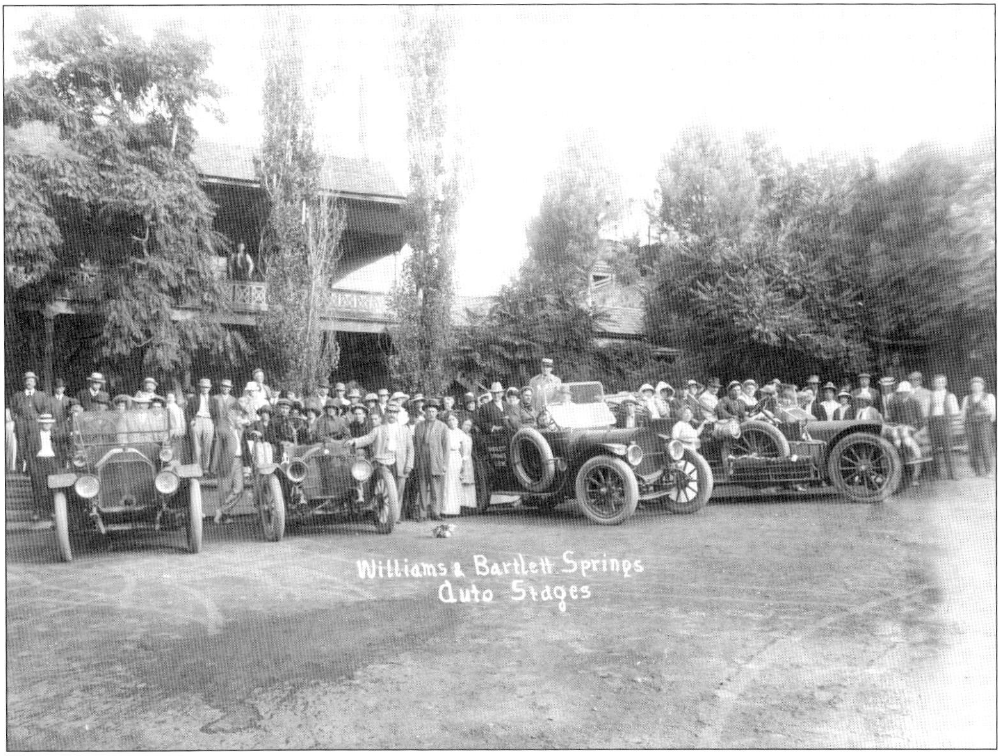

Around 1910, horse-drawn stages were overshadowed by the horseless carriage. The one o'clock train would be met in Williams by the Bartlett Stage lines, and the touring cars were loaded with people on another leg of their journey of 44 miles to the springs. This 1913 photograph shows the departing guests on their way back to Williams and parts unknown. (Sacramento Valley Museum.)

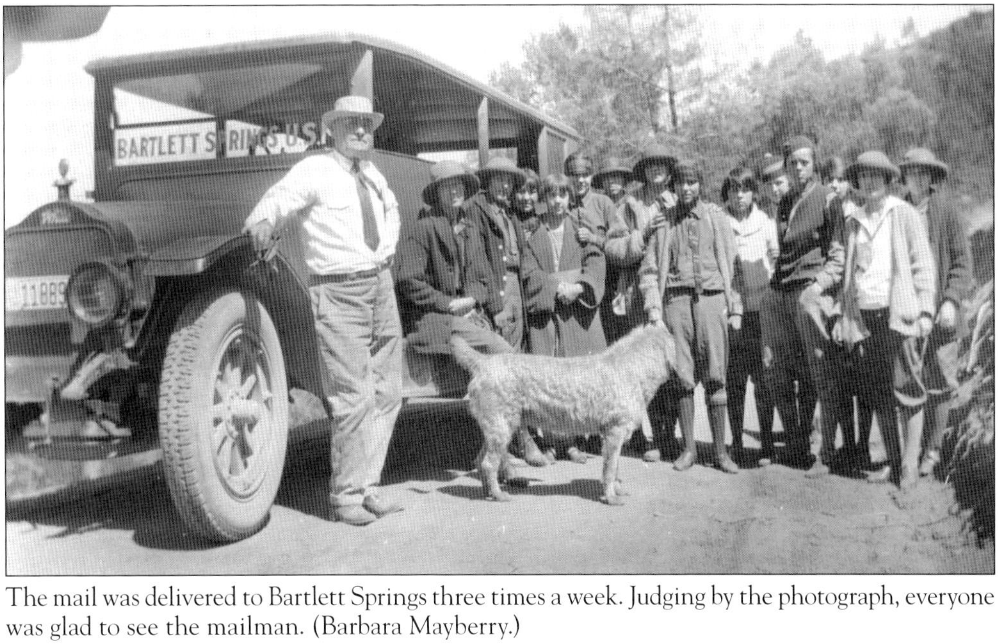

The mail was delivered to Bartlett Springs three times a week. Judging by the photograph, everyone was glad to see the mailman. (Barbara Mayberry.)

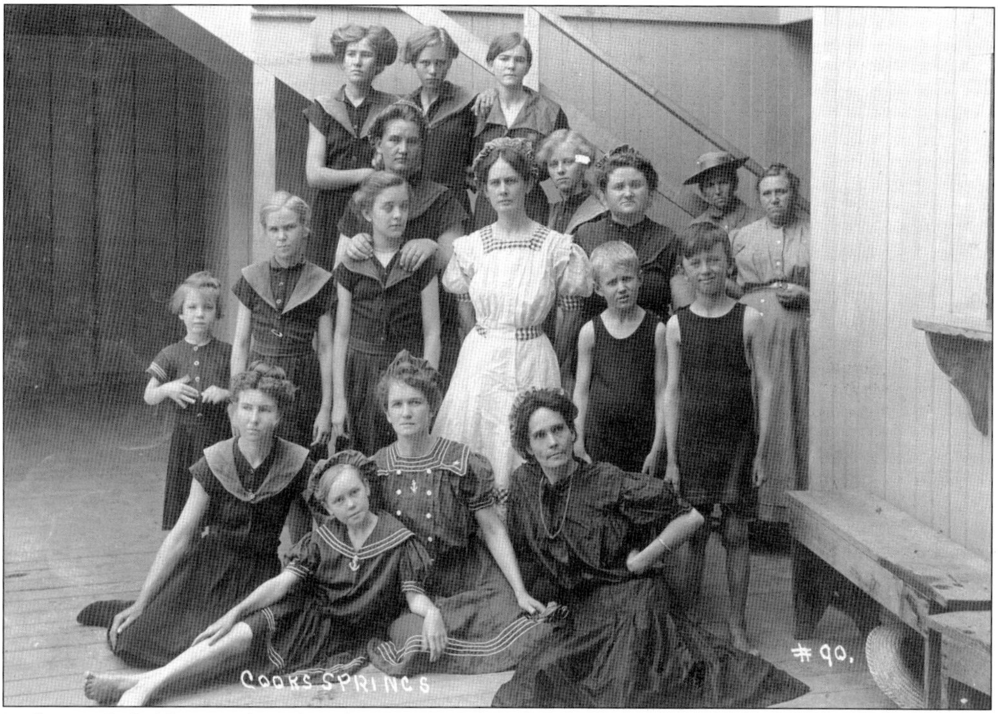

Ladies and children gathered at the Cook Springs pool to take advantage of its healing waters. There was a physician and assistant on staff with all the advantages of a hospital. The three springs were recommended for stomach, kidney, and bladder issues. The pools were also equipped with hydrotherapy equipment. (Sacramento Valley Museum.)

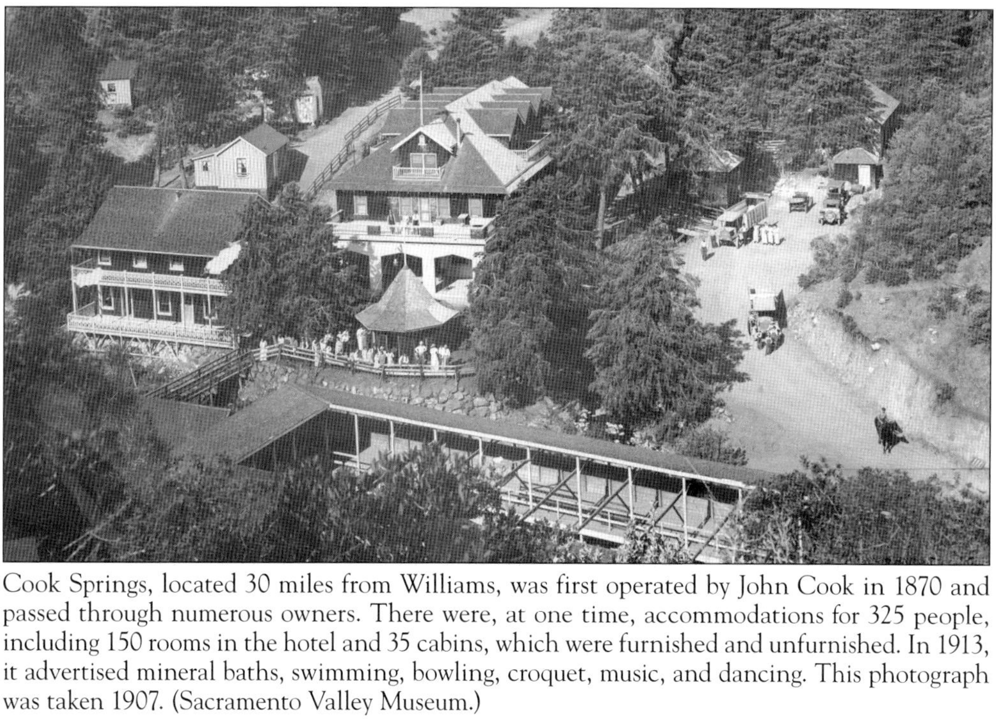

Cook Springs, located 30 miles from Williams, was first operated by John Cook in 1870 and passed through numerous owners. There were, at one time, accommodations for 325 people, including 150 rooms in the hotel and 35 cabins, which were furnished and unfurnished. In 1913, it advertised mineral baths, swimming, bowling, croquet, music, and dancing. This photograph was taken 1907. (Sacramento Valley Museum.)

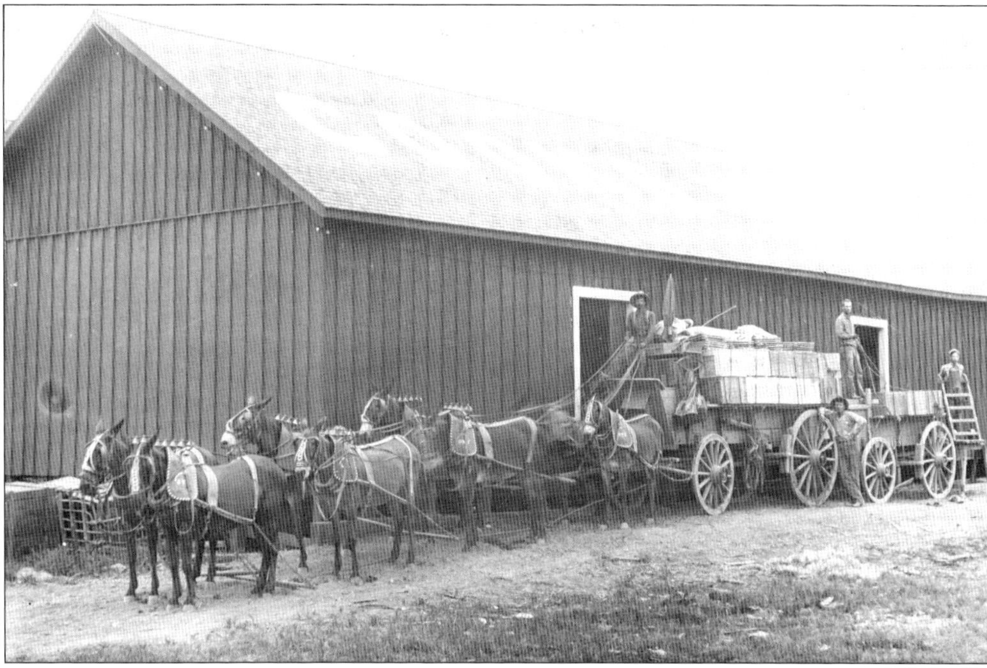

The Cook Springs Mineral Water Company was established in 1899, with U.W. Brown, I.G. Zumwalt, and A.A. Entrican as officers. The home office was located in Williams. Open from May to October with a capacity of 10,000 bottles per day, a wood-burning engine powered the steam to wash bottles, label, and run the crowning machine. The water came from 300 feet below and was then hauled 30 miles to Williams, where it was off-loaded in its own warehouses until being shipped out via rail or sold locally. It went to all parts of California and Nevada to be sold in various businesses. In 1913, Cook Springs Mineral Water Company opened its own tavern to market the water. In 1905, F.B. Hemminger had the distinction of bringing the first load of water to Williams as well as the last of the season. He made 52 trips hauling between 50–80 cases of Cook's water each trip. (Above, Marjorie Manor Marengo; below, Sacramento Valley Museum.)

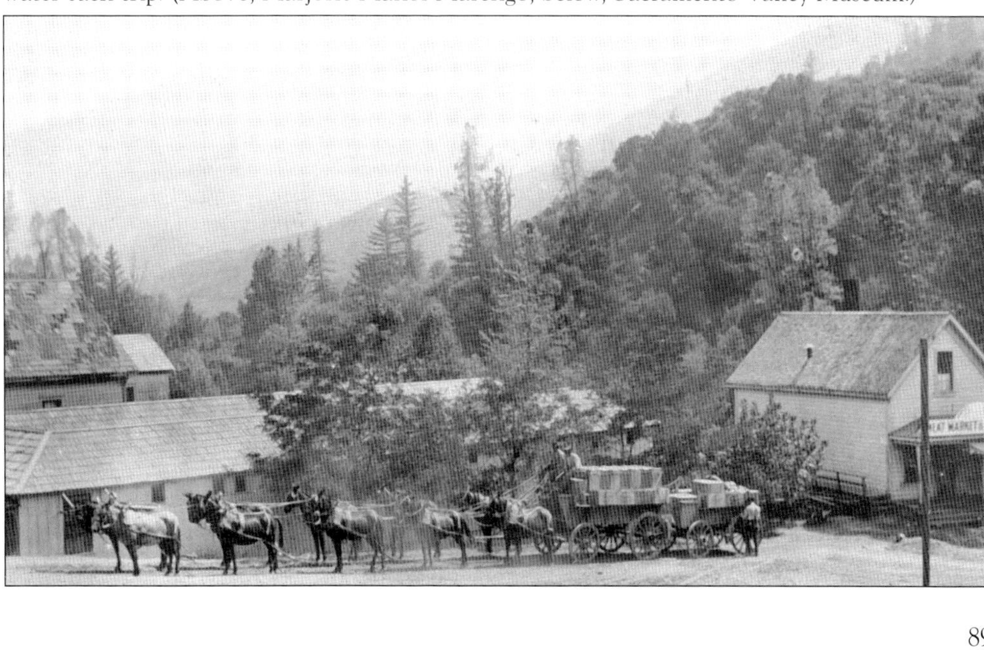

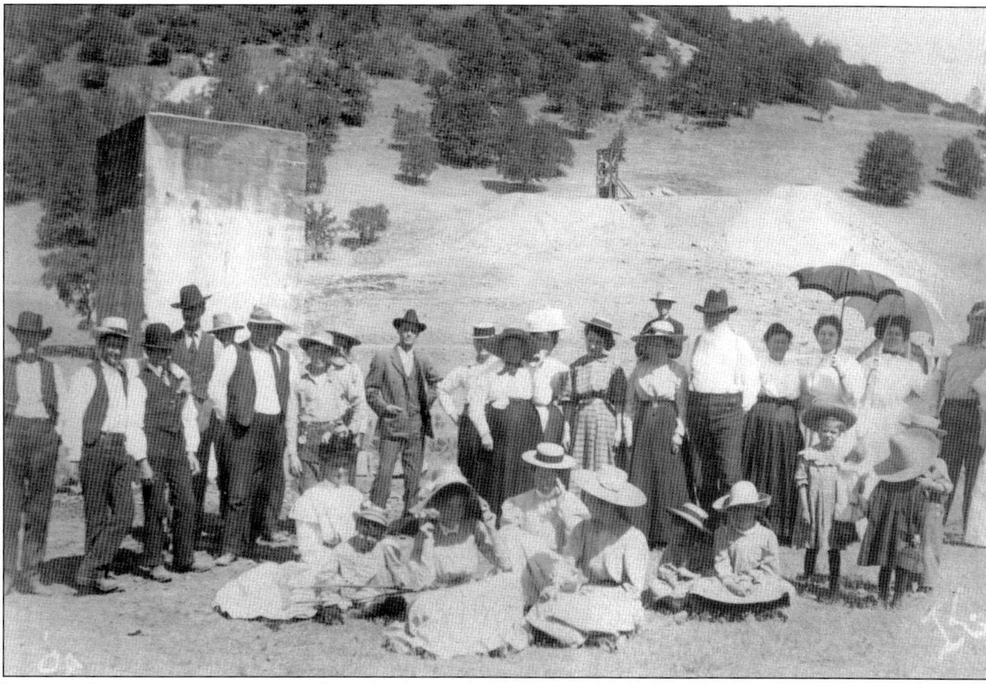

Wilbur Springs, originally called Simmons Springs, was founded in 1855. When the public discovered it, stages left every other day from Williams. In April 1915, a fire burned the hotel and dining hall as well as all other buildings, except for a barbershop and a bathhouse. Patrons of Wilbur Springs are gathered around 1910 in front of the cement tank from which the healing waters flowed. (Susan Leardini.)

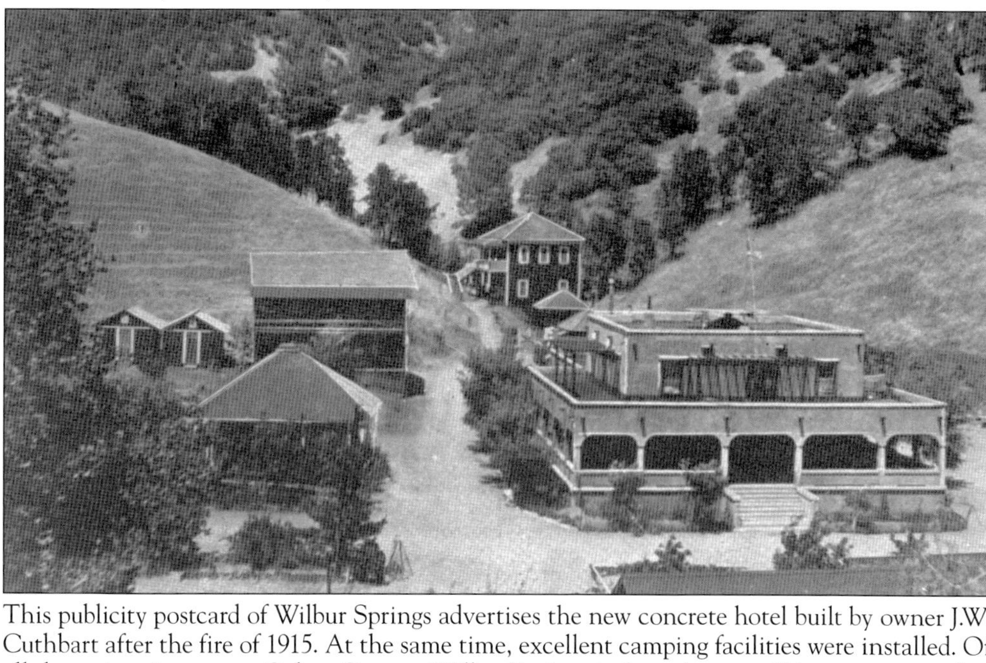

This publicity postcard of Wilbur Springs advertises the new concrete hotel built by owner J.W. Cuthbart after the fire of 1915. At the same time, excellent camping facilities were installed. Of all the springs in western Colusa County, Wilbur Springs is the only one still in operation today. (Troughton family collection.)

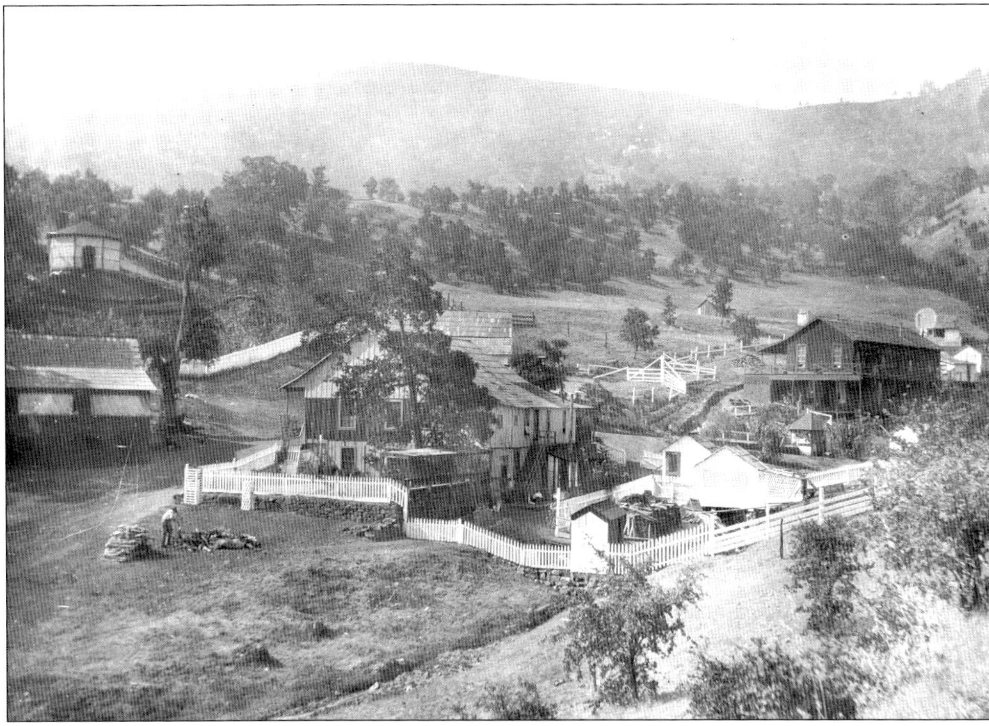

It is unknown when exactly Sulphur Creek was established, shown above in 1880, but in 1891, it is documented that there was a hotel with a general store and saloon in existence. The waters were noted for curing rheumatism, kidney problems, blood, and venereal disease. Also located in the same canyon was Jones Hot Springs, owned and operated by Tilden Jones, which began as a post office in the 1850s for the gold miners. Jones Hot Springs became known for its hot springs with water at 150 degrees. In 1915, the post office was closed, and the Wilbur Springs Company bought out the Jones Springs interests. (Above, Gilbert Allen family; below, Sacramento Valley Museum.)

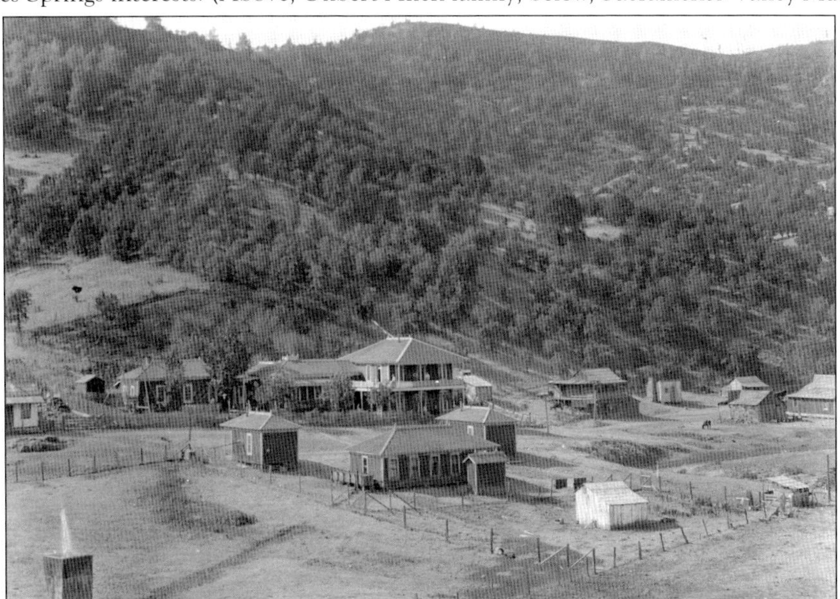

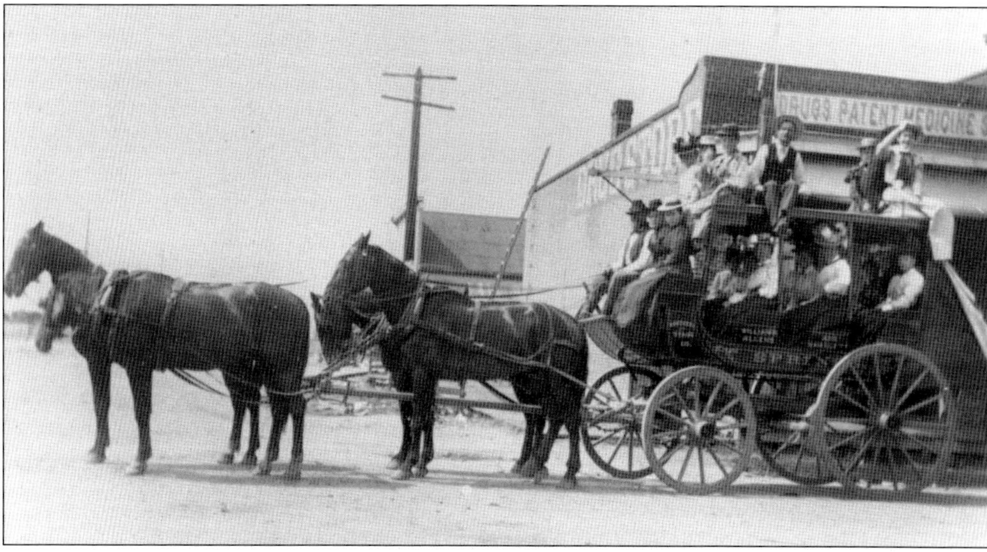

The Northern Stage Company is pictured outside of Fouch's Drugstore and is bound for Allen and Bartlett Springs while carrying 18 passengers. Regular daily stage service to Bartlett began in 1874. Roundtrip fare was $11. It was not uncommon for the passenger's luggage to follow on a freight wagon. (Gilbert Allen family.)

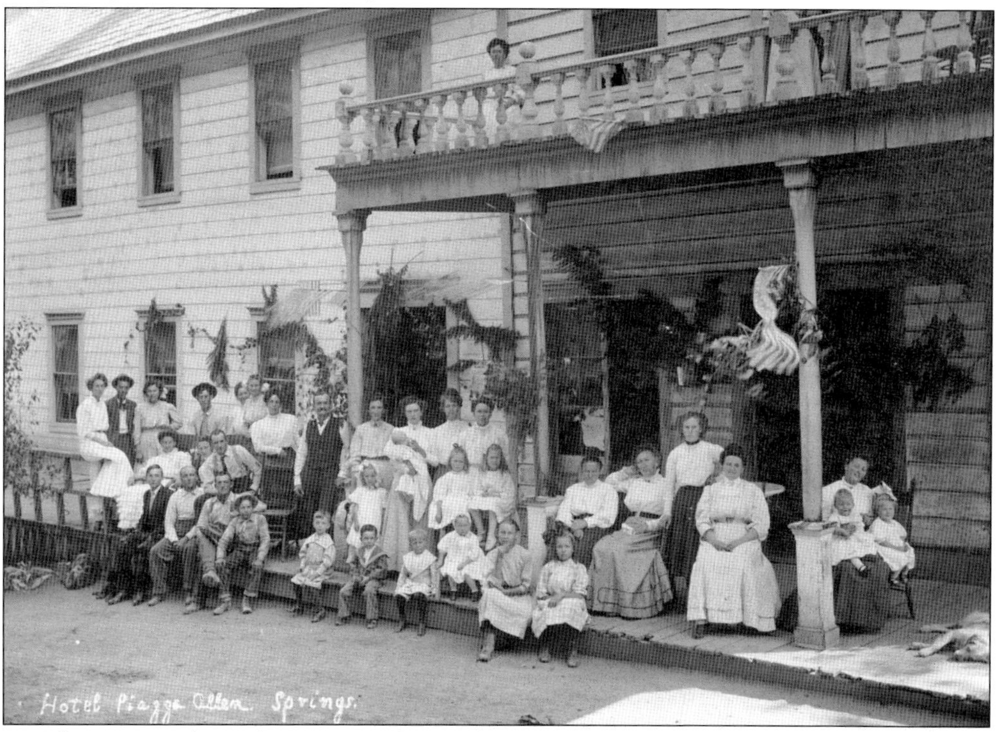

At Allen Springs, located approximately 40 miles from Williams, people could escape the heat of the summers on the valley floor and partake in the healing waters. In the early 1900s, managers Martha Crawford and her husband, Nate, had the first white baby born at Allen Springs. Shown in 1909 on the Fourth of July, Mary Gassaway is holding her infant son Elbert. The woman to her left is Sadie Gobel Bashore. (Author's collection.)

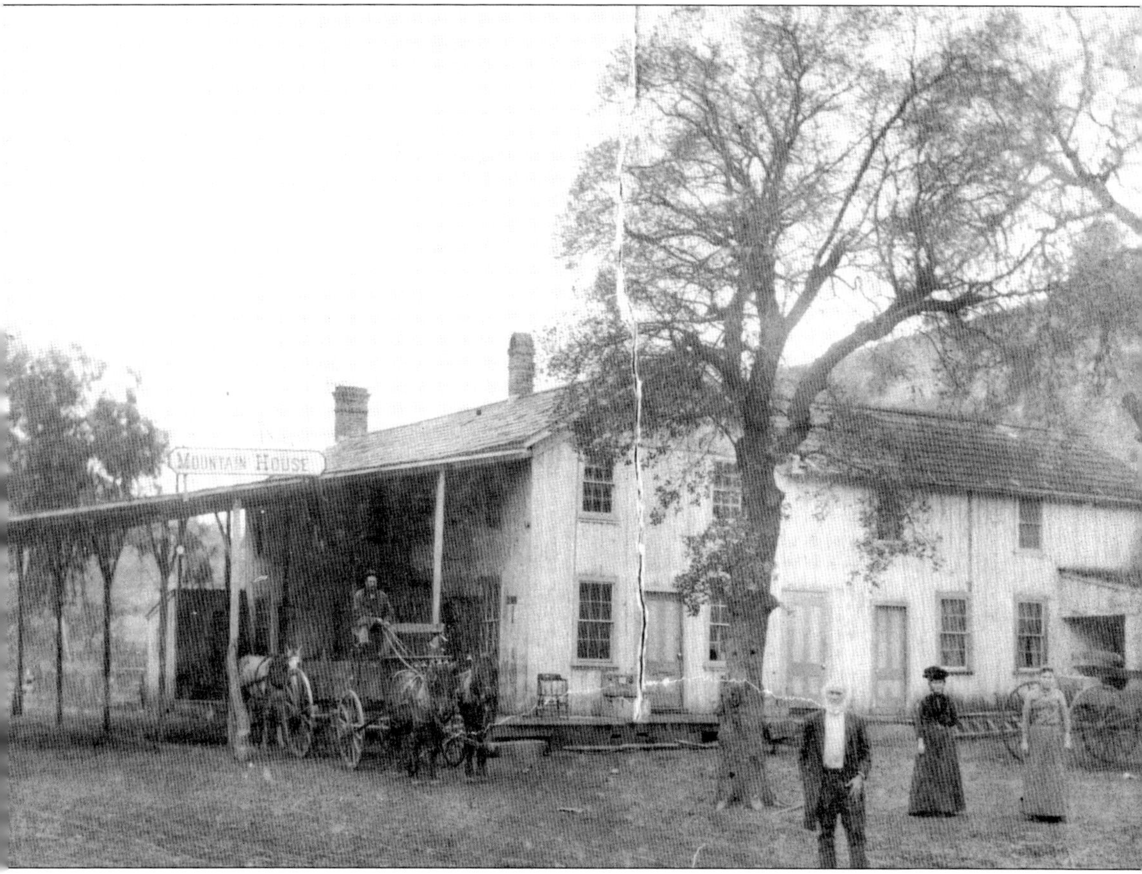

The Mountain House, located west of Williams, was a popular stage stop and a place for teamsters to change teams while on their way to the springs in the western hills. Owned in the beginning by August Schuckman, this 1893 photograph shows the original Mountain House with August and his family. In 1871, Schuckman had purchased the Twenty Mile House, and Stovall Wilcoxson Company found that it had to cross Shuckman's property to reach its other lands. The company made a deal with Schuckman to trade his property for the Mountain House plus $1,000. It was already set up to accept visitors, was on the main road to Bartlett Springs and the Sulphur Creek area, and Schuckman had always wanted to be an innkeeper, so the deal was done around 1878. He filed a homestead on the Mountain House that year. (Gilbert Allen family.)

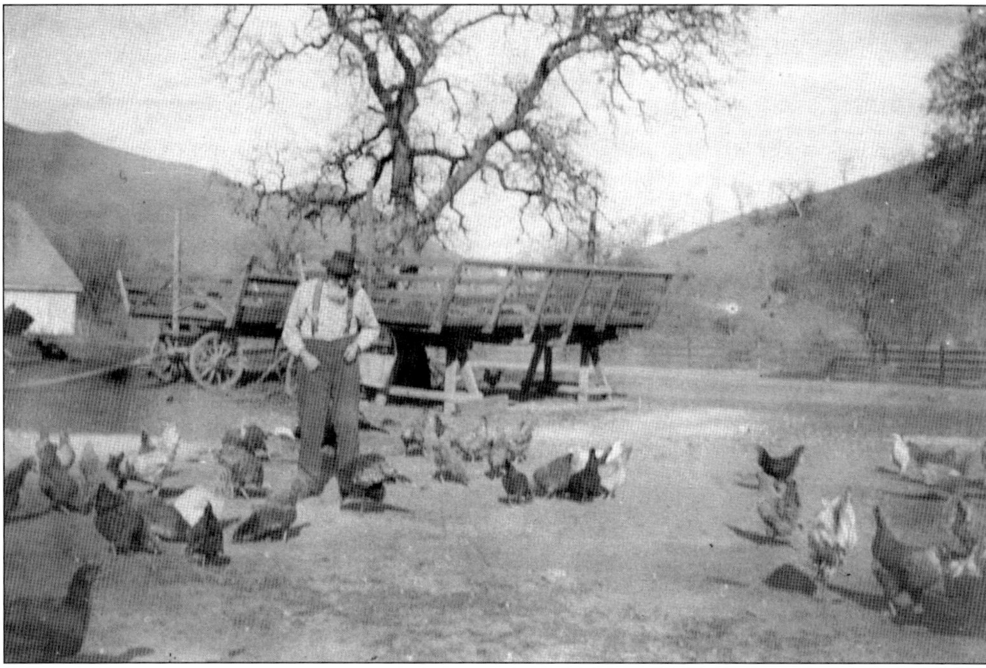

There were six children born to August and Augusta Schuckman. Their sons, Gus, Charles, and Frank, were later joined by Minnie, Emma, and Ida. Emma married Gilbert Allen, and Ida married Ed Brown, father of Gov. Pat Brown and grandfather to Gov. Jerry Brown and his sister Kathleen. Their son Frank Schuckman ran a stage line, seen here in 1898, from Williams to Sulphur Creek. Having always wanted to farm, he took over the Mountain House from his father, shown here in 1906 feeding chickens, and bought up neighboring farmlands in 1898 with financial help from August. (Both, Gilbert Allen family.)

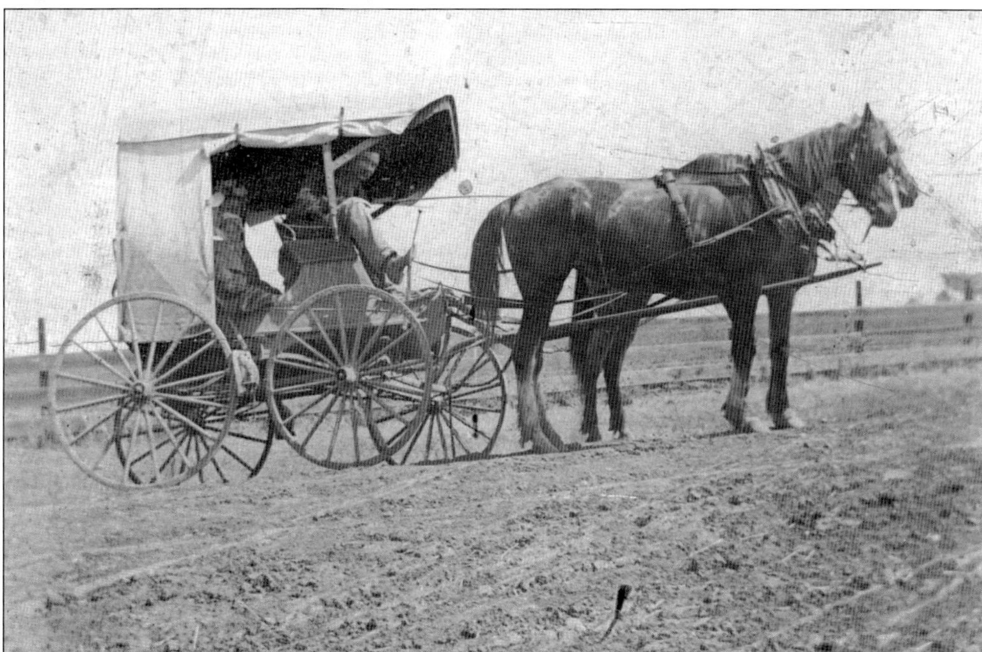

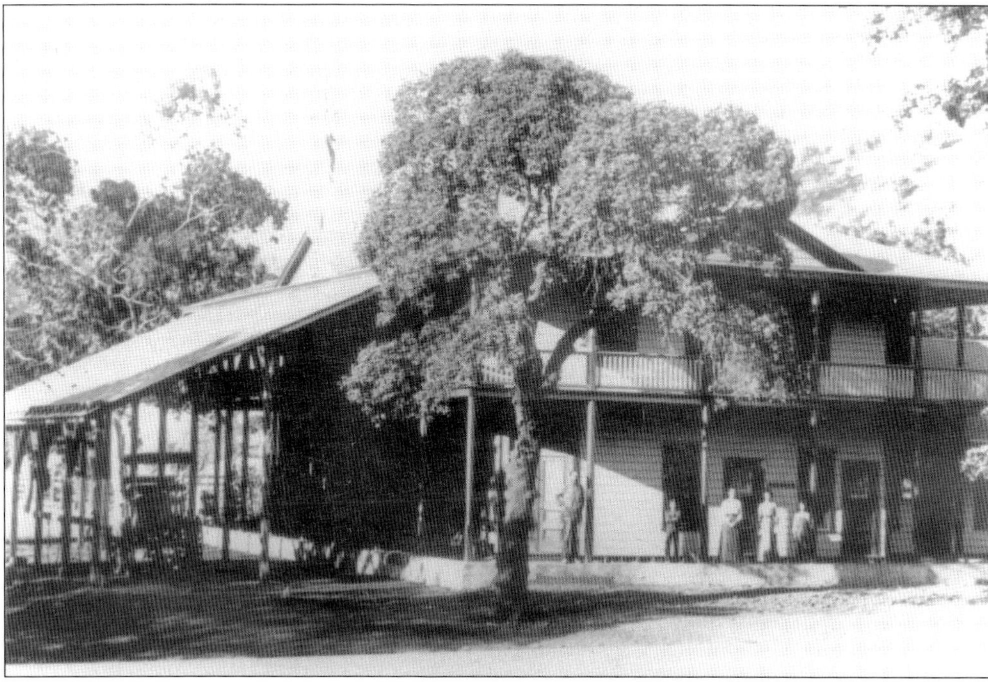

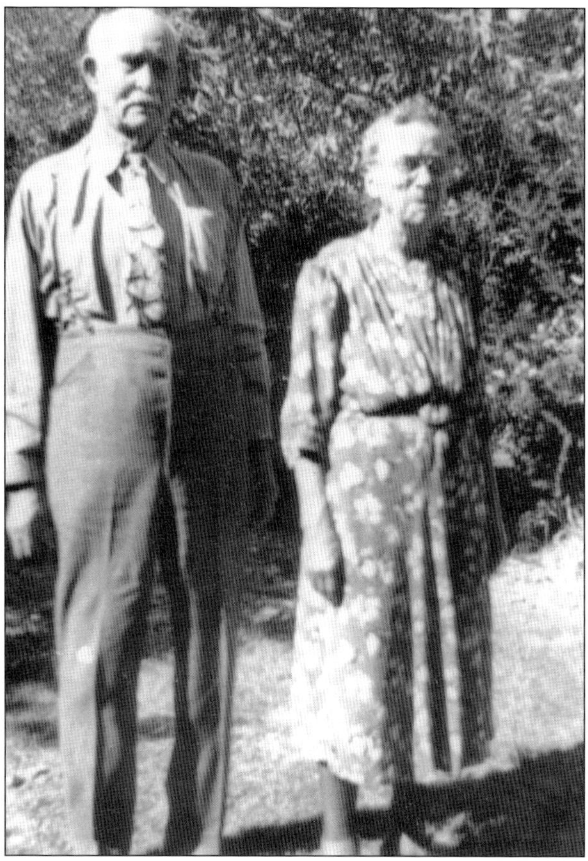

The original Mountain House was torn down and replaced in 1906. The original bar was sawed from the first building and moved over while under construction. It was said that they never missed a drink while under construction. Frank Schuckman married Margaret Henneke in 1904, and she ran the Mountain House while Frank's father, August, stayed on to tend the bar and do chores. This is the completed building in 1910. Frank went on to build the telephone line from Williams to the Mountain House and later to Leesville, Bear Valley, Sulphur Creek, and Cook Springs. Soon after, he formed a company and sold out to the Colusa County Telephone Company. In 1937, Frank furnished the bonds to the City of Williams for the building of the city hall as well as its water and street projects and helped many fledging businesses to get their start. (Both, Gilbert Allen family.)

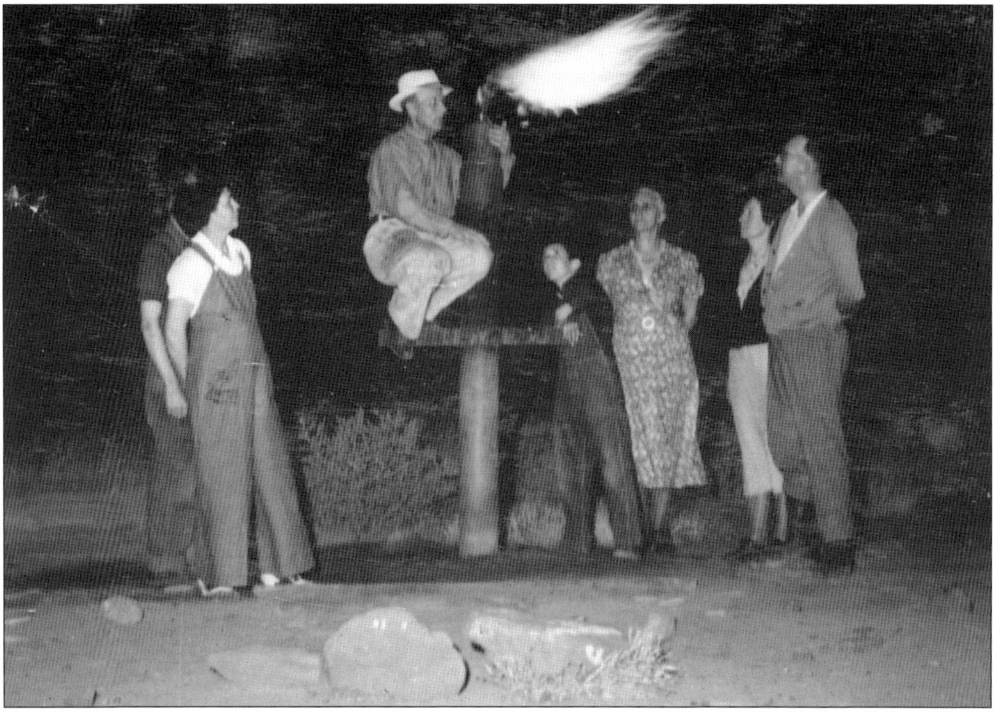

At the Mountain House in 1910, under the direction of Ira Fouch, a well was drilled and hit a gusher at 1,500 feet. The well serviced the Mountain House with enough gas to heat and light the building. In September 1941, C.M. Eagleton reopened a well on the Shuckman Ranch that was used for medicinal oil in the 1920s, and he began selling it by the ounce as a cure-all oil for $128 a gallon under the name Nutri-oil. A fire one month later destroyed the portable rig used for drilling. During the early to mid-1940s, C.M. Eagleton, his wife, Ruby, and their family lived at the Mountain House. The tanks shown are the water tanks with the oil floating to the top, and C.M. is pictured on top of the well outlet with Ruby to his right in overalls. (Both, Eagleton family collection.)

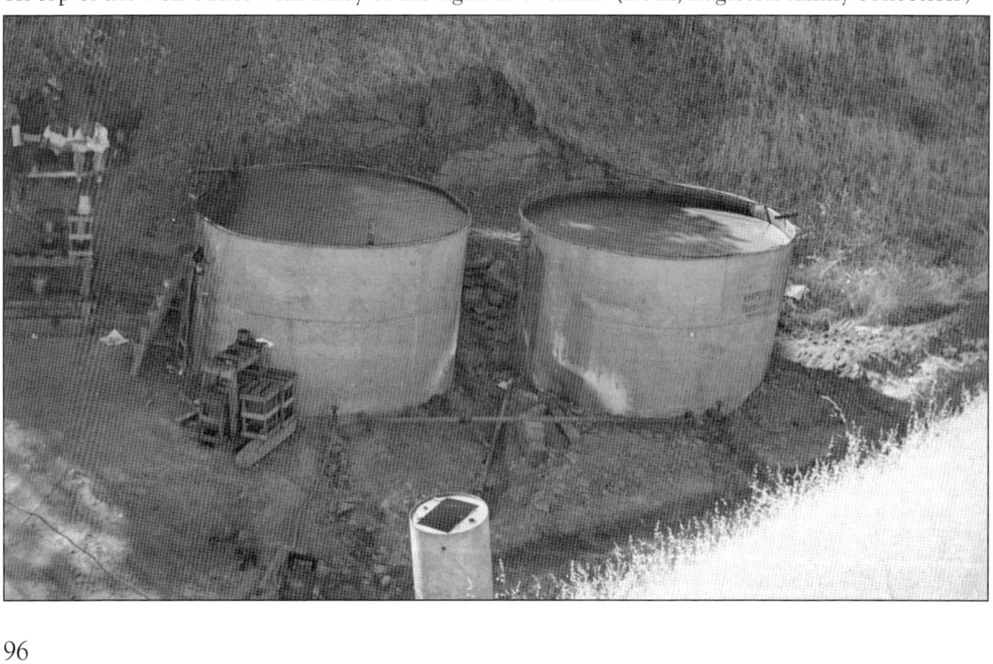

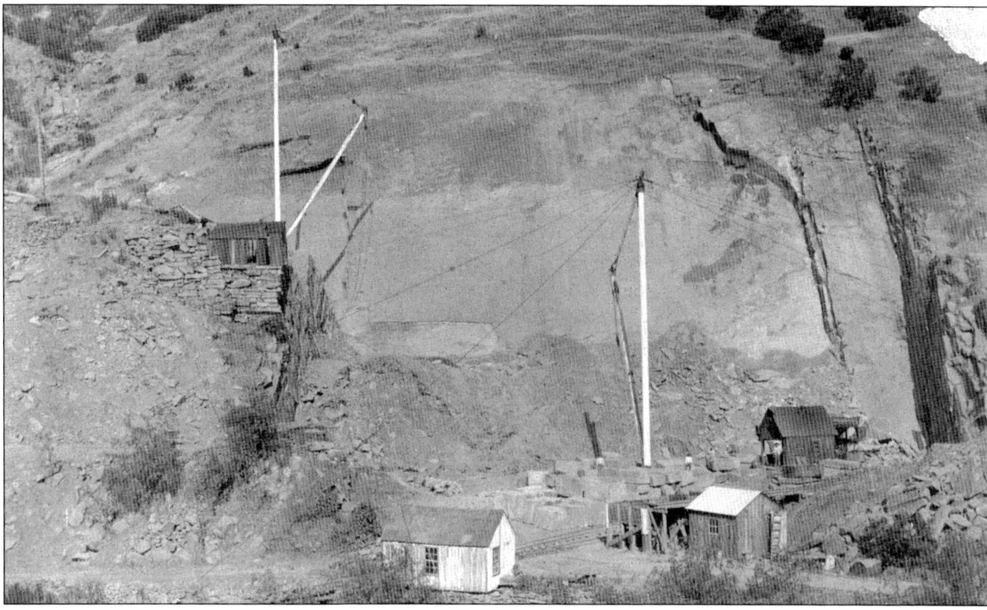

Located northwest of Williams were the stone quarries that ran from 1894 and until 1917. The quarries became overcrowded with orders and yielded stone valued at $1,488,000. In 1904, there was a reported $290,000 worth of sandstone that passed through Williams by rail on its way to San Francisco for the building of new, modern buildings. In 1906, not one building built with the stone was displaced during the earthquake. It was shipped to San Francisco for such notable buildings as the Ferry Building, the Emporium, the Spreckles Building, the Hall of Justice, the Shreve Building, and the pillars at the entrance of the St. Francis Hotel as well as other local buildings. (Both, Sacramento Valley Museum.)

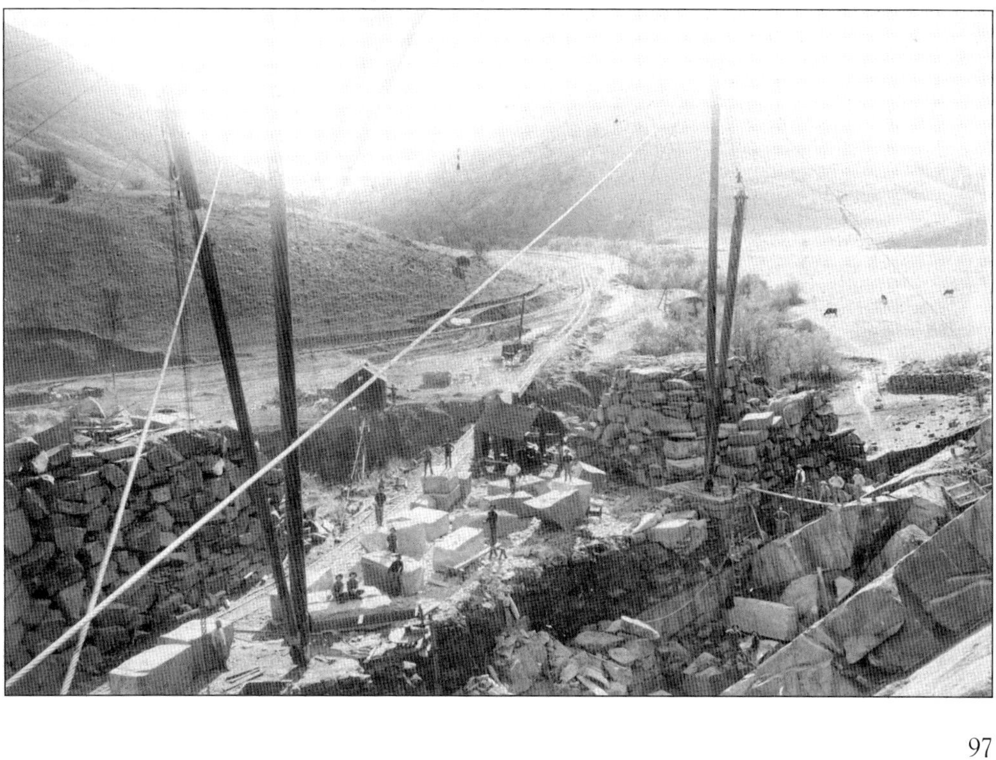

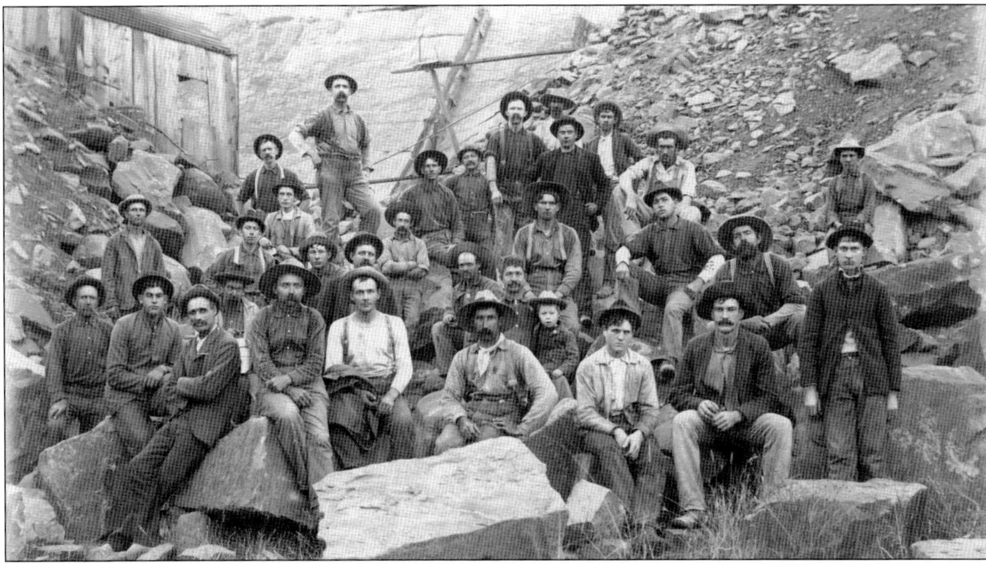

In no specific order, the workers identified at the then-McGilvery Quarry are John Nordyke, Milt Woodward, Sturrok Son (superintendent), John Heigel, Frank Heigel, and Dan Chisolm; the man front and center with his hand on his upper thigh is Placido Valley. Inside the cutting room of the quarry, they had different saws for the size of stone they needed. In 1957, there were 100 tons of rocks removed to use in the construction of a church in San Francisco. The Goforth Brothers of Williams did the hauling for Henry Kron, then-owner of the quarry. It took two men 10 days to cut the stone to the requested size. Many people watched as the work was done, stirred by the memories of when the quarry was at its peak. (Both, Sacramento Valley Museum.)

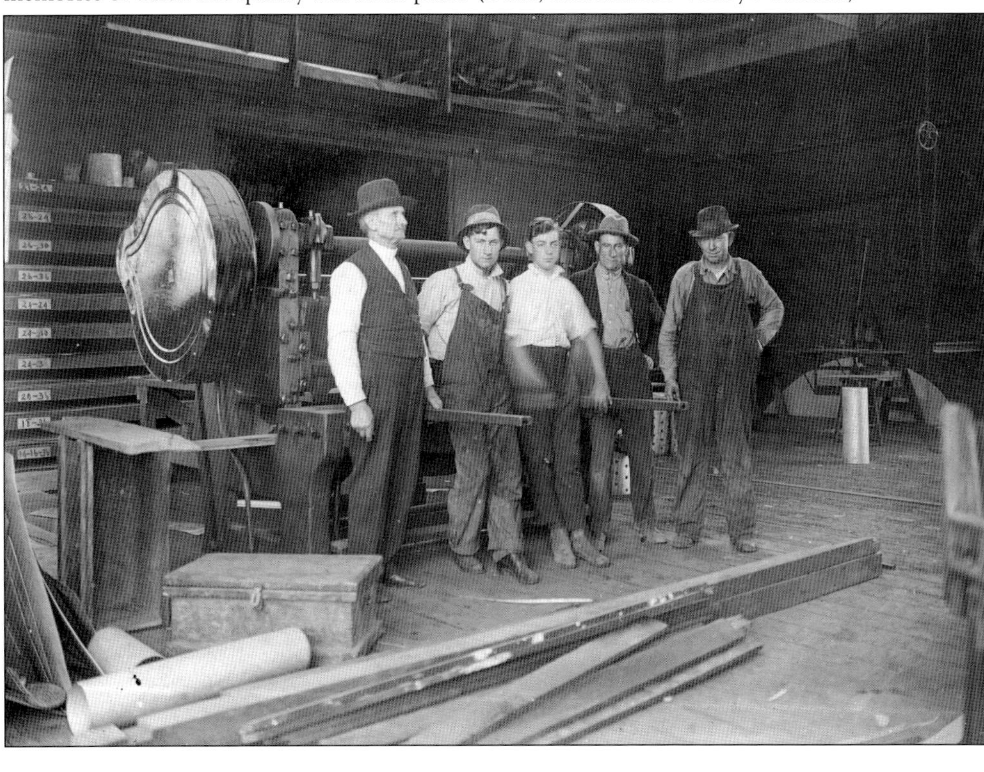

Seven

Farming during the First 100 Years

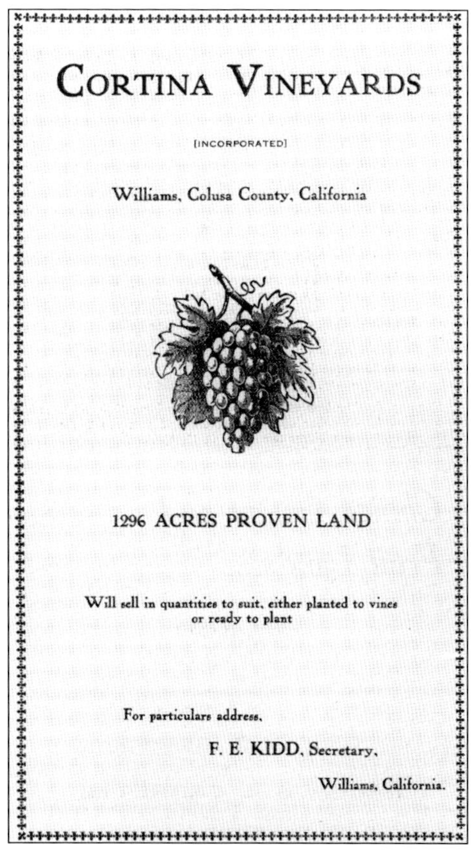

The Cortina Vineyard was incorporated in 1906, and C.L. Schaad was president. It was capitalized for $50,000 and held an option to purchase and bond on Weinstock, Lubin Company's land consisting of 1,296 acres situated southwest of Williams. They received 54,000 cuttings and 18,000 rooted vines of Zinfandel and Petite Syrah sorts. In 1923, the grapes tested very high for sugar, and the 15-railcar loads of Zinfandels were shipped out to New York. It was thought that they would bring in a $100 a ton. (Author's collection.)

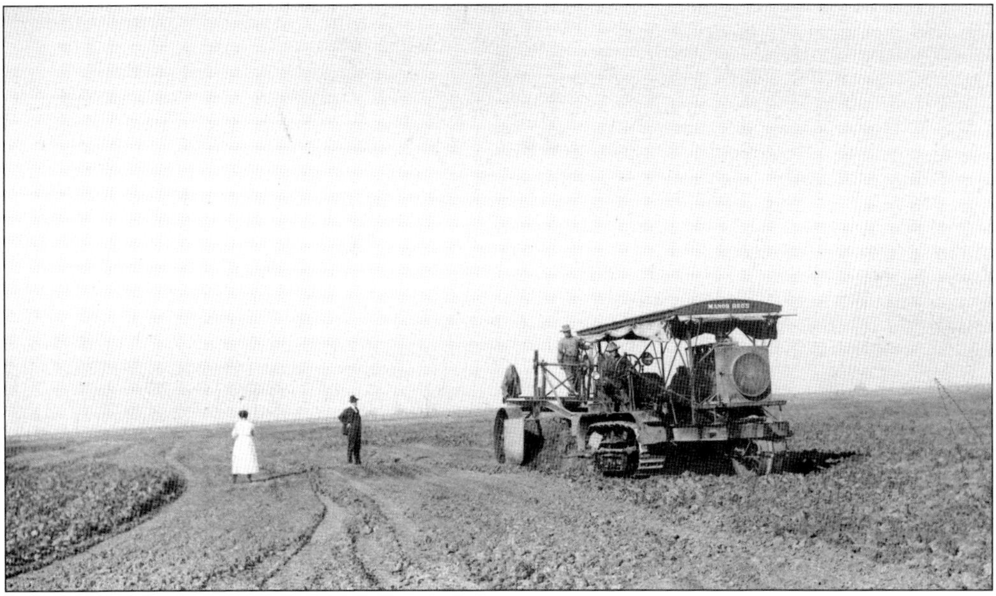

Working the ground for the next crop is Bill Tallman (standing) and Guy Manor (driving the tractor) as Belle Williams Moore and her husband, Stanley, look on in February 1920. Stanley Moore died in 1927 at the age of 46. (Marjorie Manor Marengo.)

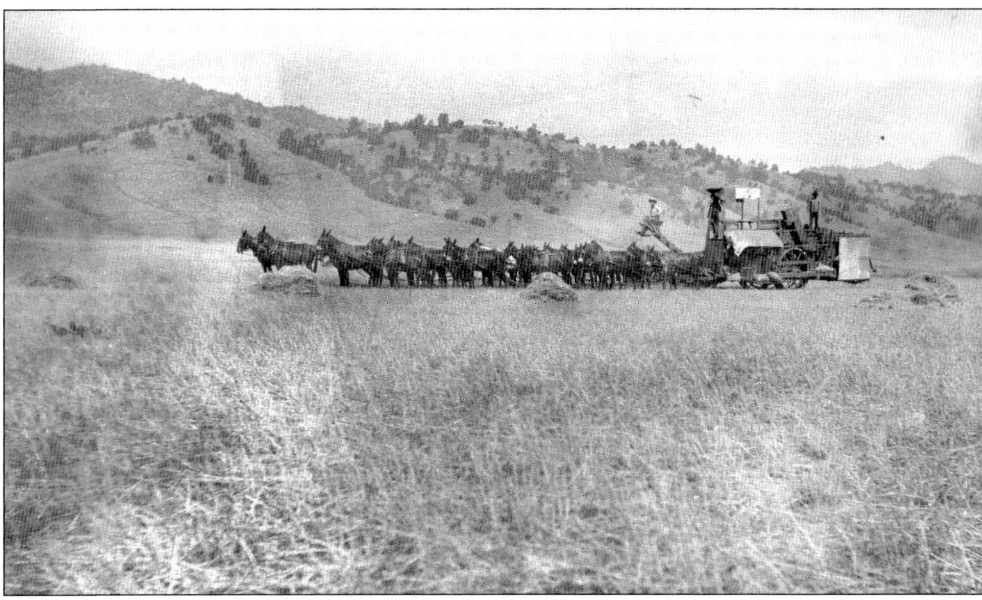

At the Britton ranch in Spring Valley, this mule-driven harvester shows the skinner sitting on top of the Jacob's ladder. With nerves of steel and using his whip, he would direct the mules and call them by name. Each mule knew his name and responded accordingly, and the driver was subject to eating the mules' dust and would get the dust as well as the chaff in a tailwind. (Author's collection.)

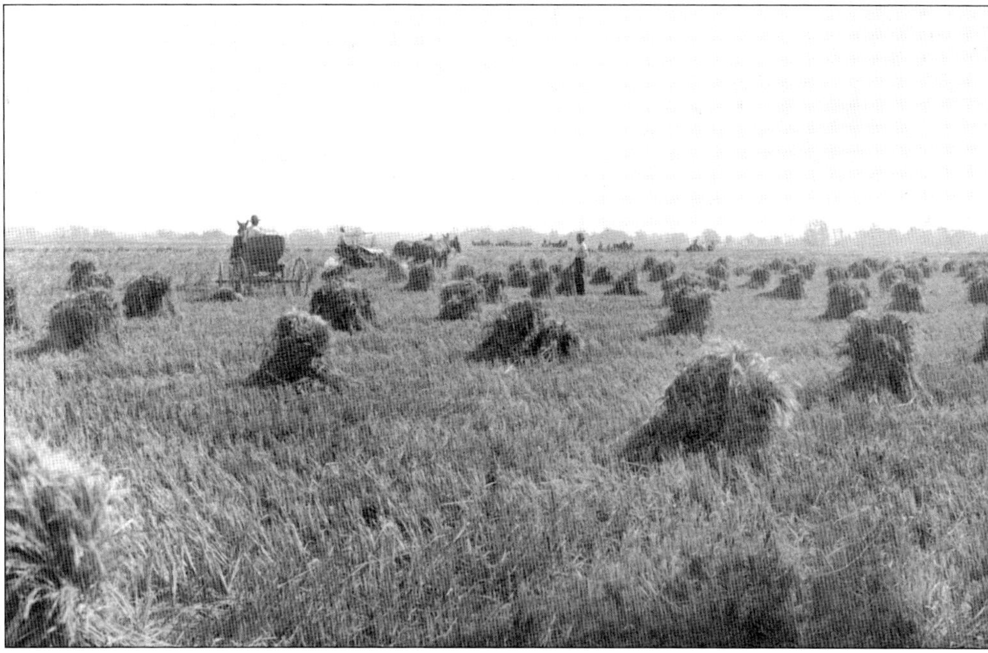

Grain has been shocked and left in the field ready to be loaded on the wagon before going to the stationary harvester. It was then fed into the separator, where the jig man would load it into the sack. The sack-sower would sow the burlap bag closed, and then the sack buck would stack it. (Doug Gassaway.)

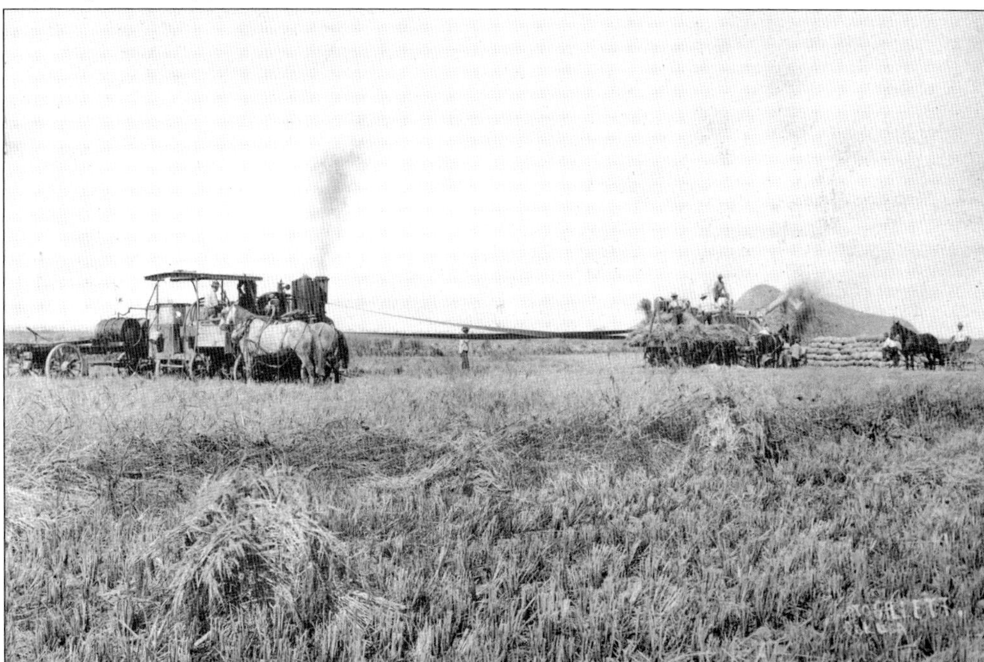

This photograph shows the steam tractor driving the separator by a belt. It is then off-loaded, and the chaff is then shot out the pipe to the side. The grain is then sacked, sown, and shown waiting to go to the warehouse. (Doug Gassaway.)

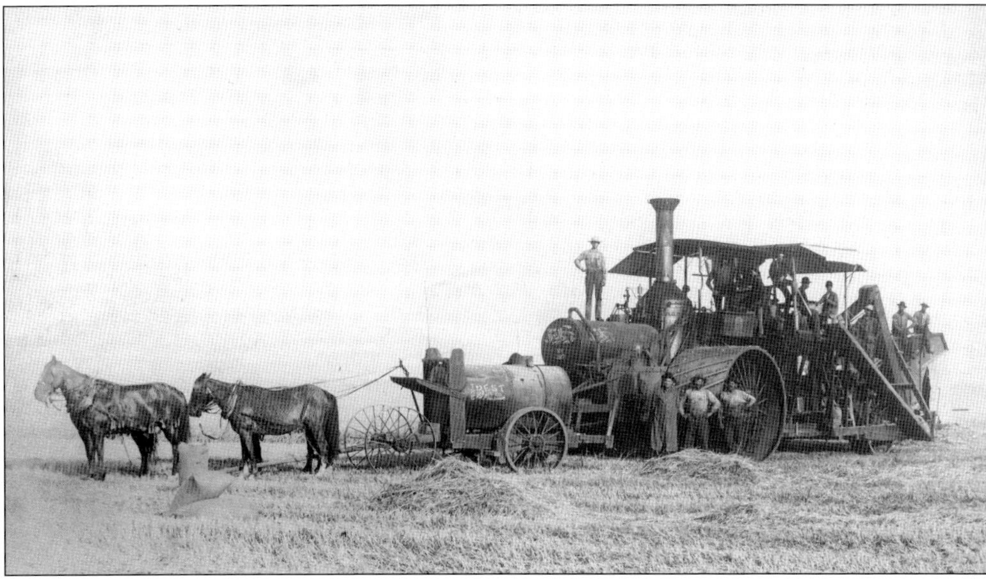

This harvest crew, photographed in 1907, is showing off the Best steam-driven tractor and harvester. Standing on the tank is Arch Matzka. Others pictured are, from left to right, (on the ground) Siem Callen, Charles Myers Sr., and Harry Manor; (on the farm machinery) L.G. Manor, L.A. Manor, Davis Forsythe, Frank Boynton, Ernie Manor, and Bob Ostrander. The two men on the far right are unidentified. (Author's collection.)

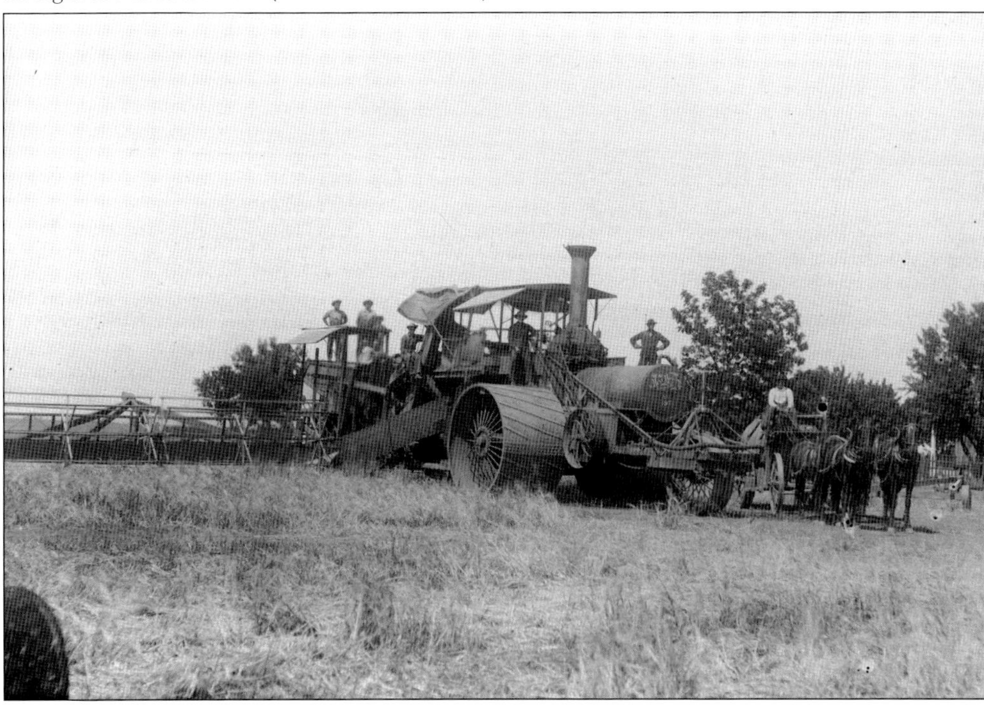

This steam-driven harvester is about to take on water. It took a minimum of five to operate the harvester. There was the engineer, the separator man, the header tender (sometimes referred to as the header punch), the sack jig, and the sack sower. Often, there were more than one sower on board. (Marjorie Manor Marengo.)

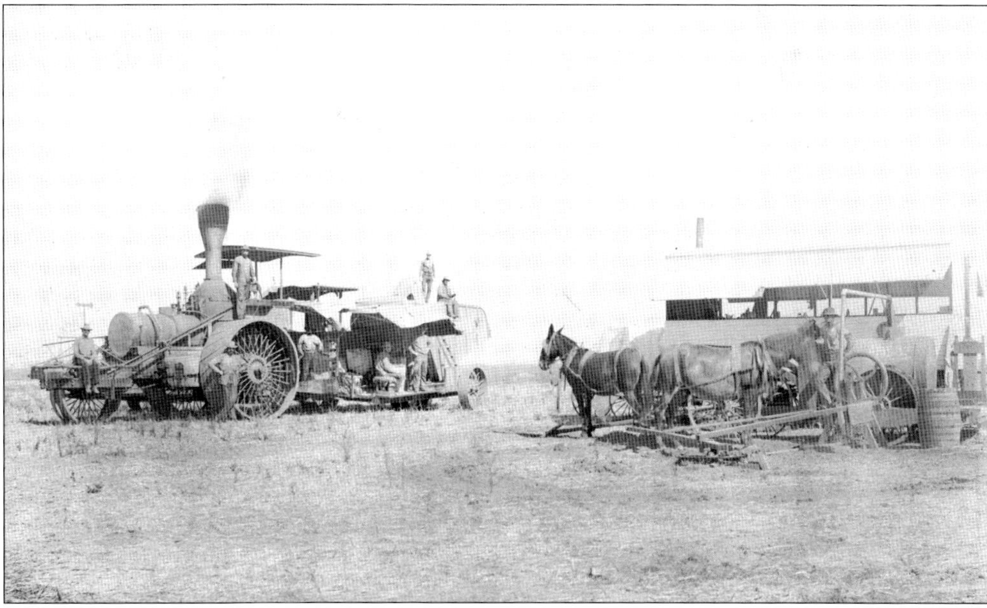

Shown above is L.G. Manor on the Crocker Ranch. A very important member of the harvest crew was the camp cook, who traveled in a modest cook shack to feed the crew, as seen here. They fed the crew morning, noon, and night and loaded down the table with meat, potatoes, pies, and things that seemed impossible, given what they had to work with. (Marjorie Manor Marengo.)

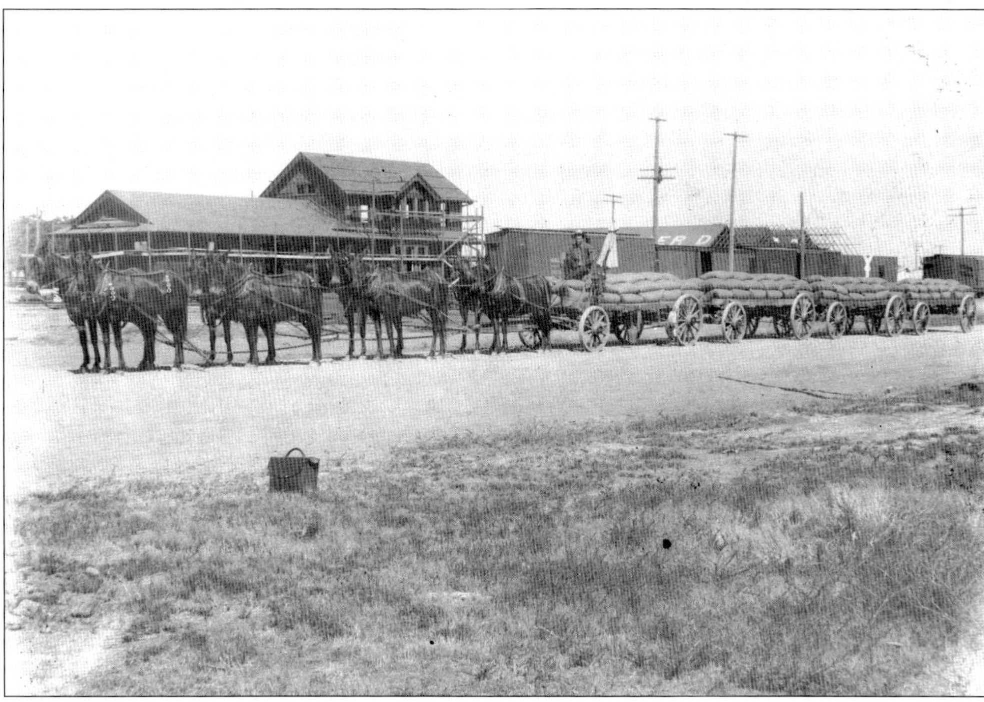

Once the railroad was up and running, the building along the railroad tracks began to flourish. This photograph shows a set of four wagons of grain en route from the Harry Manor ranch to the Stovall Wilcoxson Warehouse with the railroad depot under construction in the background. George Murray is the team driver. (Marjorie Manor Marengo.)

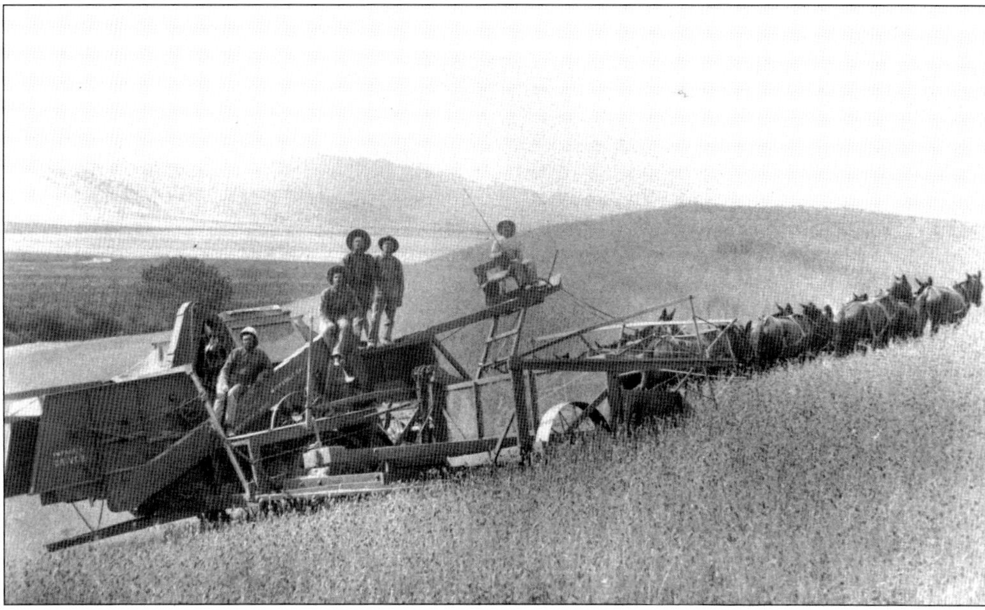

Working on a hillside proved to be a feat in itself. Developed in 1891, Holt Harvester advertised its side-hill harvester as the "wonder of the twentieth century" in 1905. They advertised the regular two-wheel side hill as well the junior side hill machine. The wheel on the downhill side was adjustable, keeping the machine level. (Marjorie Manor Marengo.)

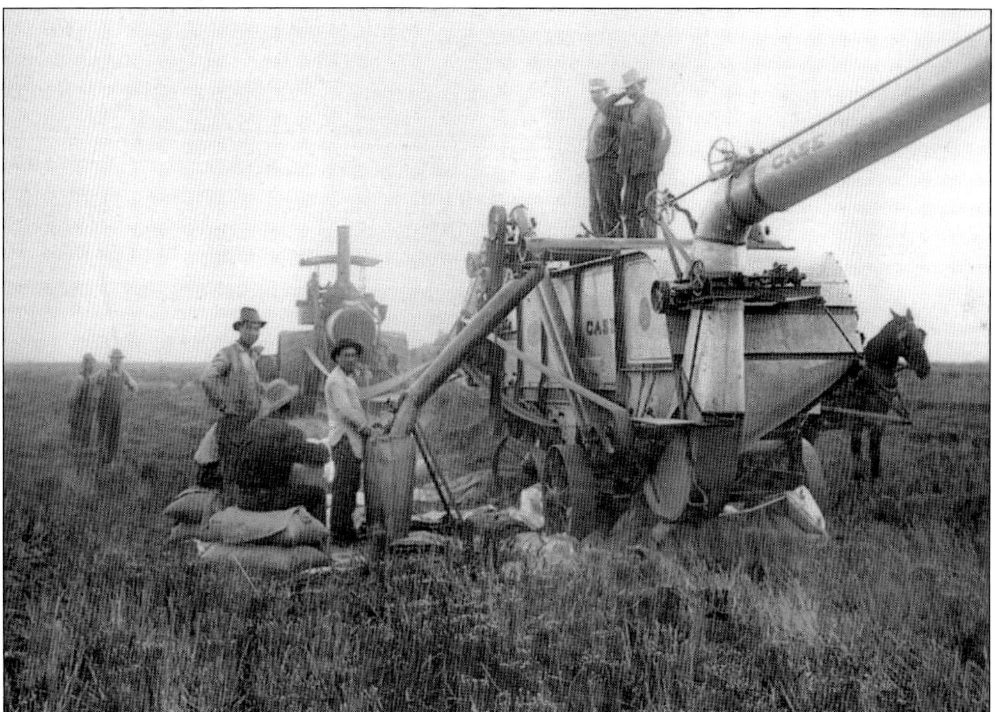

Showing the stationary separator by Case, the man with the sack is the sack jig, settling the sack before handing it off to the sack sower working behind him. Again, the steam-driven tractor in the background can be seen supplying the power to run the separator. (Bill Barrett.)

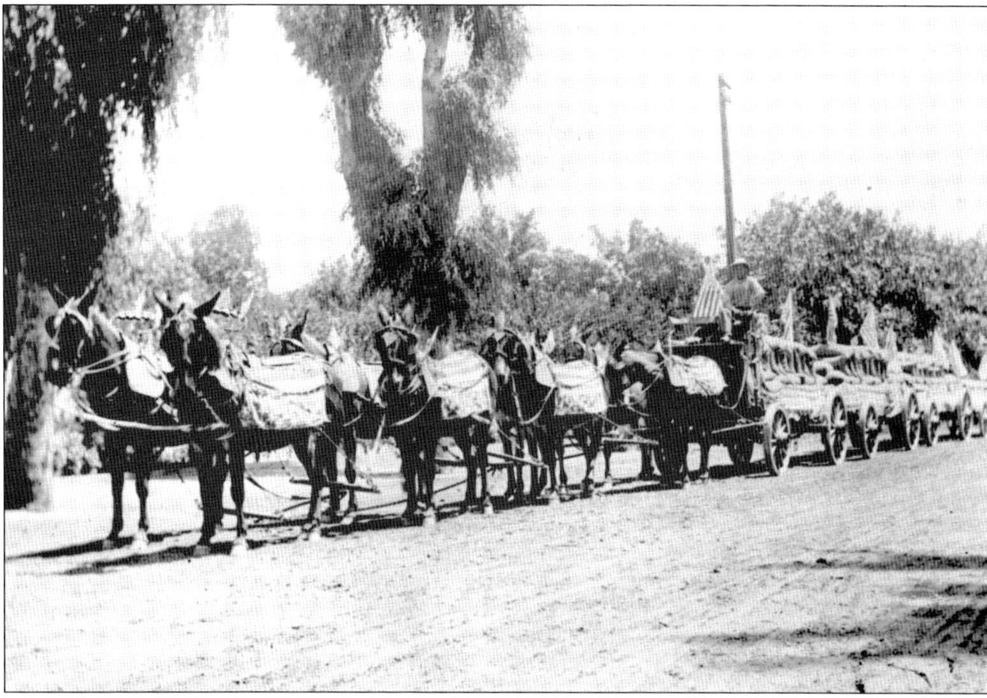

A Fourth of July event was a great excuse for proud farmers and teamsters to show off their teams and crops. Here, August Schaad is proudly showing his patriotism, which has been so typical of the people of Williams throughout the years. (Henry W. Rhoades family.)

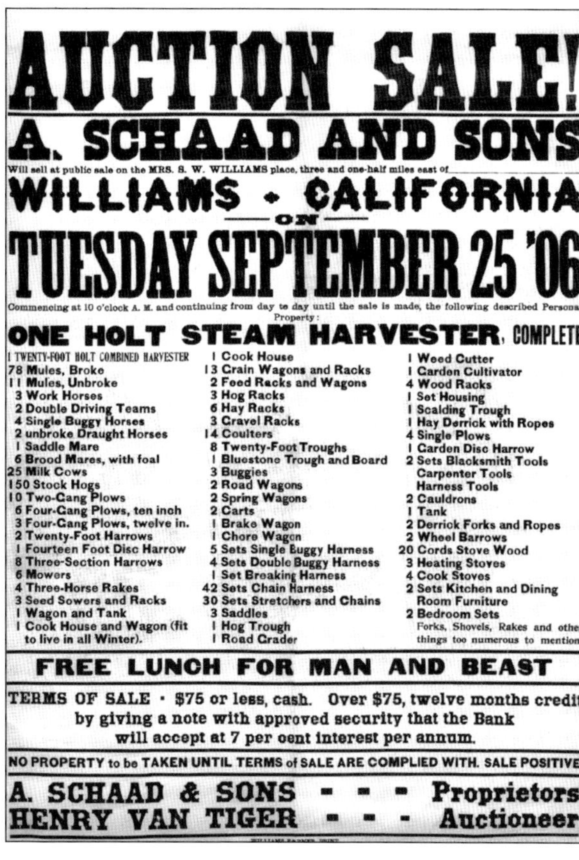

AUCTION SALE!

A. SCHAAD AND SONS

Will sell at public sale on the MRS. S. W. WILLIAMS place, three and one-half miles east of

WILLIAMS - CALIFORNIA

ON

TUESDAY SEPTEMBER 25 '06

Commencing at 10 o'clock A. M. and continuing from day to day until the sale is made, the following described Personal Property:

ONE HOLT STEAM HARVESTER, COMPLETE

1 TWENTY-FOOT HOLT COMBINED HARVESTER
78 Mules, Broke
11 Mules, Unbroke
3 Work Horses
2 Double Driving Teams
4 Single Buggy Horses
2 unbroke Draught Horses
1 Saddle Mare
6 Brood Mares, with foal
25 Milk Cows
150 Stock Hogs
10 Two-Gang Plows
6 Four-Gang Plows, ten inch
3 Four-Gang Plows, twelve in.
2 Twenty-Foot Harrows
1 Fourteen Foot Disc Harrow
8 Three-Section Harrows
6 Mowers
4 Three-Horse Rakes
3 Seed Sowers and Racks
1 Wagon and Tank
1 Cook House and Wagon (fit to live in all Winter).

1 Cook House
13 Grain Wagons and Racks
2 Feed Racks and Wagons
3 Hog Racks
6 Hay Racks
3 Gravel Racks
14 Coulters
8 Twenty-Foot Troughs
1 Bluestone Trough and Board
3 Buggies
2 Road Wagons
2 Spring Wagons
2 Carts
1 Brake Wagon
1 Chore Wagon
5 Sets Single Buggy Harness
4 Sets Double Buggy Harness
1 Set Breaking Harness
42 Sets Chain Harness
30 Sets Stretchers and Chains
3 Saddles
1 Hog Trough
1 Road Grader

1 Weed Cutter
1 Garden Cultivator
4 Wood Racks
1 Set Housing
1 Scalding Trough
1 Hay Derrick with Ropes
4 Single Plows
1 Garden Disc Harrow
2 Sets Blacksmith Tools
Carpenter Tools
Harness Tools
2 Cauldrons
1 Tank
2 Derrick Forks and Ropes
2 Wheel Barrows
20 Cords Stove Wood
3 Heating Stoves
4 Cook Stoves
2 Sets Kitchen and Dining Room Furniture
2 Bedroom Sets
Forks, Shovels, Rakes and other things too numerous to mention.

FREE LUNCH FOR MAN AND BEAST

TERMS OF SALE - $75 or less, cash. Over $75, twelve months credit by giving a note with approved security that the Bank will accept at 7 per cent interest per annum.

NO PROPERTY to be TAKEN UNTIL TERMS of SALE ARE COMPLIED WITH. SALE POSITIVE

A. SCHAAD & SONS - - - Proprietors
HENRY VAN TIGER - - - Auctioneer

This poster advertising the sale of August Schaad and Sons equipment in 1906 even lists a free lunch for man and beast. (Henry W. Rhoades family.)

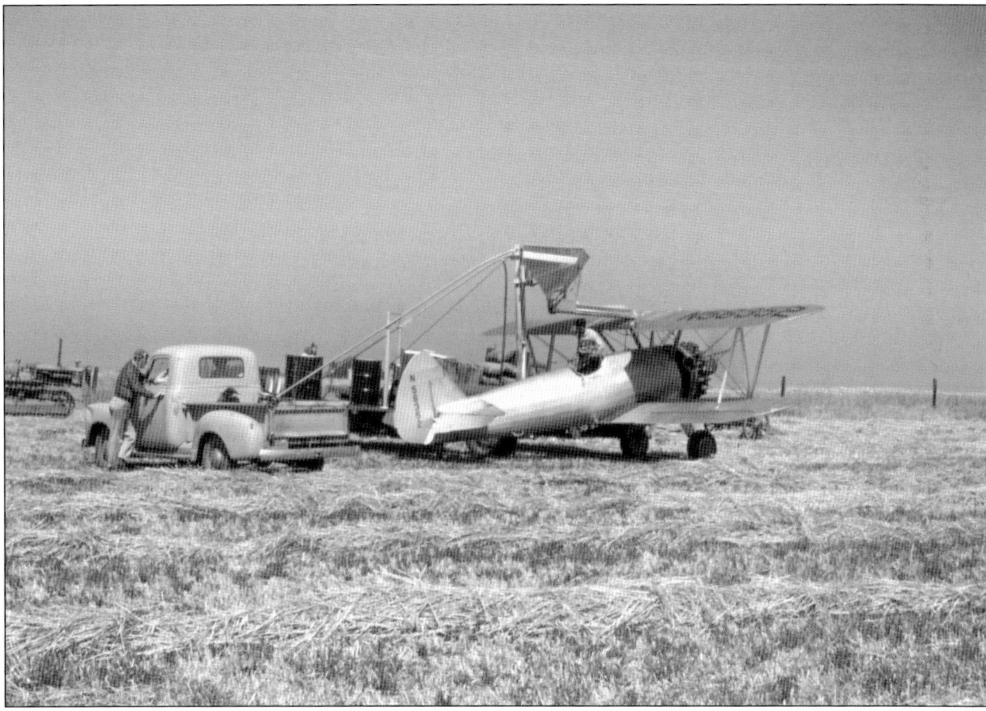

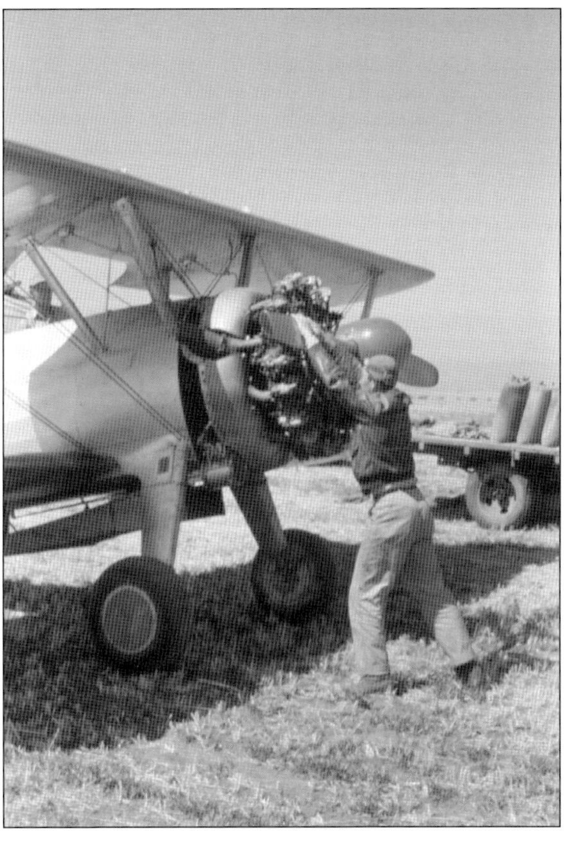

When the seed was sown for the field, it was found that aerial sowing was the most efficient. The seed was fed from into the hopper of plane, and the last-minute discussion between the farmer and pilot was taken care of before the pilot hand-cranked the propeller for takeoff. These photographs, taken on the Schaad Ranch, are showing Harold "Pete" Peterson as the pilot. Pete commanded a B-29 in World War II and developed an agricultural aviation service in 1947. At one time, he owned six 450-horsepower Stearmans to do the job. After logging in 14,000 hours, he sold the business in 1968. (Both, Henry W. Rhoades family.)

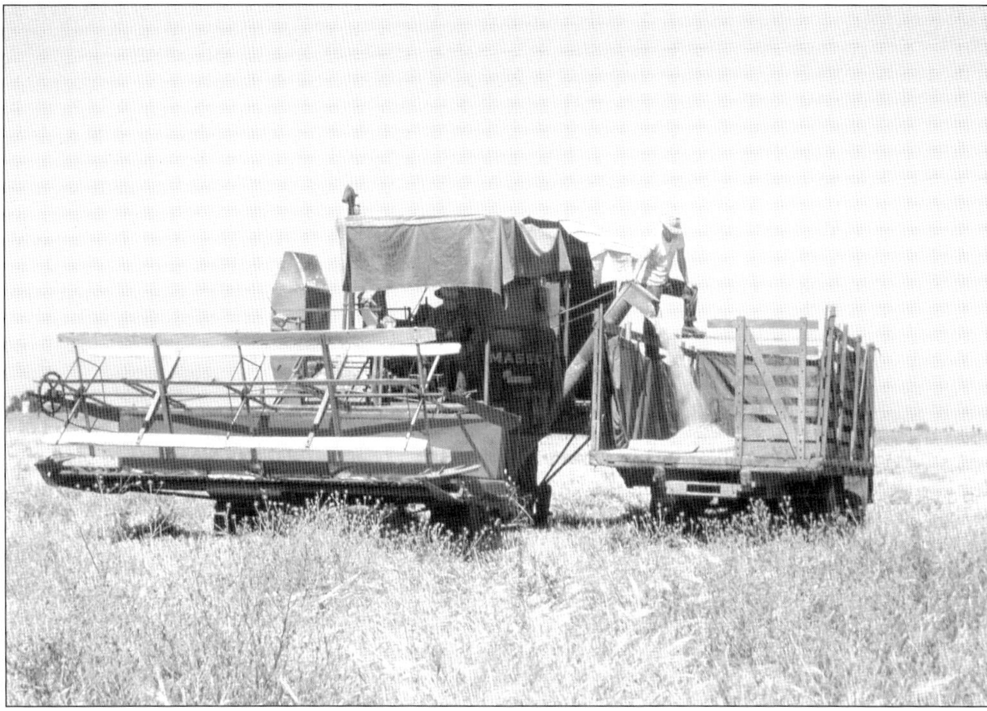

Grain harvest in August 1949 on the Schaad Ranch has Roy on the harvester unloading into a truck to be sacked and sown. (Henry W. Rhoades family.)

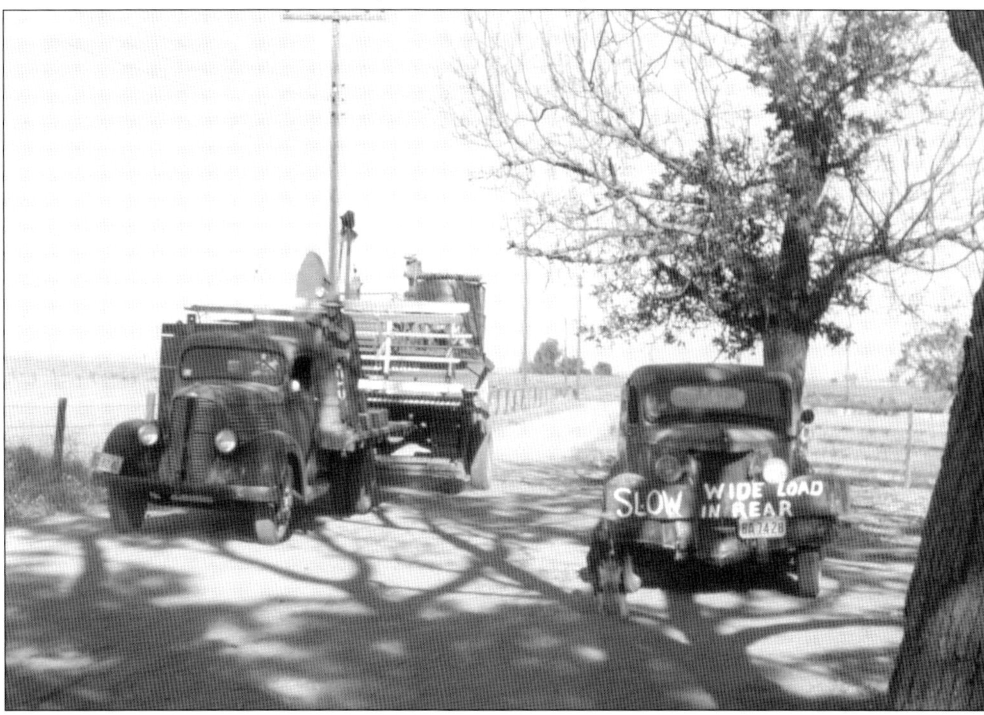

This is a wonderful 1949 photograph of moving equipment on the Schaad Ranch with Roy Schaad on the back of the truck. (Henry W. Rhoades family.)

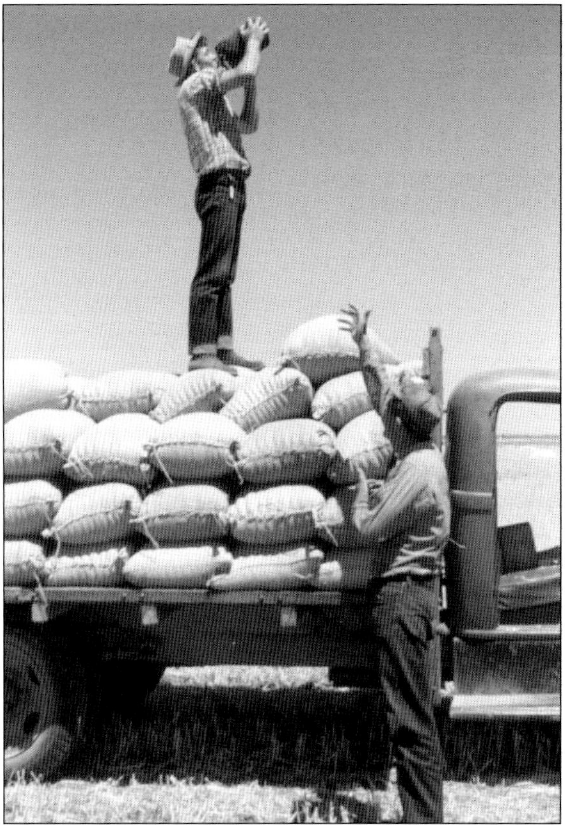

This iconic photograph shows young Parker Wallace, probably as a sack buck, in 1949. The water jug he is holding was considered a fixture in those days. Men would wrap a glass gallon jar in layers and layers of burlap and soak the burlap-covered bottle in water when they came in from the fields. Soaking it, in theory, was to help keep the water in the jug cool. (Henry W. Rhoades family.)

Trucks loaded down with sacks of grain make their way to the Depue Warehouse from the Roy Schaad Ranch in the 1940s. The Depue was originally the Stovall Wilcoxson Warehouse and dated back to the 1880s. Each sack was filled, sown, and closed by hand and loaded onto the truck. (Henry W. Rhoades family.)

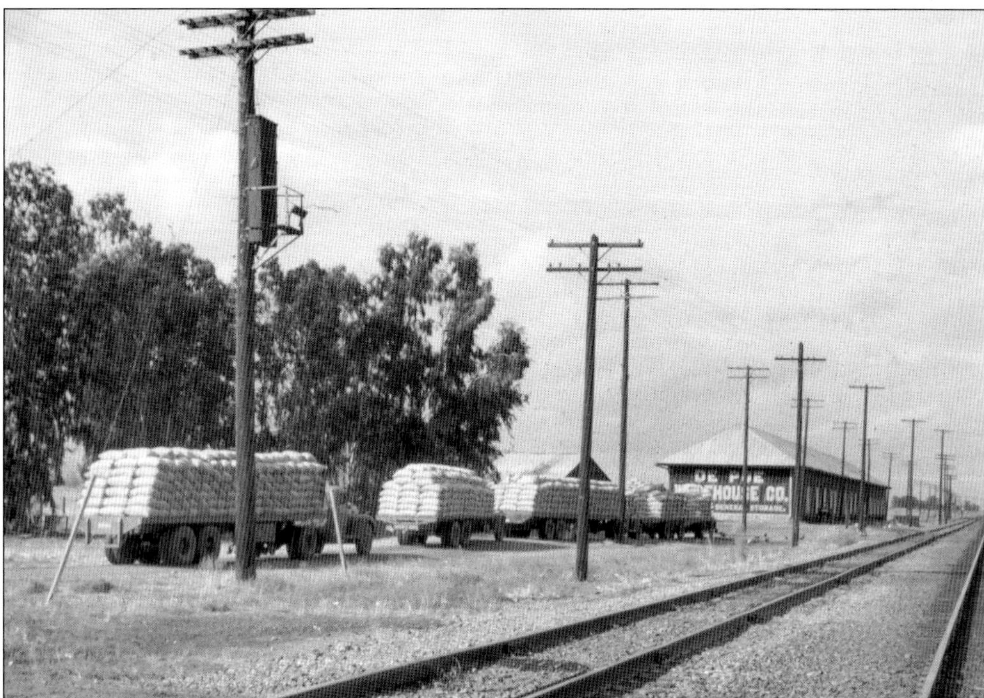

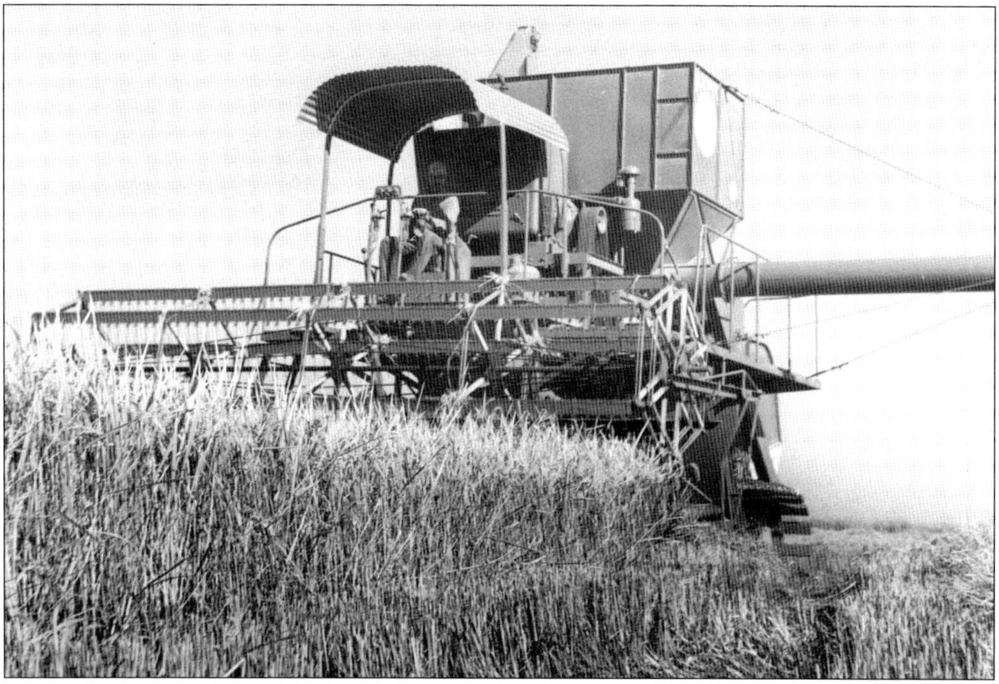

One of the biggest changes in rice harvesting came with the invention of the Hardy Harvester in 1948. Designed by Jess Hardy of College City in Colusa County, the harvester was known to be a workhorse in muddy, less-desirable conditions. Palmer Cheney purchased the first harvester and was able to help farmers who were unable to get their machines into the fields because of mud. In 1954 or 1955, the second Hardy order was taken. Story has it that the design of the harvester resulted from drawings on a cocktail napkin, and with that idea, it changed rice harvesting in Colusa County. Hardy Harvester No. 1 is still in operation today and owned by Doug Gassaway of Williams. Kelly Ornbaun of Williams owns Hardy No. 2. (Both, Tim and Jim Morrow.)

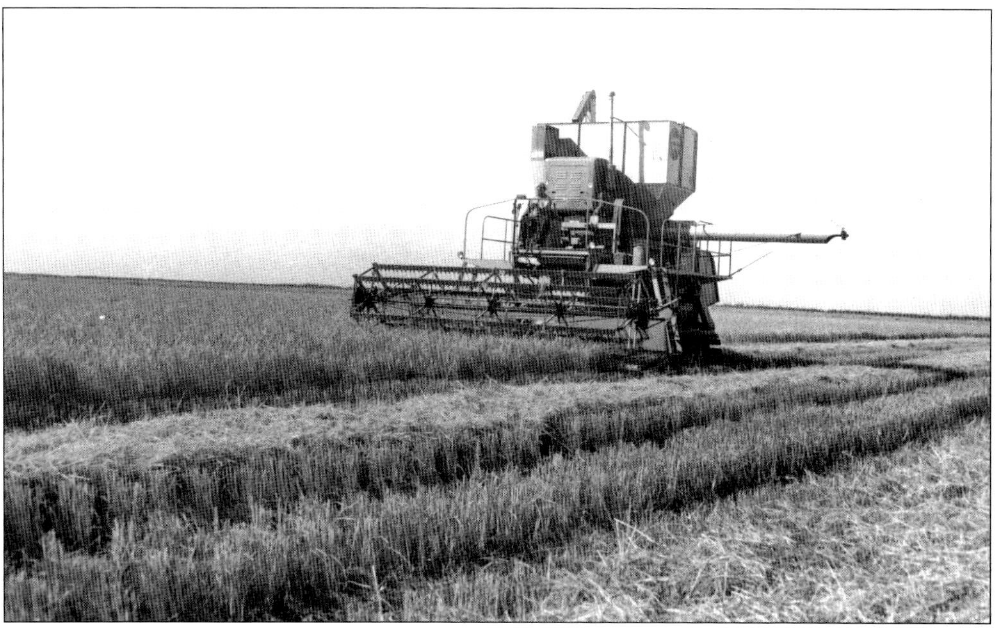

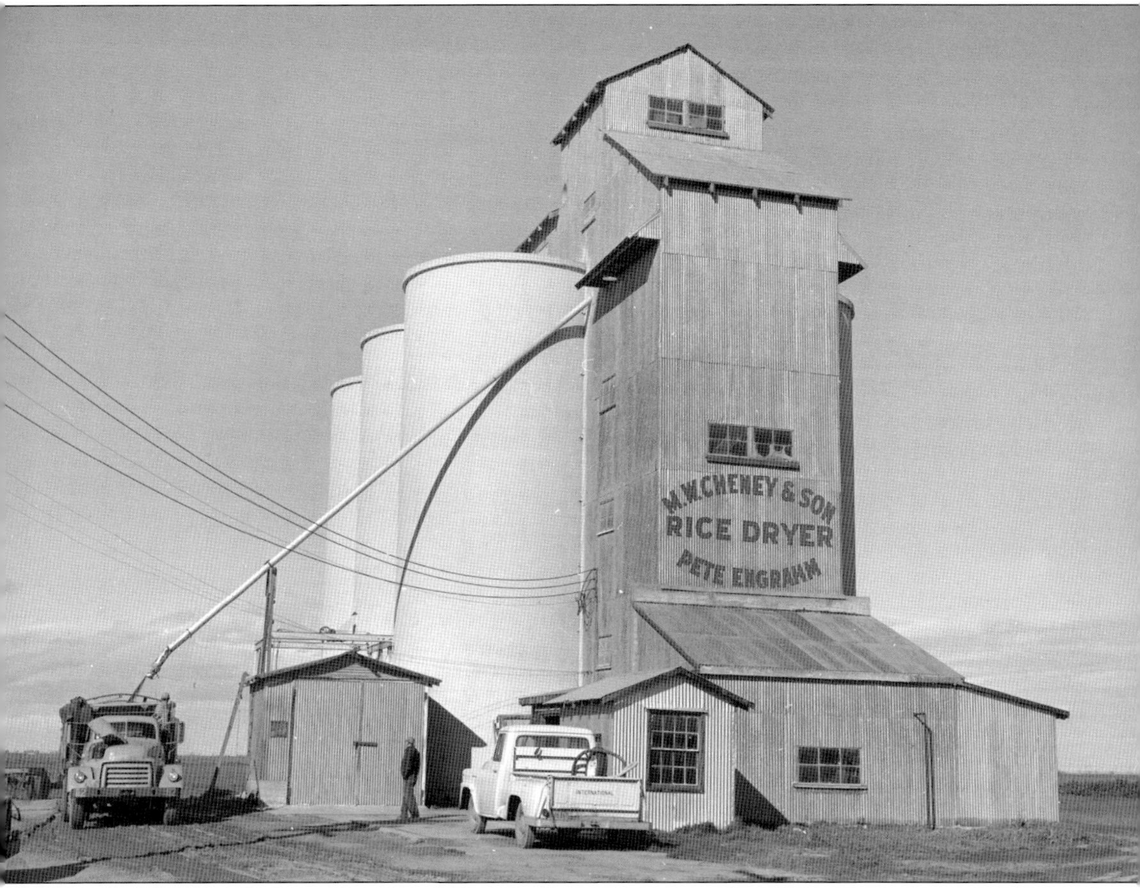

After the rice is off-loaded from the harvester, the rice is then driven to a drier, such as this one, which was owned at the time by Merrick Cheney & Son and Pete Engrahm. After the rice is cut, the farmers send it to be dried and trucked out to other storage facilities. (Henry W. Rhoades family.)

Eight

The Gibson Ranch

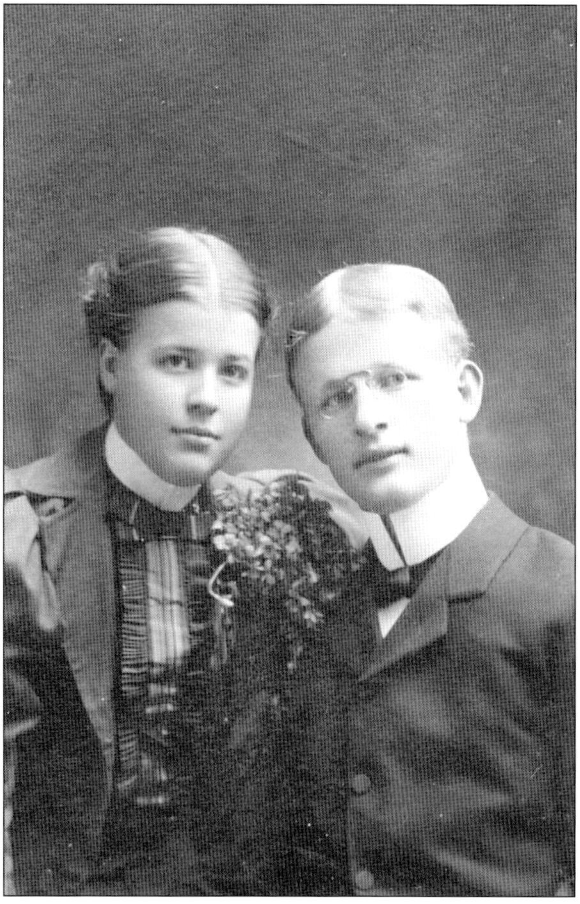

Gion Gibson and his sister Nara California Gibson, both children of Joseph and Sara, are pictured here. After the death of their father, California and Gion took on the job of running the ranch. Gion was a graduate of Stanford with a degree in engineering, and Nara California attended finishing school in Berkeley, but her heart was always with the ranch and the 1,800 acres they called home. (Gibson family collection.)

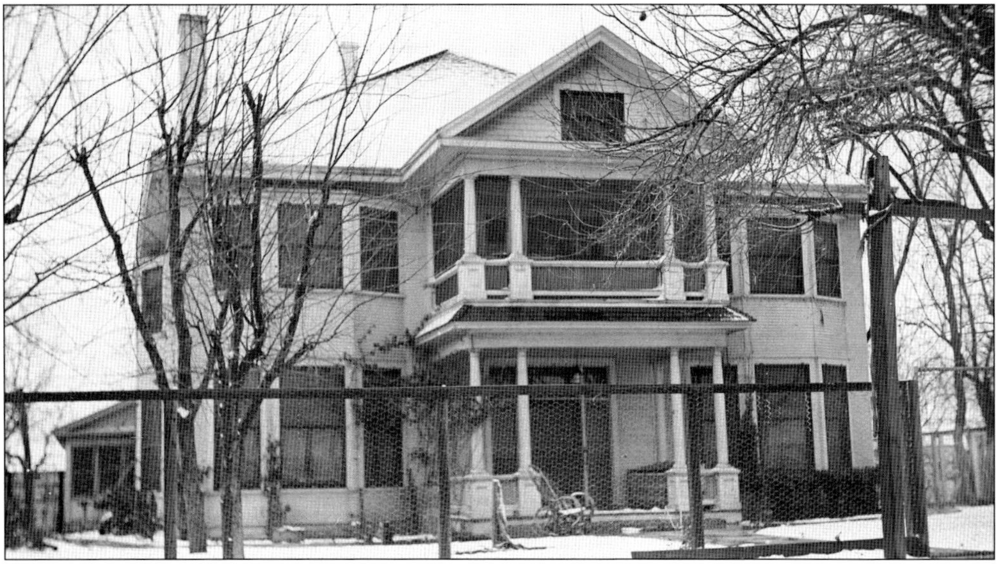

In 1869, the very first house belonging to Joseph Gibson burned with a loss of $1,500. A two-story structure was then built, and in 1905, the house was renovated into the structure shown in these photographs. A grand home in its time, it has seen several owners since the Gibsons. (Both, Gibson family collection.)

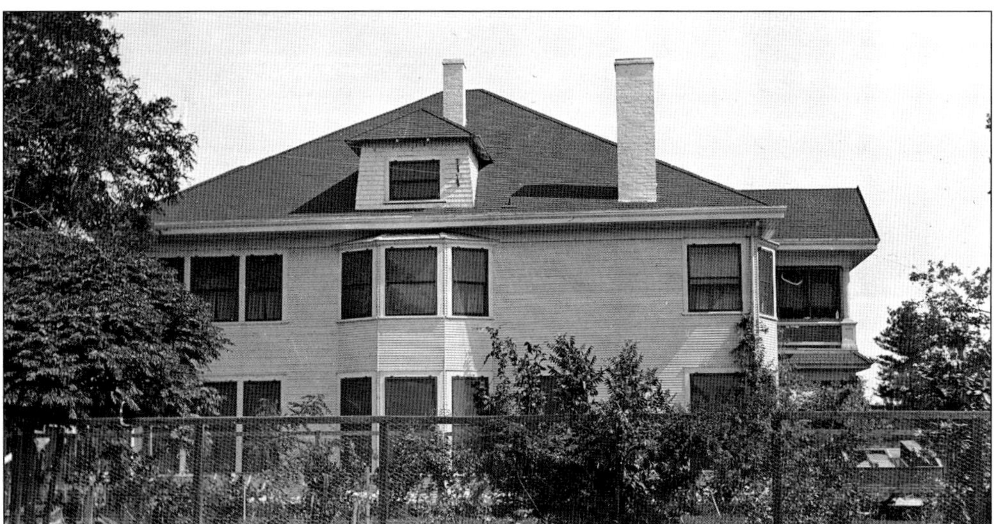

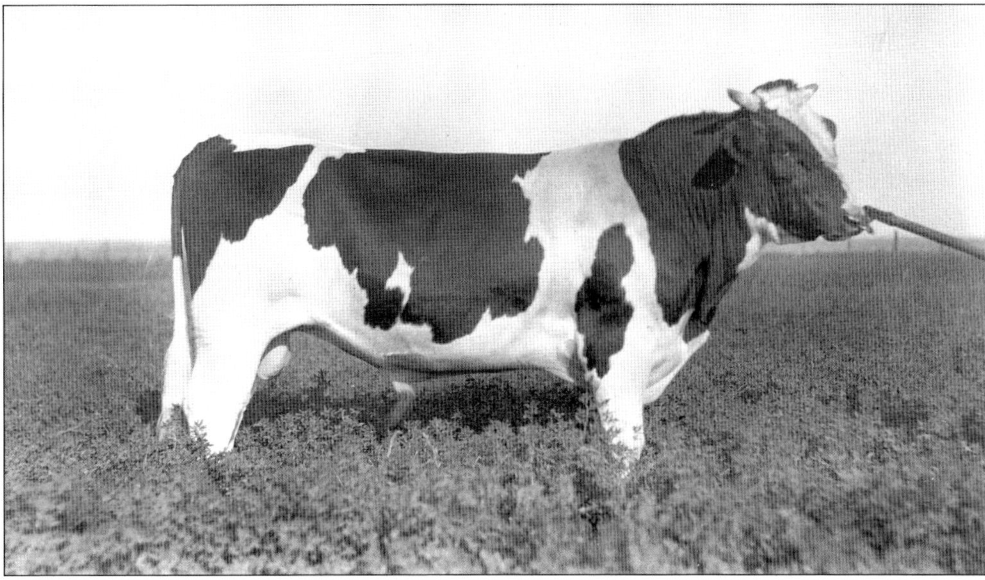

The Gibson Ranch was known for its fine pedigree stock and was always on the cutting-edge of the business. While under Gion's leadership, the purebred Holstein-Friesian line of cattle was established and bred. They were known for selling their stock by the pedigree, not by the pound, and the cows were no exception. The first cow in the world to produce over 1,200 pounds of butter from over 31,000 pounds of milk in one year was raised here along with the only herd in the state of California to produce two cows with a record of this kind. For another record, they had the only cow with a milk record of 31,000 pounds of milk in one year produce a daughter with over 28,000 pounds of milk, and one of their bull calves sold for $61,000. (Both, Gibson family collection.)

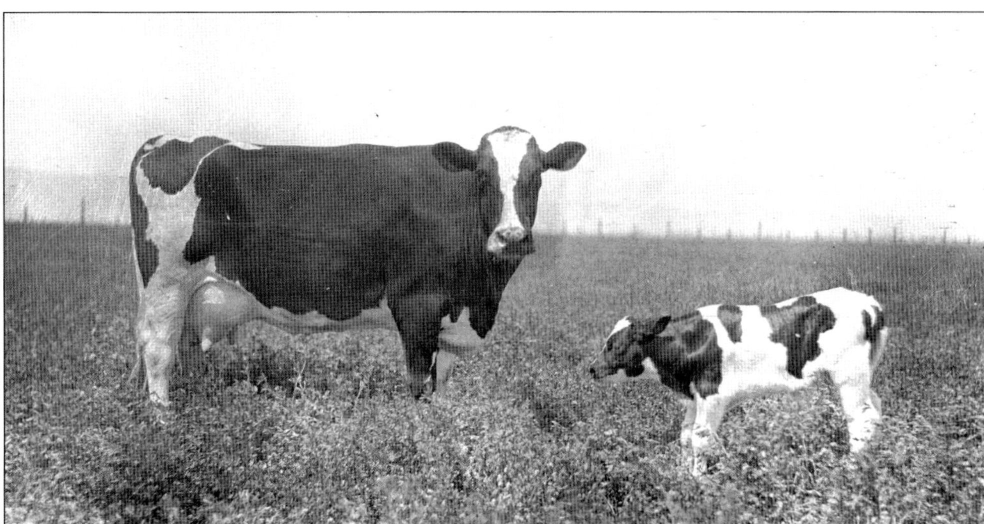

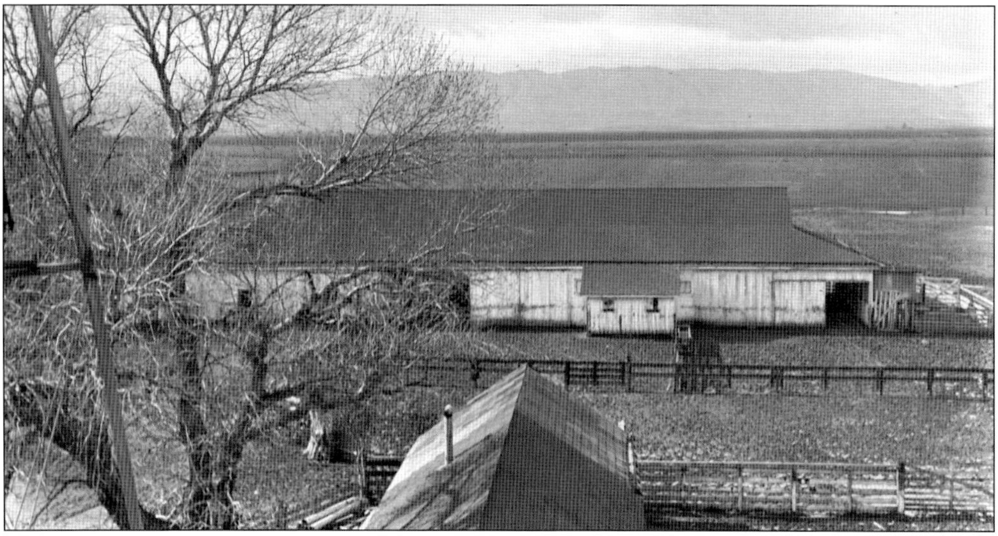

In 1913, the Gibsons built a mammoth barn to accommodate their high-grade stock and their up-to-date dairy of that era. The 148-by-64-foot structure, with a 24-foot-tall ceiling, was equipped in the very best possible way to care for the animals with minimum labor. The interior photograph of the barn shows the stalls, and because the barn was hosed out twice a day, the barns were described as all being clean and sanitary. Everything was done first class, and the ranch was considered a model for other ranches in the state. (Both, Gibson family collection.)

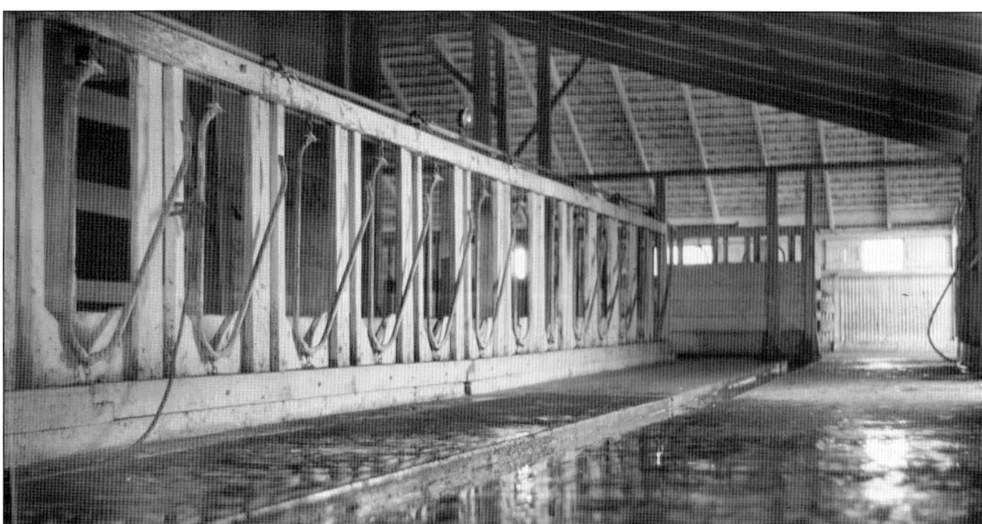

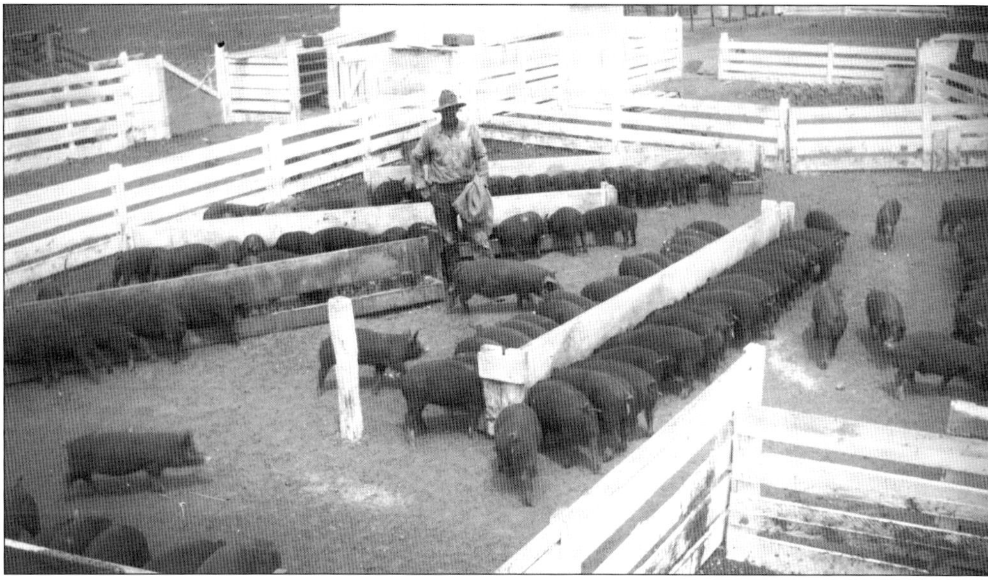

Pigs were also raised on the Gibson Ranch and were reported to be from fine nobility. Both the bovines and cows were often featured in agricultural journals. The hogs were said to be well fed and cared for in every respect. (Gibson family collection.)

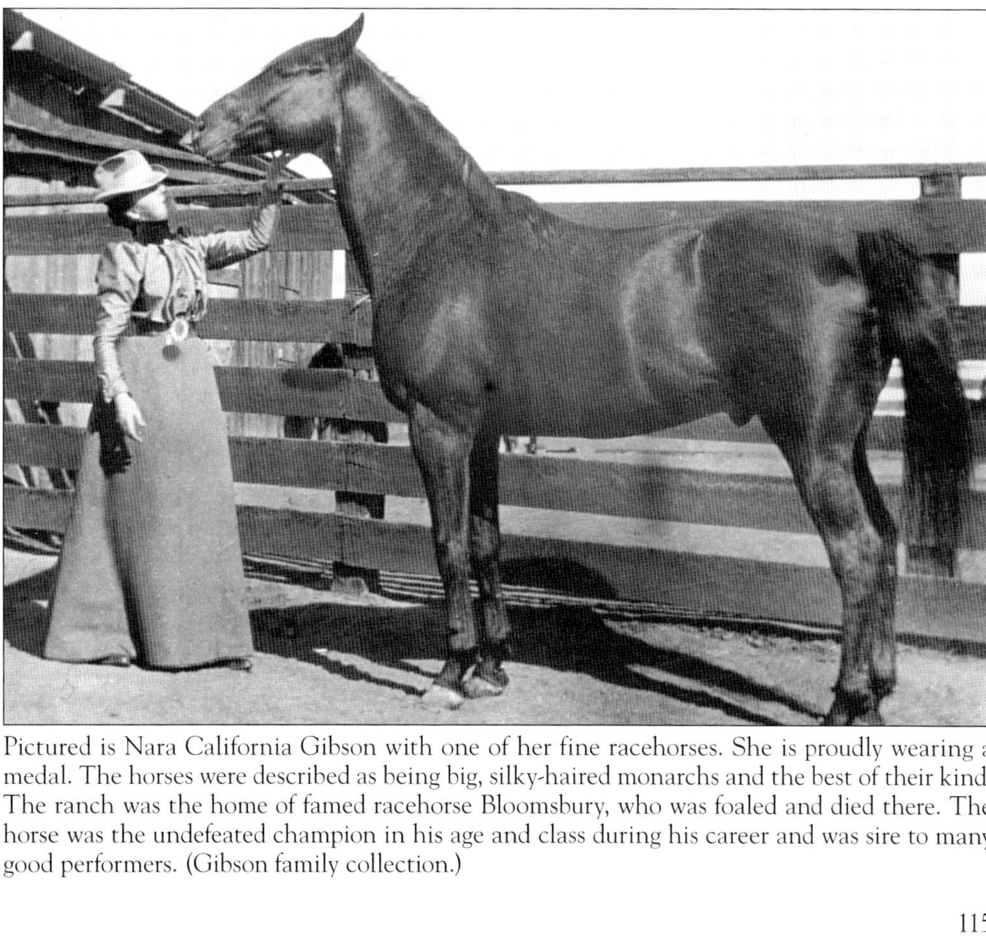

Pictured is Nara California Gibson with one of her fine racehorses. She is proudly wearing a medal. The horses were described as being big, silky-haired monarchs and the best of their kind. The ranch was the home of famed racehorse Bloomsbury, who was foaled and died there. The horse was the undefeated champion in his age and class during his career and was sire to many good performers. (Gibson family collection.)

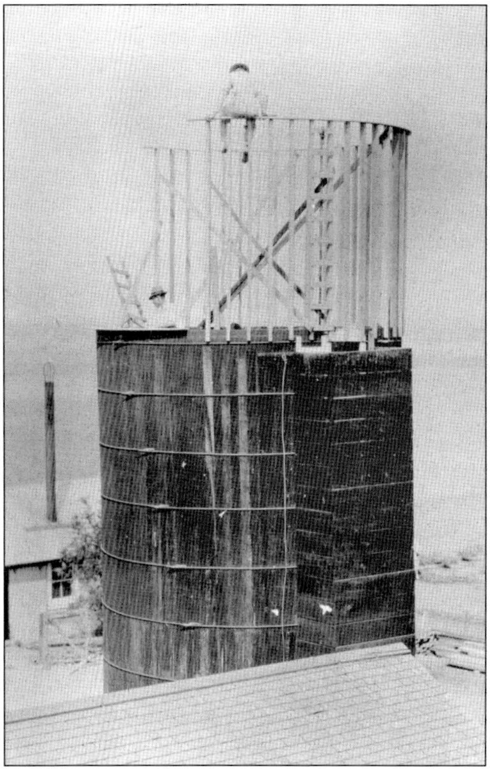

Another experimental idea that was heralded as being very innovative was the building of two silos, the only ones of their kind in the area. The silos were filled with green feed that kept the dairy herd up to the maximum milk production year-around. Building of the silos was no easy feat with each board being individually hoisted in place and then banded securely. (Both, Gibson family collection.)

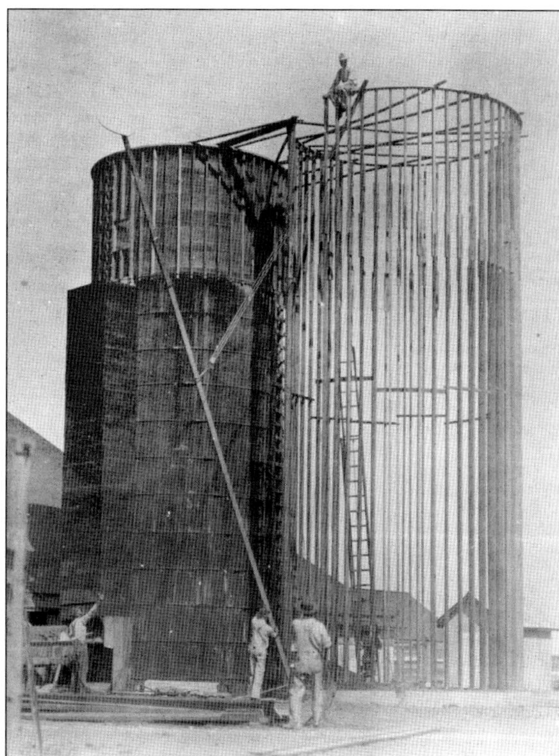

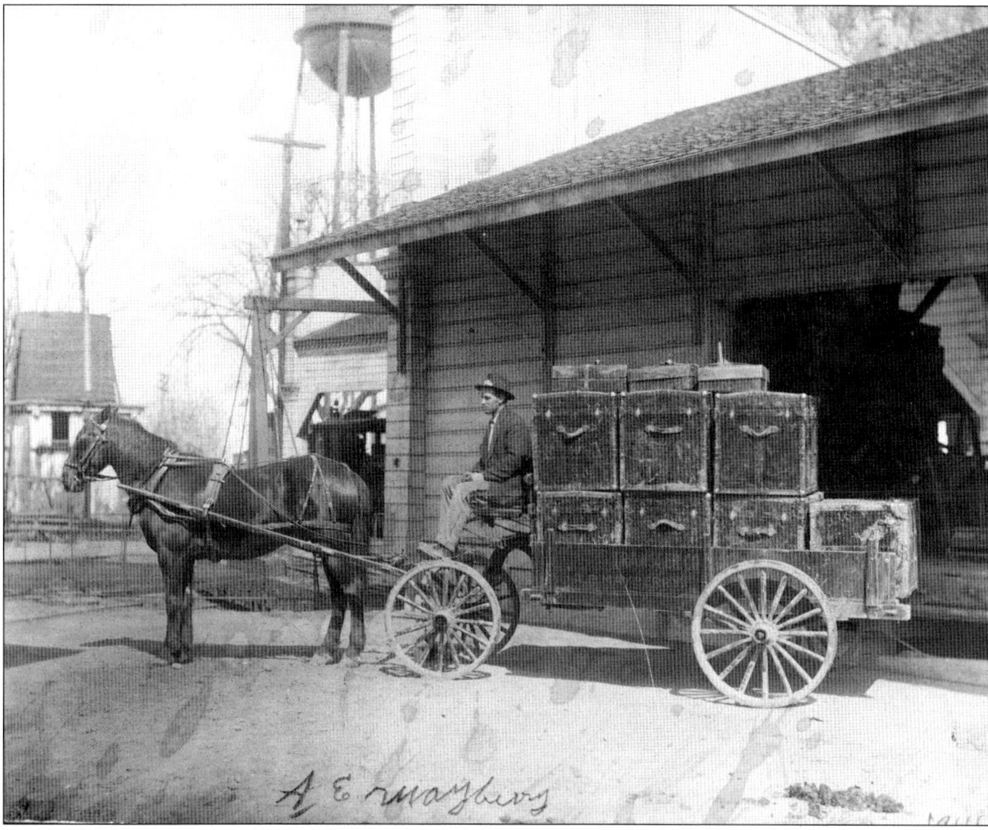

Ice was delivered to the ranch from Colusa with A.E. Mayberry seen here as the driver. Crossing the slough was dangerous, and little Verbal Mayberry was made to get off the wagon so his father could get a running start. It was a goal of Mayberry to arrive at the Gibson Ranch before lunch, because it was said that the spread put on for workers and tradesmen was the talk of the county. (Barbara Mayberry family.)

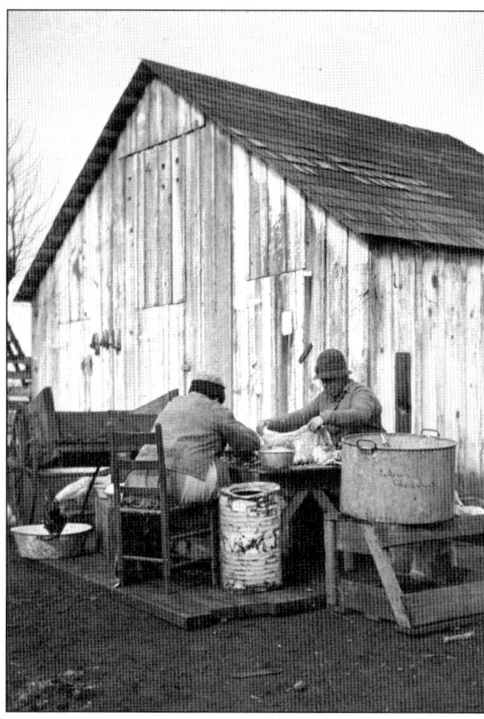

Preparing meals for a big crew was no easy task back in the day. Often, the women worked 16 to 18 hours a day in preparation and clean up. The two women here seem to have their work cut out for them in food preparation. (Gibson family collection.)

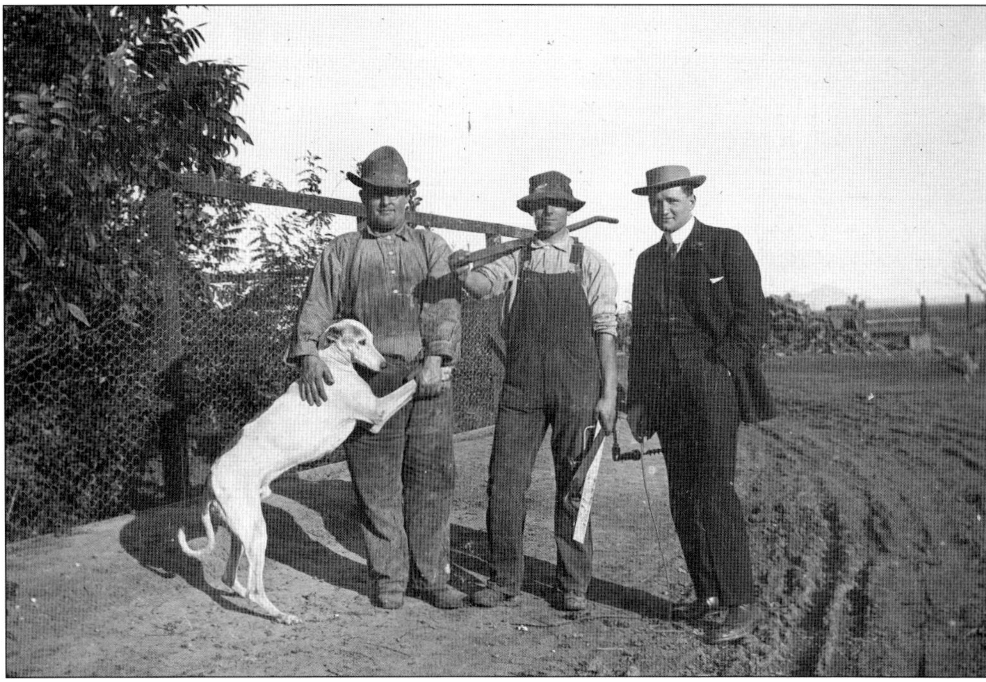

After a hard and particularly dirty day on the job, Gion (left) is shown with a young "Bunk" Wallace with carpenter tools ready to call it a day. The man on the right is unidentified. Along with everything else on the ranch, there was also a $10,000 machine shop. (Gibson family collection.)

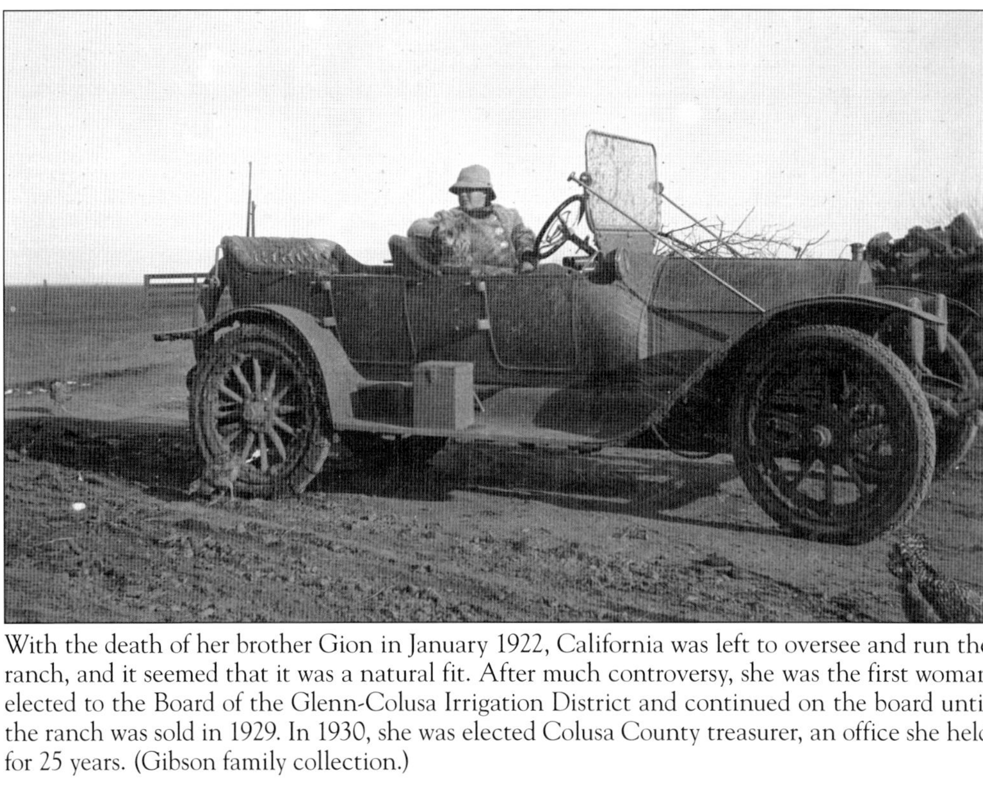

With the death of her brother Gion in January 1922, California was left to oversee and run the ranch, and it seemed that it was a natural fit. After much controversy, she was the first woman elected to the Board of the Glenn-Colusa Irrigation District and continued on the board until the ranch was sold in 1929. In 1930, she was elected Colusa County treasurer, an office she held for 25 years. (Gibson family collection.)

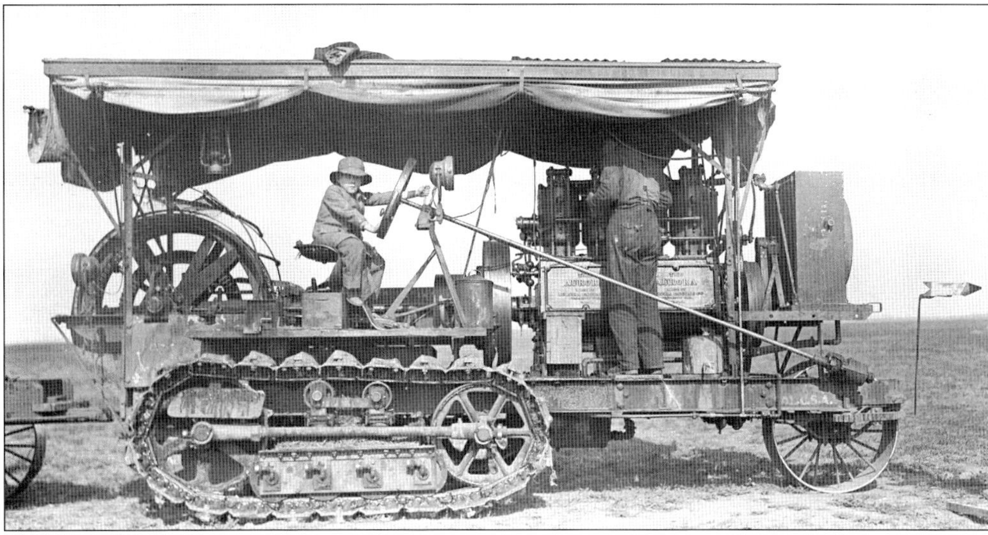

It was never too early to acquaint the children of the farm with the equipment. Shown here is little Samuel Gion Gibson, grandson of Joseph, trying out the tractor driver position. (Gibson family collection.)

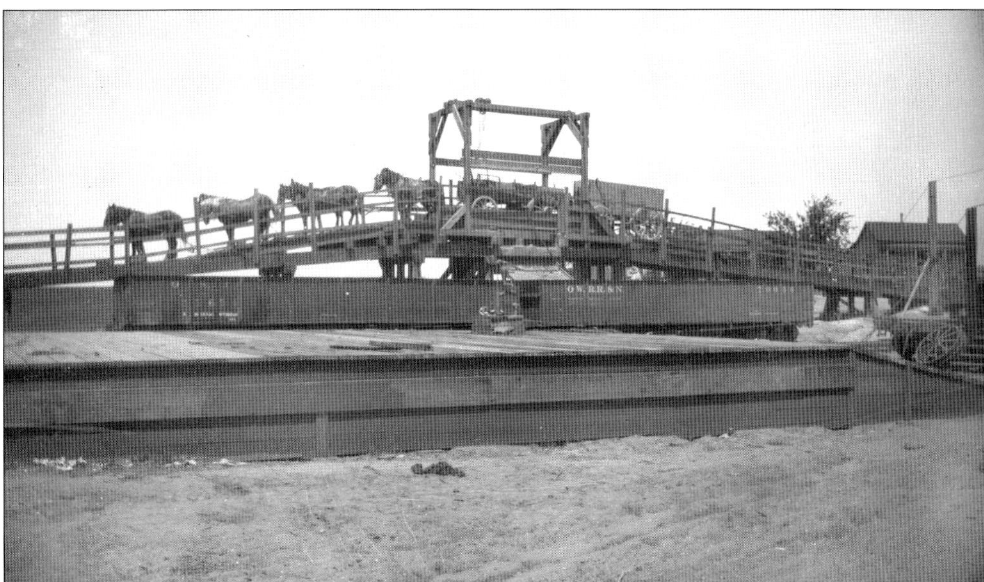

This unusual photograph shows a team being driven to a drop-off point while the product is off-loaded into the railroad car of the Colusa Lake Railroad. The team pulls forward, and the second wagon is off-loaded. The cargo is believed to be grain. The Gibson Ranch had its own railroad spur to the mainline and warehouse facilities. (Gibson family collection.)

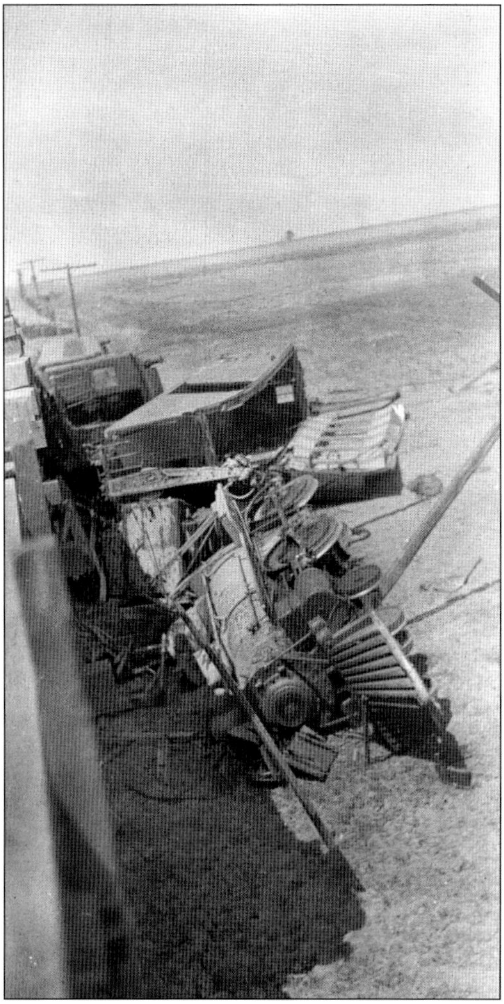

In 1913, the Colusa Lake Railroad suffered the loss of one of its three engines when the trestle gave way to the ground below just west of the long bridge. The engineer was pinned beneath the wreckage and suffered burns from the steam before he was rescued. Only two of the 12 passengers were injured, neither seriously, but they certainly had a story to tell. The Colusa Lake Railroad ran between Colusa and Sites along what is now Lurline Road, and it was hoped that one day the railroad would run all the way to Lake County and beyond, but proved too expensive to complete. (Both, Gibson family collection.)

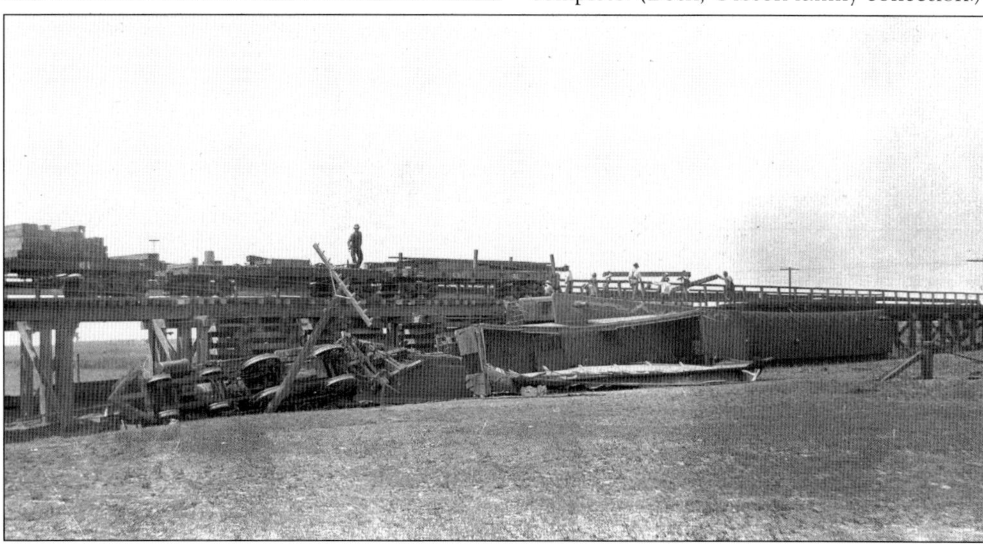

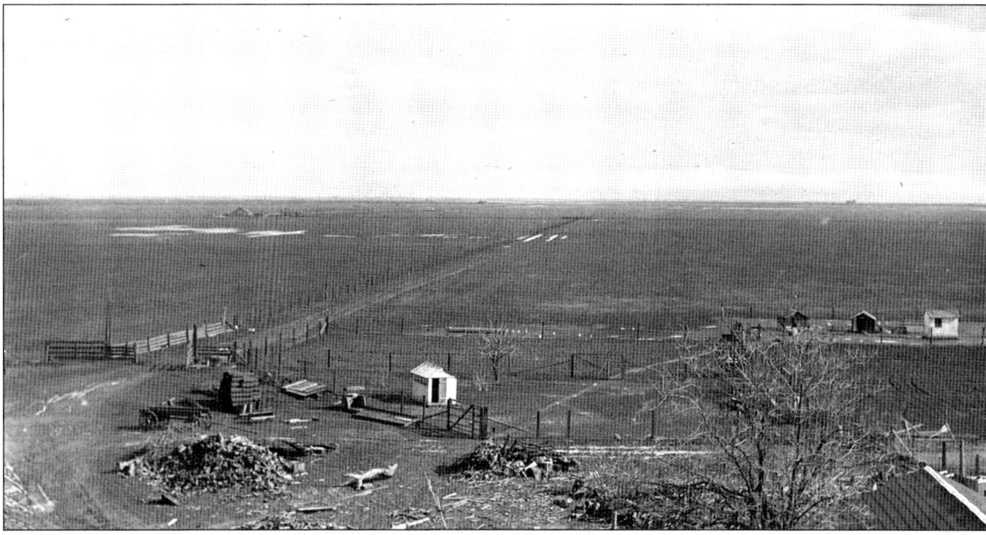

The barren land of winter will soon make way for the planting of spring and the summer harvest. This photograph shows the magnitude of the ranch and the sparse population in the vicinity. (Gibson family collection.)

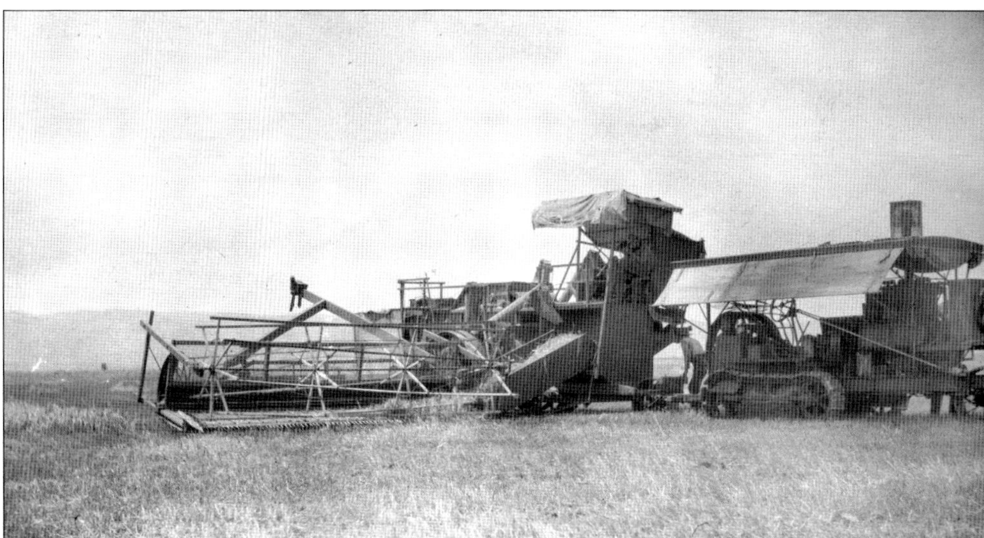

According to a local newspaper article, the Gibsons brought in, owned, and operated the first header for the harvesting of grain that was ever brought into the Sacramento Valley. This photograph shows the tractor pulling the harvester and header with the straw taken up the conveyor. Notice the man on the top of the harvester at the wheel. It is not verified that this is the harvester spoken of above. (Gibson family collection.)

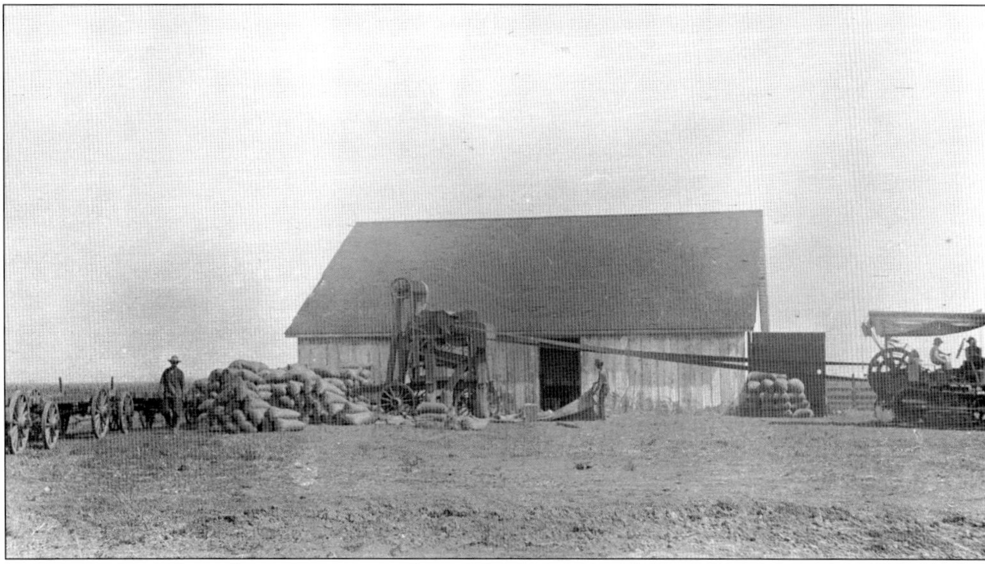

Once the grain was harvested, it was time to separate the grain and put it into sacks. The sack-sowing job was tedious, and the worker had to be fast to keep up with the pace of the grain. Often earning less than $1 a day, the men would work 12 hours or more. The workers seem to be taking a well-deserved break, with the one man ready to have the sack filled. (Both, Gibson family collection.)

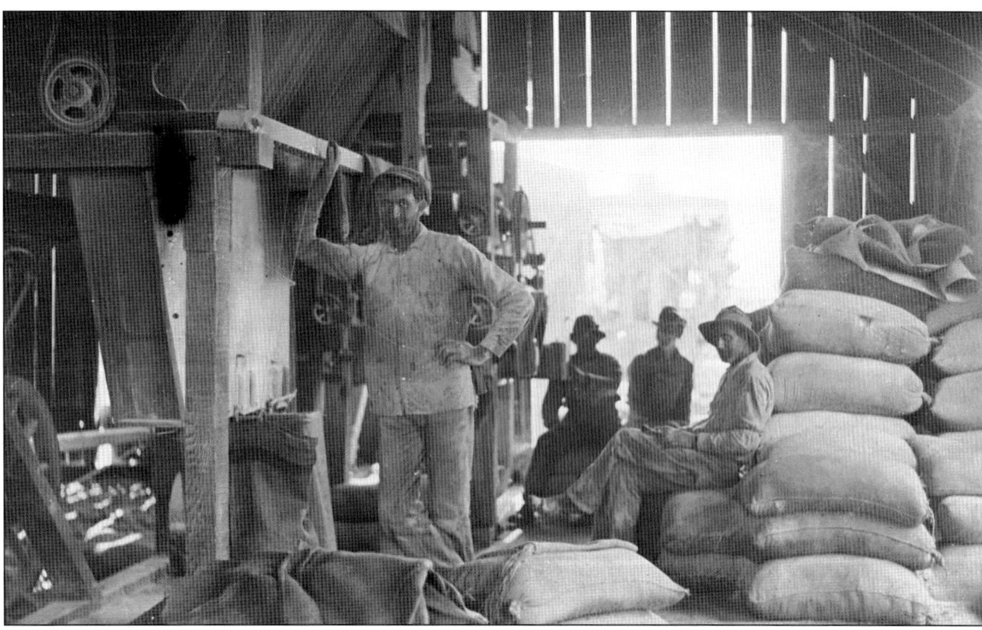

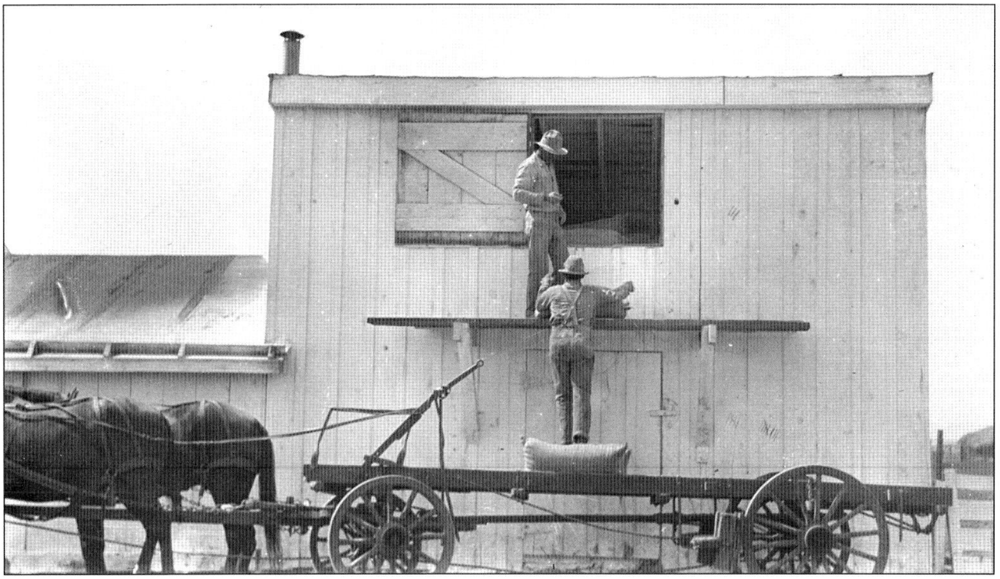

After the sacks were sown, the job was far from done. The sacks then had to be loaded on a wagon and distributed to the different storage facilities on the ranch. The work required a strong back and for men to be in top condition. (Gibson family collection.)

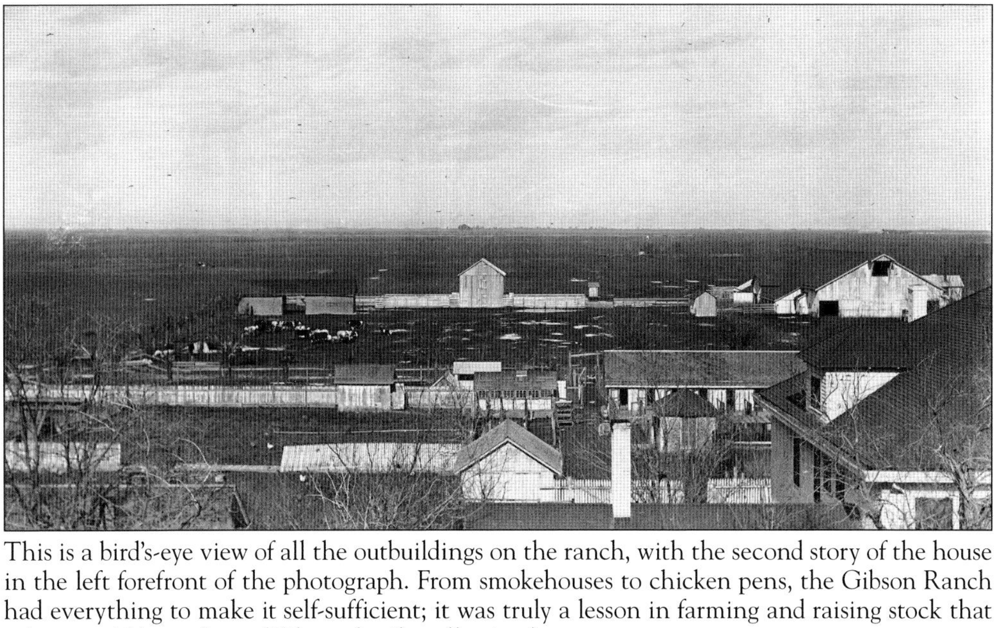

This is a bird's-eye view of all the outbuildings on the ranch, with the second story of the house in the left forefront of the photograph. From smokehouses to chicken pens, the Gibson Ranch had everything to make it self-sufficient; it was truly a lesson in farming and raising stock that others could learn from. (Gibson family collection.)

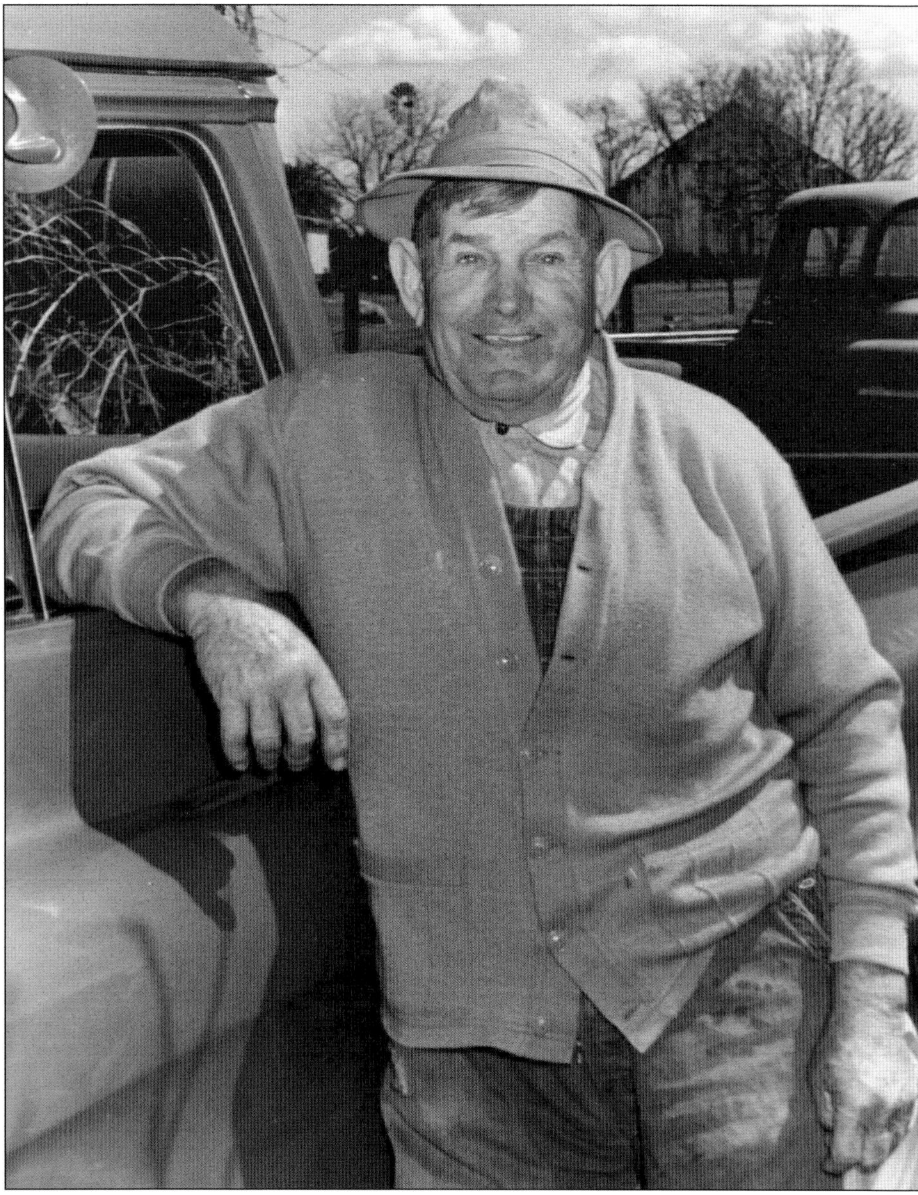

One of the early Gibson Ranch employees was Malion "Bunk" Wallace, shown here in his trademark bib overalls, who worked for Gion in his youth and before he enlisted in World War I. Bunk wrote to Gion while in France and purchased part of the subdivided Gibson tract for his family when he returned. While there, his daughter June was born, and as a tribute to his friend Gion Gibson, he named his youngest son Parker Gion Wallace. Bunk served years on both the Central one-room schoolhouse board as well as on the Williams Union High School Board. He worked harder than many men and always shared what he had, sometimes giving when he did not have anything to give. The world could learn a lot from Bunk. He was a patriot until the very end, helping to organize the American Legion when he returned from war and never missed a chance to attend the Memorial Day Services, single-handedly putting flags on each of the graves of local veterans. From a pioneering Central family, he exuded what Williams was built on: hard work, giving until it hurts, and respect for one another. (Henry W. Rhoades family.)

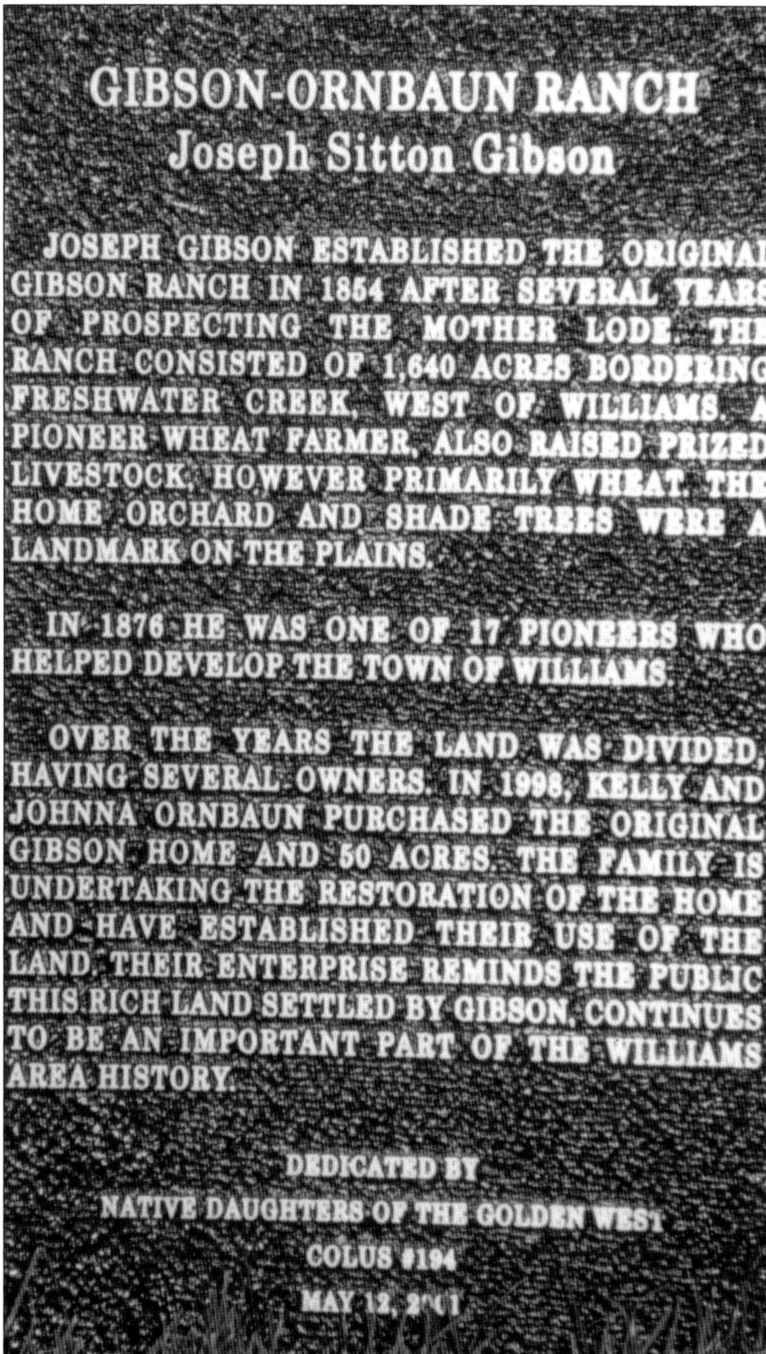

After the Gibsons, the ranch had several owners, many of whom were unlucky and lost the ranch through foreclosure. The ranch now consists of 50 acres after being parceled and sold in sections. Kelly and Johnna Ornbaun currently use the ranch as educational premises to teach people about agriculture and farming. In 2000, the Native Daughters awarded the property a plaque for its historical significance. The Ornbauns are in the process of renovating the old home. (Kelly and Johnna Ornbaun.)

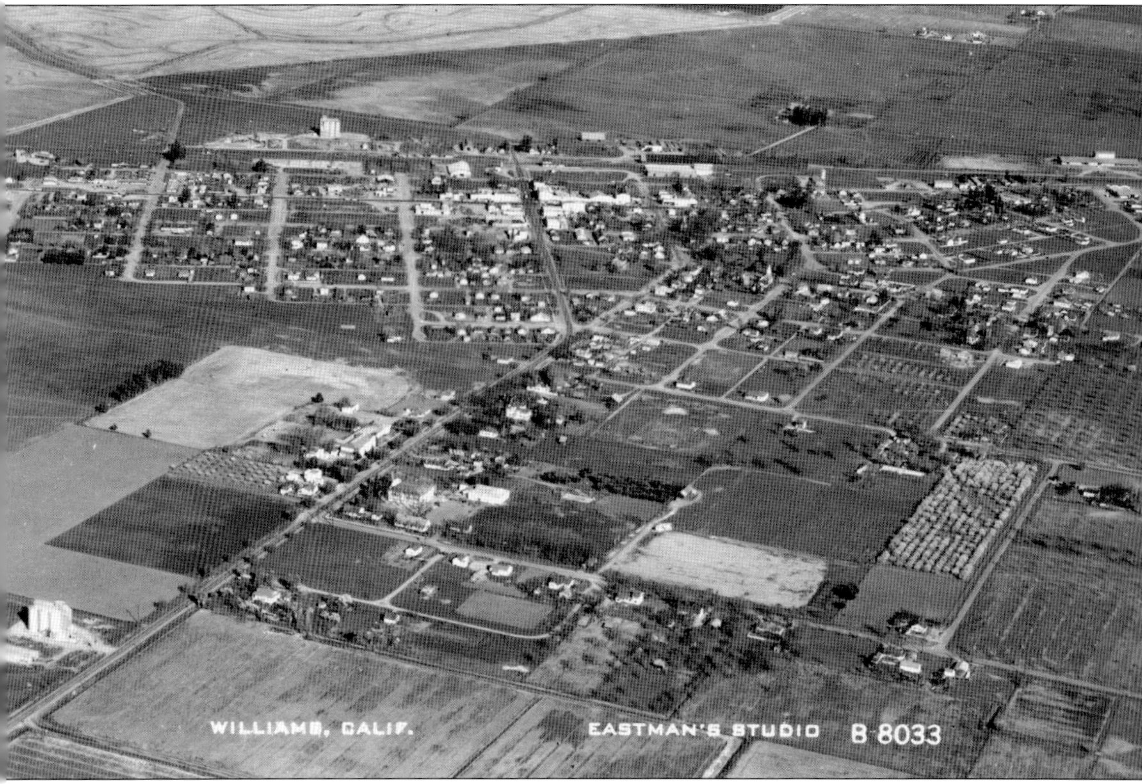

This is an aerial photograph of Williams before 1949. (Mike Ferraiuolo.)

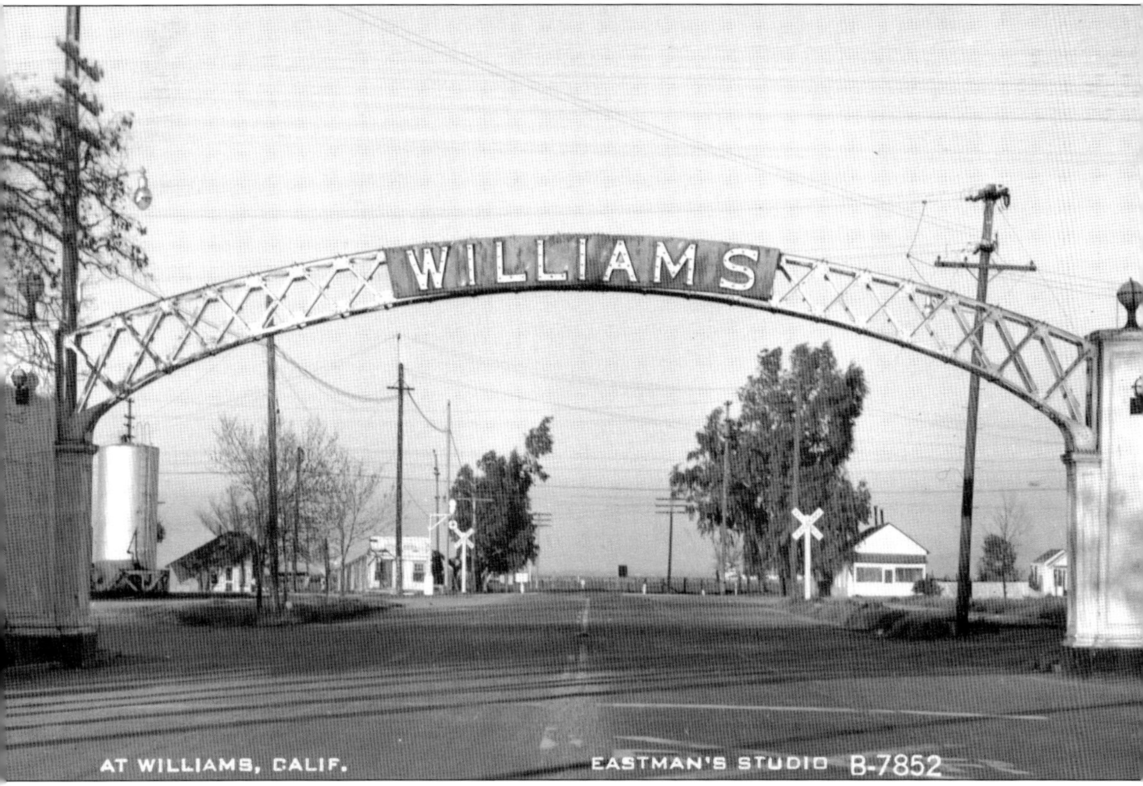

Thanks for visiting Williams. Come back soon! (Bill Barrett.)